THE AESTHETICS OF EXCESS

SUNY series in Aesthetics

Mary C. Rawlinson, editor

The Aesthetics of Excess

ALLEN S. WEISS

State University of New York Press

Published by
State University of New York Press, Albany

Printed in the United States of America

For information, address State University of New York Press, State University Plaza, Albany, N.Y., 12246

Library of Congress Cataloging in Publication Data

Weiss, Allen S., 1954-
The aesthetics of excess / Allen S. Weiss.
p. cm.—(SUNY series in aesthetics and the philosophy of art)
Includes index.
ISBN 0-7914-0052-2.—ISBN 0-7914-0053-0 (pbk.)
1. Aesthetics. 2. Critical theory. 3. Modernism (Art) I. Title. II. Series.
BH39.W39 1989
111'.85—dc19
88-39379
CIP

10 9 8 7 6 5 4 3 2 1

For my mentors.
(In chronological order.)
Samuel Cherniak
Darrell Taylor
Don Ihde
David Allison
Alphonso Lingis
Annette Michelson

All that you cast off through the centuries as refuse is now speaking out through me.

Witold Gombrowicz
Diary

la KKKKultur

Marcel Proust
Le Temps Retrouvé

Contents

Preface

The prohibition against the use of the word "I" in the critical or theoretical text is a curious restriction, not completely unlike those literary games of *Oulipo* where, for example, an entire text must be written with the systematic suppression of the letter "e".[1] But while the latter seeks a sheerly aesthetic effect, the former reveals a certain moral or psychological, if not metaphysical, imperative. Is it the expression of the author's narcissism that is feared, or could it rather be the very inauguration of a more subtle ontological disturbance that is to be avoided?

Classical rhetoric was an art of mastery—and not least of all, an art of self mastery, through the "masterful" control of "one's own" language. The structural aspects of the rhetorical field—*inventio* (invention), *dispositio* (composition), *elocutio* (style)—form the major axes of a discipline of expression, where locutory pleasure is a secondary effect, and intellectual control of the interlocutor the prime objective. (We must remember the Aristotelian distinction between rhetoric and poetics; in our terms, the great Sophist Isocrates is not so distant from the great philosopher Socrates, except that the latter insisted on the pretention of a logic as the basis of the proper use of rhetoric.)

But we have learned that writing and speech can entail either mastery or dispossession—the dispossession of the self. This risk in speaking is due to the fact that the linguistic system far surpasses the limits of our expression: language is the space of excess of our speech. Our discourse is always threatened by the universalizing properties of language, our words always escape us, our meanings are constantly subverted—to the point where in certain psychotic discourse language is perceived as a strange, disquieting, alien body. The "I" is the other of language, an empty linguistic shifter where each change of speaker entails the forgetfulness of what language otherwise articulates. Might not the fear of this dispossession be precisely the fear of the "death of the author," the terror of finding nothing at the base of our narcissism—the very end of interiorization, the impossibility of any further subjective impulse? The death of the author (*ressentiment* against narcissism) entails the objectification of authorial modes and practices, where rhetoric is finally subsumed as one more function of a universal and universalizing *actio*, beyond all truth value. (This would be an *actio* beyond its rhetorical significance as "body language," and rather of the body traversed by the libido.)

Our narcissism is thus simultaneously revealed and betrayed by speech. Does silence, then, offer a refuge? To be silent may signify either knowledge or ignorance. One or many silences? The silence imposed by the Nietzschean Eternal Return is a wisdom without preconceived object (or subject!); the silence of Bataille's night of eroticism is an effect of the body's transgressive powers; the silence so desired by Schreber and Artaud is the need to rid the unconscious of the final remnants of a theological monomania in an epoch where God is dead, and where mystical expression is thus categorized as psychopathology and relegated to the asylum. The mystical silence before God—answered by the very silence *of* God—is now replaced by the desire to silence God once and for all. Negative theology or pathology?

An exceedingly ironic moment in the history of rhetoric was the publication of *L'Art de se taire (The Art of Keeping Silent)* in 1771 by the Abbé Dinouart.[2] In the century where D.A.F. Sade's texts—in which *everything* is to be said—reached the zero-degree of rhetorical and narrative subtlety, Dinouart proposed exactly the inverse. In the negative, reactionary expression of rhetoric as pure *actio*, *L'Art de se taire* proffers a program whereby silence before God is replaced by silence as a social strategy. Silence is henceforth to be expressive, performative, cunning. Dinouart catalogues the different modes of silence (just as the classical rhetoricians catalogued the different modes of speech): prudent, guileful, complaisant, mocking, spiritual, stupid, approbative, scornful, political, humorous, capricious.

These silences are not nonsensical: quite to the contrary, they permit the body and the face to "speak." Through this gestural or "body" language all of the classic tropes and figures of rhetoric are manifest: the figures of rhetoric are doubled by the positions, or figures, of the body. Thus we find the double, often parallel, constraint upon meaning—semiotic/somatic—whereby communicable structures of exchange and incommunicable phantasms coalesce in that magma of expression which we are pretentious enough to call "meaning."[3]

If each rhetorical figure has its corporeal double, might not each trope and each gesture permit a correlative silence? One or many silences? Perhaps there is a silence for each passion. Descartes enumerated the varied "passions of the soul;" Sade listed 600 passions (simple, complex, criminal and murderous); Fourier counted no less than 1620 passions; for Nietzsche, the number was as limitless as the multifarious manifestations of the Will to Power. In a sense, rhetoric as a discipline (and as a hermeneutic) has all the answers and none: all on the structural, conceptual register; none on the passional, corporeal register. Rhetorical analysis provides an explicitation of the linguistic armature of expression and meaning, but is incapable of providing an account of the libidinal economy which underlies and motivates expression. Finally, rhetoric is not merely an aesthetic pretense, nor a pseudo-concept, but rather the very slippage of meaning that underlies all conceptuality.[4] Tropes proffer not the figures of meaning, but rather the very conditions of figurability.[5] The impurities of rhetoric are not inherent in any deviation from literalness: rather, tropes are "impure" insofar as they indicate those primary process activities which underlie their own generation, those libidinal charges which subtend all transference, and thus all communication, all signification. It is within this rhetorical "excess" that the trace of the body remains, as evidence (or prolegomena) for all future hermeneutics (or metaphysics). The libido is the site of the interchange between the psychic and the somatic; rhetoric, the foundation of style, bears the traces of this procedure, of this movement between *logos* and *corpus*.

Speech, too, bears the traces of this psychic/somatic transfer. At the threshold that separates meaning from nonsense, we find rhythm, melody, harmony—the pure expression of the body in language. Speech is "worked" at one extreme by metaphysics, and "played" at the other extreme by music: logocentrism versus melocentrism.[6] Such *musication* (the purest figure of elocution, which underles all rhetorical figuration) is a function of absolute rhetorical differences, while conceptuality is a function of the dissimulation of such rhetorical differences. This separation, this threshold, is perhaps what might be called poetics, where the renunciation of truth values entails the creation of entire systems of expression for the sheer pleasures that they produce. Ultimately, at some level, this "poetics" is to be found at the interior of every metaphysical system—the construction and utilization of a *mathesis universalis* is not without its own pleasures, and all mathematical forms are, *a fortiori*, musical.

Every text is potentially a supplement of all other texts, a fragment of an infinite, universal text that unfolds with every moment of every discursive act. Any text can be grafted on to any other text, to every other text; every text can serve as a cognitive paradigm, can be used as a hermeneutic device, can operate as a moment of narration, can be a fragment of poetry. And every text is the object of a partical identification on the part of the reader. Thus Nietzsche, in claiming that, "I am every name in history,"[7] not only figures, and prefigures, his own madness, but also indicates the ultimate program of reading and writing. Yet finally, this becomes the question of a very few names: as all writers create their predecessors, all projects create their antecedents—hermeneutics is the genealogical study of such kinships, and of the passions which underlie them.

This current work, my own, is no exception; I am no exception. If this book reveals the form of a "Chinese" or Borgesian encyclopedia, it all the same reveals, in that very disorder, the partial logic of a series of partial identifications, within the incompleteness that haunts every "unity."

We read here: Nietzsche (for the non-Pascalian silence of that fearful circle of the Eternal Return, and for his genealogical method by means of which we can at least hope to become unique, the avatars of this *gaya scienza*); Sade (for showing that the body is no less complex than the figures of speech, for speaking the passions, and for those terrifying silences through which are revealed the depths of our own monstrosity); Schreber (for creating yet another theology, fabricated from the psychological fragments of everyday life); Artaud (for having once and for all exorcized God from the unconscious, and for the poetry that this conflict produced); Klossowski (for having been the last to struggle with interiority, from which arose our discourse of phantasms and simulacra); Deleuze (for the purity and heterogeneity of surfaces); Bataille (for his praise of baseness, eroticism, perversion); Freud (for having understood all of the above, and none of the above.)

In an epoch marked by the transition from one totalizing power (the absolute monarchy) to another (the Terror), the rhetoric of silence proposed by the Abbé Dinouart bespoke a certain practical wisdom, despite the historical irony in which it was cast.[8] He intended his book as a guide which would aid us not to govern others (the ancient task of the rhetorical arts), but rather to escape the others' grasp (the mark of a new rhetoric.) Likewise, I do not want this present book to be a trap for the neuroses of others, nor a site for the return of the repressed. Rather, it should be the locus of an active forgetting; these texts should be enjoyed, used, forgotten. Here, rhetoric should serve as the incitement to think, write, speak within the very thickness of language, always opposed to the metaphysical deontologization of speech. The rhetorician (thinker, writer, reader) is to become an *"ingénieur de l'occasion,"* seeking not a fundamental language, but the very traces of immediacy inherent in all expression. Here, the *actio* of rhetoric is to be a sign of *disengagement,* where the other—with all of its differences, with all of its *barbarisms*—is left to speak.

Acknowledgments

"Possession and Dramatic Perversity" is a previously unpublished text.

"Impossible Sovereignty" was originally published as, "Impossible Sovereignty: Between *The Will to Power* and *The Will to Chance*" in *October* #36 (MIT Press, Spring 1986).

"A Logic of the Simulacrum" was previously published as, "A Logic of the Simulacrum, or The Anti-Roberte" in *Phantasm and Simulacra,* a special issue of *Art & Text* #18 (July 1985).

"A New History of the Passions" was originally published in *October* (MIT Press, 1989).

"Structures of Exchange, Acts of Transgression" is a previously unpublished text.

"Demented, Deoedipalized, Deconstructed" is a previously unpublished text.

"The Errant Text" first appeared as "Ideology and the Problem of Style: The Errant Text" in *Enclitic* #14 (Fall 1983; appeared in 1984).

"L'Amour fou, L'Amour unique" first appeared in *Art & Text* #20 (February-April 1986).

"The Other as Muse" was originally published as "The Other as Muse: On the Ontology and Aesthetics of Narcissism" in *Psychosis and Sexual Identity: Toward a Post-Analytic View of the Schreber Case,* eds. David Allison, Prado de Oliveira, Mark Roberts, Allen S. Weiss (Albany, State University of New York Press, 1988).

"Psychopompomania" first appeared in *Art Brut: Madness and Marginalia,* a special issue of *Art & Text* #27 (December-February 1988).

"Cartesian Simulacra" was originally published in *Persistence of Vision* #5 (1987).

"On the Art of Fascination" was originally published as, "An Eye for an I: On the Art of Fascination" in *SubStance* #51 (1986).

"Frampton's Lemma, Zorn's Dilemma" first appeared in *October* #32 (MIT Press, Spring 1985).

"Between the Sign of the Scorpion and the Sign of the Cross" was first published as, "Between the Sign of the Scorpion and the Sign of the Cross: *L'Age d'or*" in *Dada/Surrealism* #15 (1986); this essay was reprinted in *Dada and Surrealist Film*, ed. Rudolf E. Kuenzli (New York, Willis Locker & Owens, 1987).

(All articles have been revised.)

Part I

NIETZSCHE REDIVIVUS

1

Possession Trance and Dramatic Perversity

Dionysus arrives as a stranger, enigmatic, disquieting, contagious, spreading an epidemic of mania leading to impurity and death. That moment when tragedy was only chorus and not yet drama, when the god Dionysus was only imagined and not yet represented, witnessed a creative, participatory will already in the process of transfiguration from festival to art. Why, then, the need to *represent* the god, so that the audience, excited by the dithyrambic chorus, would see this masked figure as, "a visionary figure, born as it were from their own rapture,"[1] a rapture henceforth organized by the theatrical scenario? In becoming drama, a private excitation and passion is transformed into a public, communal vision or sign. But why was it Dionysus, whose epiphany is a function of sacrificial violence, who was so honored (and perhaps, ultimately, debased)?

Sacrifice is a form of communication, and a primal precondition for community. Within a theological system, the symbolic is inaugurated by the violence of sacrifice which transforms the body into a signifier, bound to circulate within a restricted economy of significative exchange. The restriction—the cognitive limitation—of such a system is determined by the relation between God and death, which is the foundation of value and meaning whereby all other signifiers in the system—expecially "man" and "woman"—receive their meaning and value. It is precisely this significative, hieratic organization that grounds the *natural order* of things, an "order" which dissimulates the general contradiction between the human and the divine. This relationship, this mystery principle of existence, demands a resolution, manifest in sacrilege as an attempt to transcend both the limits of individuality and the boundary between humanity and God.[2] Wisdom, thus, is a function of blasphemy, abomination, monstrosity, transgression and crimes against nature.

As Nietzsche asks, if gods exist, how can one not desire to become a god? The boundary between the human and the divine may be transgressed in two ways: (1) the individual becomes one with God (a mimetic, identificatory apotheosis—a condition of *being*); or, (2) one can encounter God in some manner (from the scopophilia of visionary experience to the sadistic horror of deicide—a condition of *having*.) Such transgressions, which Bataille recognizes as the summit of human existence, entail that combination of horror and delight, of anguish and ecstasy, characteristic of all fetishism.[3]

The Dionysiac festival, and its dramatization in Greek tragedy, provides one scenario whereby the spectator may assist in such transgression. The world of the stage is a manifestation, a vision, of the satyr chorus, "the Dionysian chorus which ever anew discharges itself in an Apollonian world of images."[4] Within this scenario, the reveler is transfigured into a satyr who participates in the violence of that mass hysteria whereby the *diasparagmos* of the god is effected. The function of the drama is to transform the state of Dionysian *intoxication* into an Apollonian *vision* or *dream*, to transform libido into sign. Sacrificial death transfigures the subject into object, the sign-maker into sign.

Bataille's work, accomplished in what he felt as community with Nietzsche—and perhaps even in identification with Nietzsche, since the parallel identifications of Bataille/Acéphale/Dionysus and Nietzsche/Dionysus entail the indentification of Bataille and Nietzsche) derives its major themes directly from the Nietzschean discourse on Dionysian intoxication. For Bataille, sovereignty is a function of excess, trangression, "an exhuberance of forces which leads to the maximum of tragic intensity."[5] Such transgressive exhuberance is manifest in eroticism, drunkenness, laughter, sacred sacrifice, poetry, and madness. Compare Nietzsche's text on Dionysiac frenzy from *The Will to Power*:

> The states in which we infuse a transfiguration and fullness into things and poetize about them until they reflect back our fullness and joy in life: sexuality; intoxication; feasting; spring; victory over an enemy, mockery; bravado; cruelty; the ecstasy of religious feeling. *Three* elements principally; *sexuality*,

> *intoxication, cruelty*—all belonging to the oldest *festal joys* of mankind, all also preponderate in the early "artist."[6]

The goal of such expenditure of libidinal energy, of such a will to power, is to attain the "whole man,"[7] by overcoming fragmented individuality; the *principium individuationis* is overcome within Dionysian frenzy.[8]

In the famous section of *Twilight of the Idols*, "Toward a Psychology of the Artist," Nietzsche assimilates these conditions of intoxication to the source of artistic creativity, where the indispensable element is frenzy:

> Frenzy must first have enhanced the excitability of the whole machine; else there is no art. All kinds of frenzy, however diversely conditioned, have the strength to accomplish this: above all, the frenzy of sexual excitement, this most ancient and original form of frenzy. Also the frenzy that follows all great cravings, all strong affects; the frenzy of feasts, contests, feats of daring, victory, all extreme movement; the frenzy of cruelty; the frenzy in destruction; the frenzy under certain meteorological influences, as for example the frenzy of spring; or under the influence of narcotics; and finally the frenzy of will, the frenzy of an overcharged and swollen will. What is essential in such frenzy is the feeling of increased strength and fullness. Out of this feeling one lends to things, one *forces* them to accept from us, one violates them—this process is called *idealizing*. Let us get rid of a prejudice here: idealizing does not consist, as is commonly held, in subtracting or discounting the petty and inconsequential. What is decisive is rather a tremendous drive to bring out the main features so that the others disappear in the process.
>
> In this state one enriches everything out of one's own fullness: whatever one sees, whatever one wills, is seen swelled, taut, strong, overloaded with strength. A man in this state transforms things until they mirror his power—until they are reflections of his perfection. This *having to* transform into perfection is—art. Even everything that he is not yet, becomes for him an accasion of joy in himself; in art man enjoys himself as perfection.
>
> What is the meaning of the conceptual opposites which I have introduced into aesthetics, *Apollinian* and *Dionysian*, both conceived as kinds of frenzy? The Apollinian excites the eye

> above all, so that it gains the power of vision. The painter, the sculptor, the epic poet are visionaries par excellence. In the Dionysian state, on the other hand, the whole affective system is excited and enhanced: so that it discharges all its means of expression at once and drives forth simultaneously the power of representation, imitation, transfiguration, transformation, and every kind of mimicking and acting. The essential feature here remains the ease of metamorphosis, the inability *not* to react (similar to certain hysterical types who also, upon any suggestion, enter into *any* role). It is impossible for the Dionysian type not to understand any suggestion; he does not overlook any sign of an affect; he possesses the instinct of understanding and guessing in the highest degree, just as he commands the art of communication in the highest degree. He enters into any skin, into any affect: he constantly transforms himself.[9]

Dionysus is the body marked by difference, disorder, the unformed, disintegration, forgetting; Apollo is the body traced by the Gestalt of "good form," by identity, order, memory.

Note that in the *Birth of Tragedy* the tragic chorus is understood as, "the mirror in which the Dionysian man contemplates himself,"[10] while in the later generic aestheticization of the figure of Dionysus (*Twilight of the Idols; The Will to Power*) Dionysian intoxication is the state in which, through art, "man enjoys himself as perfection." Here, *narcissistic autofiguration is contemporaneous with mimetic communication*: the distiction between self and other is effaced. In Greek tragedy, communication and community are inaugurated by the sacrifice of the god Dionysus within a ritualistic mimetic ceremony; through the Dionysian frenzy of the artist, communication is a function of sacrificing the ego within an expressive mimesis, a metamorphosis of the self. The origin of drama is the epidemic loss of self and transformation into alterity.

In an early text, the "Nietzschean Chronicle," Bataille—identifying Nietzsche with Dionysus just as Nietzsche himself did at the moment of the onset of his madness—conflates the figures of Dionysus and Apollo. Writing of *The Birth of Tragedy*, Bataille claims that, "The very first sentences of Nietzsche's message come from 'realms of *dream* and *intoxication*.' The entire message is expressed by one name: *DIONYSUS*."[11] By reducing the Apollonian to the Dionysian, he also conflates their respective characteristics, in claiming that Dionysus, "demands that a *brilliant will* return the earth to the divine accuracy of the dream."[12] (This in turn reduces the Dionysian to the Apollonian.) Thus Bataille has Dionysus appear in the guise of Apollo, an ironic, hyperbolic instance of representing Dionysus as the god of misunderstanding. Identity is always mistaken identity: identification is thus always false, tragic; possession by Dionysus is demonic, leading to the loss of self-identity, to madness.

In *Sur Nietzsche*, consistent with this earlier misidentification of Dionysus, Bataille writes:

> I believe that we must, in this sense, invert the meaning of the Eternal Return. It is not the promise of infinite repetitions that tears one apart, but rather the fact that the moments grasped in the immanence of the Return suddenly appear as ends. It must not be forgotten that in all systems those instants are envisioned and assigned as means. Every moral system says: "let every instant of your life be *motivated*." The Return *demotivates* the instant, freeing life from ends, and thereby begins by ruining life. The Return is the dramatic mode and the mask of the whole man; it is the desert of the man whose every instant is henceforth unmotivated.[13]

Insofar as the Eternal Return appears to Bataille in the "dramatic mode," it remains a function of representation—of Apollonian formalism. The sovereign, demotivated subject is indeed transformed, but it is nevertheless asserted as *dramatis persona*. As such, it remains a symbol, the mere simulacrum of subversive, transgressive demotivation.

Finally, one might add that this reading is prefigured in an earlier text, Bataille's "The Obelisk:"

> What Nietzsche experienced when his thoughts suddenly resulted in the ecstatic vision of the Eternal Return cannot be compared to the feelings habitually linked to what passes for profound reflection. For the object of the intellect here exceeds the categories in which it can be represented, to such a point that as soon as it is represented it becomes an object of ecstasy—the object of tears, the object of laughter . . . The *toxic* character of the "return" is even of such great importance that, if it were set aside for an instant, its formal content might appear empty.[14]

Clearly, the celebration of creativity and ecstasy beyond the limits of rational thought is founded upon *intoxication* as demonic possession by Dionysus. Bataille is absolutely correct in stressing the *toxic*, poisonous effects of this *intoxication*, of this delirium which demands catharsis. This is perfectly in accord with the dual nature of Dionysus, as examined by Marcel Detienne in his recent *Dionysos à ciel ouvert*.[15] Dionysus is a dual god, bearing both the illness of madness and the consequent cathartic purification. It is in this cathartic moment, the moment of passage from illness to cure, from delirium to understanding—the moment of solving the enigma—that we may locate the key to the tragic emotion.

To exceed the categories of representation—what Bataille sees as being the Eternal Return's effect upon thought—would be to reach that limit of sublimation called the *sublime*. But wouldn't such an aesthetic be diametrically opposed to Bataille's *desublimatory* ontology? Is not the "hypertrophy of the impossible"[16] of which Bataille speaks yet another term for the enigma of existence revealed in the Nietzschean enunciation of the Eternal Return, which in turn may reveal the inability to surpass the paralogisms of Kantian epistemology?

It would seem that this need for dramatization, objectification, and representation is a sign of weakness of will. Yet isn't such a weakness, (albeit, in the context of Bataille's writings of the period, the manifestation of a decisive political position) at the very core of Bataille's project? And isn't a weak, passive will precisely a necessary precondition for the state of possession, of intoxication?

Bataille insists that Nietzsche misunderstood the relation between sovereignty and the will to power, insofar as, "Sovereignty is rebellion; it is not the exercise of power. Authentic sovereignty refuses . . . ."[17] Bataille renounces the idealizing willfullness whereby we transform things, the world, ourselves. Rather than a *will to power*, he insists upon the *will to chance*, which is a counterwill, entailing the renunciation of volition. The ultimate limit of this hypertrophy is the death of the subject, a sacrifice which gives "an obsessive value to communal life,"[18] even if this community be without a leader, of those "bound together by the obsessive image of a tragedy." Such death, modelled on Dionysian ritual, is both the ultimate test of sovereignty and the ultimate joy. But are not the will to power and the will to chance both constituent factors of such a Dionysian aesthetic and ethic? Is not the Dionysian aesthetic itself already rift in two, between a reactive expression of mimesis, representation, figuration, *and* a transformative, creative process of metamorphosis, literally of *disfiguration*?[19] And this obtains *before* the manifestation of the Apollonian supplement to Dionysian excitation.

In *Music and Trance*, Gilbert Rouget exhaustively examines how possession is fundamentally a theatrical phenomenon: music does not cause the trance, but rather serves as one of the conditions that forms the context in which possession trance is effected and becomes meaningful. Possession trance signifies a change of identity, recognizable by means of a collective representation, and marked by a stylization of gesture. Such gestures signify the particular god which possesses the subject, in conjunction with the music serving as the god's "theme." Possession is thus a "theatricalization of identificatory behavior;"[20] the music associated with possession trance is identificatory, and not simply emotional, invocatory or incantatory. It is thus a socializing factor, a mode of ritual integration of the individual into the community and the cosmos.

Analyzing the relations between music and trance in ancient Greece, Rouget shows that Plato already recognized this function: ". . . telestic *mania* as described by Plato is indeed possession trance in which the subject identifies himself with the god possessing him."[21] Yet the expression, the manifestation, of such possession in dance occurs in two major modes:[22] (1) an *abstract style*, void of any figurative function, representing nothing but the dancers' passions; hence a convulsive, frenzied sort of "*danse furieuse;*" and (2) a *figurative style* of hysterical mimesis, executing symbolic and imitative gestures of the possessive gods; hence a stylized, collective form of communication through identification.

The symbolic efficacy of possession trance, integrating the self into community and cosmos, is a function of *both* types of dance, such that possession serves a therapeutic role by "curing" the subject of the malaise of individuality. As Detienne claims, it is kinesatherapy as homeopathy.[23] Ecstatic joy is placed in the service of community.

This difference of style is also manifest, as we have seen, in Nietzsche's model of Dionysian aesthetics, in the division between Dionysian and Apollonian aesthetics (this division being but a projection of the already rift being of Dionysus himself.) This is the difference between disfiguration and figuration, between metamorphosis and representation. Consistent with Rouget's analysis, in *The Birth of Tragedy* Nietzsche already maintains that possession by Dionysus entails a fusion of the subject with primal being, where music itself is a copy of the primal unity, its very sign.[24]

> In the Dionysian dithyramb man is incited to the greatest exaltation of all his symbolic faculties . . . The essence of nature

> is now to be expressed symbolically; we need a new world of symbols; and the entire symbolism of the body is called into play . . . .[25]

Vigorously opposed to the Apollonian dicta of the Delphic oracle—"Know thyself" and "Everything in moderation"—Dionysus teaches that, "Excess revealed itself as truth. Contradiction, the bliss born of pain, spoke out from the very heart of nature."[26] Yet, as we have seen, this contradiction is double: the difference that separates Dionysus from his Apollonian projection (two modes of frenzy) is already marked out as the contradiction within Dionysus himself. Thus, as Detienne emphasizes, we must contrast *Dionysus of Thebes* (bringing misunderstanding, madness, murder, and finally catharsis) with *Dionysus of Attica* (who is prudent, benevolent, and who introduces viniculture to the region). Homologizing these observations, these contradictions, with Rouget's analysis of the two modes of possession trance, we may conclude that in possession the body functions symbolically either as the *pure expression of libido* or as an *identificatory sign.* We find ourselves once again within the classic antinomy of modern thought: the body as *subject* or the body as *object;* the body *producing signs* or the body *acting as sign.* The non-sense of the body, reacting to pure contingency, gives rise to the *will to chance;* while the mimetic, identificatory function of sacrifice and loss founds the symbolic and the communal, giving rise to the *will to power.* Both modes of the will are manifest in possession rites, through the different apparitions of Dionysus.

The people of Corinth celebrated the apparition of Dionysus in his duality (madness/catharsis) by presenting in the agora two absolutely identical statues of gilded wood decorated with vermillion, distinguished only by their names: *Dionysus Baccheios* and *Dionysus Katharsios* or *Lysios.*[27] To forget the expiatory effects of the latter is to portend the worst. Perhaps as an allegory of madness as exile from the self, we might consider the fate of Cadmus, who was condemned by Dionysus in punishment for the sins of his descendants. Exiled, lost amongst the barbarians, he was doomed to return at the head of a barbarian army and, ironically, desecrate the most sacred places of the Greeks: the altars of the gods and the tombs of his ancestors. This culminated in the highest sacrilege: the pillage of the Panhellenic temple of Apollo.[28] The vengence of Dionysus reaches the extreme limit of destroying the sign of that other divinity—Apollo—which, centuries later, Nietzsche will recognize as the very projection of Dionysus. Can we not see in this tale a parable of Nietzsche's own fate? Guilty of his epoch's deicide, a scapegoat, he falls into madness, oblivious of the cathartic possibilities of *Dionysus Katharsios.* Apollo forgotten, there remains only Dionysus the Crucified; there remain only the empty gestures of one we call mad, one who perhaps was only nostalgic for a different order of things, for the possibility of sacred sacrifice, for that different joy which marked the origin of our culture.

2

Impossible Sovereignty

The predilection of strength for questions for which no one today has the courage; the courage for the *forbidden;* the predestination to the labyrinth. An experience of seven solitudes.

Friedrich Nietzsche

He has no need to erect a labyrinth when the whole world already is one.

Jorge Luis Borges

Strange gods, which must be forgotten so that we may live; strange obsessions, for which we are prepared to sacrifice ourselves; strange desires which determine our discourse. While every god bears witness to that transcendence which pervades our existence, what god isn't somehow blasphemous, what god isn't somehow a provocation? Yet occasionally a god appears which repudiates the reduction of human existence to transcendence. One such god was evoked by Georges Bataille during the period of his rupture with the Surrealist group, whose "pretentious idealist aberrations" he contested with a base, anti-idealist, nonteleological materialism that was to remain central to his thought. The god evoked in this project, in "Le bas matérialisme et la gnose" (1930), is characterized as an "acephalic god crowned with two animal heads," which appears on a third or fourth century Gnostic stone, an abraxas. This symbolizes, for Bataille, matter as an active principle, whose existence is autonomous from spiritual being. "Base matter is exterior and foreign to ideal human aspirations and refuses to let itself be reduced to the great ontological machines which result from those aspirations."[1] This acephalic god is thus, within Bataille's mythopoeia, that curious oxymoron of an atheological god which denies the transcendental, logocentric formations presented by Western deities.

The acephalic god was to reappear six years later in Bataille's work, as the central figure of the journal *Acéphale*, founded by Bataille and Pierre Klossowski, and mainly devoted to the work of Nietzsche. Yet it was to appear transformed: the new Acéphale is truly headless, the Janus-like heads of the Gnostic god having been suppressed. Such a deletion is a sign of willful forgetting: Janus, the god of origins and transitions, is a guarantor of identity and continuity; his elimination entails the exclusion of any quest for origins and the eradication of all identity.

The second Acéphale, conceived by Bataille and drawn by André Masson, is a headless human form; the head reappears as a skull, a death's-head, in the place of the genitals; in its raised right hand, where the earlier god held a pomegranate, is a flaming heart; its raised left hand bears a sword; and the abdomen is opened to reveal the intestines in the form of a labyrinth. The Acéphale is a contestation of the Platonic body politic, where reason, seated in the head, rules the lower spirited and appetitive forces of the body. It is also a condemnation of the ideal form and perfect proportions of the human figure as the measure of all things, celebrated since the classic age of Greece, especially during the Renaissance. The Acéphale is, rather, pure body, irreducible to idealizing, intellective operations; headless, it lacks identity, and thus reveals its universality in a negative manner, where all identity is false identity, mere fiction; and, headless, it is also speechless, so it escapes the ontotheological rule of Logos.

The living, speaking head, transformed into a death's-head, displaced to the genitals, turns the Acéphale into a *memento mori*, confounding life, death, and eroticism as the excessive limits of human existence, limits inscribed upon the base materiality of the body. "The death of god is produced not as a metaphysical debasement (bearing on the common measure of being), but as the absorption of a life avid with a joy imperative in the face of the weighty animality of death," he writes earlier in "Sacrifices."[2]

As a pomegranate, which is said to have sprung from the heart of Dionysus (with whom the later Acéphale is equated), the object in the right hand of the earlier gnostic god is a sign of death as well as of eternal rebirth. Presented as the flaming heart held by the later Acéphale, it evokes the mystical theology of the sacred heart, where the desires of the flesh are transformed into mystical passion. Only for Bataille, it is conversely the sacred which is made manifest in the excesses of the flesh. This is a sign of libidinal wastefulness, where desire is materialized and expended, where sexual disorder and death decompose the coherent forms of life.

The sword in the left hand signifies violence and power, which makes possible that sacrifice, that self-mutilation, that *diasparagmos* of the god (Acéphale, Dionysus, Christ) by means of which the other symbols gain their significance, and by means of which a community of believers may be founded. It is the sword which decapitates the god, cuts out his sacrificial heart, and lacerates the abdomen to reveal the labyrinth of the bowels within. While Dionysus was torn apart by the Maenads, the Acéphale sacrificed itself, beheaded itself; the will is turned back upon itself, interiorized, which is for Bataille a precondition of sovereignty.

The death of God, which for Nietzsche entailed the transvaluation of all values, secured for Bataille the foundations of an atheological thought. In the Catholic Eucharist, the separation of the blood and the flesh of Christ serves as a sign of His death; this sacrifice is a precondition of the universal internalization of spiritual values. The dogma of transsubstantiation and the sacrament of the Eucharist reveals how the Spirit is perpetually present and subject to interiorization and appropriation. Klossowski shows how, quite to the contrary of this dogma, Bataille's atheology proposes a sort of counter-sacrament,[3] what Bataille parodically speaks of as hyperchristianity where a "generalized incarnation" is effected by means of the "fall of the universal into humanity" and the fall of humanity into sheer chance. But the Acéphale, whose blood (heart) is also separated from its flesh, is a suicide, a monster, which indicates not a transcendental divine presence, but rather the very limit of interiority: death. It is this death which effects the impossible communion (of Bataille and Nietzsche; of the members of the secret society of Acéphale; of Bataille with his readers) of those without community, the communion of sovereign individuals.[4] Only by risking the self, by exposing it to the exigencies of alterity, can this community be achieved; yet the self is ultimately thrown back upon its own life, its own body, as the guarantor of its sacrifice. Within a theological system, the symbolic is inaugurated by the violence of sacrifice which transforms the body into a signifier, whose destiny is to circulate within a restricted economy of exchange; conversely, in an atheology, the violence of sacrifice disrupts the symbolic by offering the body as non-sense, as the nexus of possibility and mortality, hence as pure contingency.

The paths of chance are indicated in the very center of the figure of the Acéphale, where the intestines in the form of a labyrinth are revealed. The labyrinth, equivalent to the Nietzschean sign of the Earth, is an all-encompassing signifier, embracing every possibility from the chaotic to the structured, chance to necessity, the sacred to the profane, life to death, as well as every contradiction. It is pure difference itself, hence it is no longer of the symbolic register, which collapses as the labyrinth absorbs all possible symbols and signifiers and offers nothing in return, nothing in exchange. It collapses under the weight of the totality of the signifieds which it assumes, destroying willful intentionally and announcing intensive libidinality.

Appropriately, the labyrinth is represented in an indefinite variety of forms. In, "The *Dodécadédale,* or in Praise of Heuristics,"[5] Pierre Rosenstiehl is correct in claiming that the labyrinth is neither symbol, myth, nor metaphor, since it is too charged a figure, a sort of black-box which generates numerous metaphors. Yet his demonstration is antithetical to these conclusions: he investigates only a specific type of single-line labyrinth, the *dodécadédale,* a form common to Christian theological symbolism, even if its precise meaning is not determinable. This is a labyrinth of stable form, with characteristic and specific rules of the organization, doubling and alternation of its ribs, its paths. Yet as such, it remains an oppositional and diacritical system, and is thus fully describable and calculable. It is an object. As must be the case for all single-line labyrinths, there is only one path to follow, and one inevitably arrives at its center. It is impossible to get lost in it, and the return is no more difficult than the quest. Thus it is hardly terrifying or enigmatic, and is at best an indication of difficulty and perseverance, where risk is at a minimum and chance is eliminated.

In *Le livre des labyrinthes,*[6] Paolo Santarcangeli provides a taxonomy of labyrinths which more fully documents the variety of possible forms: (a) natural, artificial, mixed; (b) fortuitous, accessory, intentional; (c) unique path or mutliple paths; (d) geometric or irregular; (e) fixed, irregular or mixed schema; (f) rectangular, rounded or mixed turns; (g) rectangular, circular or of another form; (h) symmetrical or mixed; (i) compact, diffuse or mixed; (j) acentric, monocentric or polycentric; (k) bi-dimensional or tri-dimensional; (l) simple or complex branchings (with all of the possible inherent complexities of crossings, knots, returns and impasses); (m) one or many centers; (n) one or many entries.

As a final degree of complexity, Gaston Bachelard writes of dynamic labyrinths, and Denis Hollier describes a particularly Dionysian mode of such dynamism by claiming that labyrinthine space is drunken space.[7] How do we situate ourselves in this labyrinth of labyrinths? Who among us will serve as *haruspex* and examine the sacrificed Acéphale?

The labyrinth exposed as the bowels of Acéphale (a labyrinth which, in stylized form, served as the logo for the journal *Acéphale*) is a static, acentric, one-line labyrinth. It signifies a transformational system whereby what enters from above is changed into base matter, excrement, the ultimate anti-idealist symbol. Such a metamorphosis signifies materialism as scatology, where the end product is nothing but a sign of decay, of death. The intestine as labyrinth proffers a miasma; out of its chaos, its pure heterogeneity, meaning is generated, but a meaning which is nondialectical and totally insubordinate. In an earlier article, "L'anus solaire," Bataille explains that:

> Since sentences circulate in brains engaged in reflection, a total identification had been instituted, since with the aid of a *copula* one thing is connected to another by every sentence; and everything would be visibly connected if the trace left by Ariadne's thread, leading thought within its own labyrinth, would be fully disclosed in a single glance.[8]

The Ariadne's thread is here Bataille's own notes and texts, which serve as the copula connecting a community of friends and readers. And the labyrinth serves as a sort of linguistic black box, within which thought (and by extension the self) is continuously transformed, and where the very structure of thought is catastrophic, led to affirm the sovereignty of the self by moving from excess to excess within the limits of experience: eroticism, drunkenness, laughter, sacred sacrifice and poetry.

As Blanchot claims, "To be tied to Acéphale is to abandon oneself and to give oneself: *to give oneself without retrun to an abandon without limits*."[9] This Acéphale, which is more of a passion than a project (yet which gave rise to both Bataille's and Klossowski's readings of Nietzsche), is in fact identified with the self, with Bataille.

> He reunites Birth and Death in the same eruption. He is neither man nor god. He is not me but he is more me than myself; his abdomen is the daedelus in which he himself loses his way,

> misleads me along with him, and within which I rediscover myself as him, that is to say as a monster.[10]

Such monstrosity is the sign of a radical break with the rationalist tradition; it is a sign of the excessive, the incommunicable, the different. It signifies what was to become for Bataille the radical sovereignty of the inner experience, the total man. This monster is the self which must be sacrificed within the labyrinth. Is it, perhaps, identifiable with the overman?

Klossowski will discover such a "total monstrosity" in the texts of D.A.F. Sade, a writer also of great importance to Bataille. Of particular interest is the manner in which Sade and Nietzsche serve as antipodes of discursive possibility: the Sadian project, a sort of "*Summa Pornographica*," is to overload and collapse the symbolic register by saying everything, in a pastiche of the *Encyclopedia;* for Nietzsche, as we shall see, the essential is unsayable.

Barthes claimed that "The labyrinth is the typical form of the nightmare," but it would be well to remember, as Bachelard shows, that it is also a typical form of the dream and reverie. In *La terre et les rêveries du repos* Bachelard relates the story of a schoolboy responding to the question, "What would you like to be when you grow up?":

> I would like to be a sewer worker. From my youngest childhood my dream was to be a sewer worker, which seemed to me a marvellous job. I imagined that I could traverse the entire world by means of those subterranean bowels. Starting from the Bastille I would be able to travel to the devil, and then reappear in China, Japan or in the Arab lands. I would be able to see the little drarfs, ghosts and goblins of the earth. I told myself that I would voyage through the earth. I imagined that there were treasures buried in those sewers, that I would make expeditions, that I would dig in the earth and one day return to my parents loaded with gold and precious stones, and I would be able to say that I am rich, and I will buy a magnificent castle with gardens.[11]

But the boy realized, and admitted, that in fact being a sewer worker is an extremely arduous and unhealthful life, and that his idea was more of a fairy tale than a realistic project for a profession. At that point he decided to choose another profession, and, as he says, "that of a book-dealer greatly seduced me." Indeed!

This tale of exchanging one labyrinth for another (the sewer for the library) is an allegory of sublimation, and could be the story of Bataille's life, he who was in fact a librarian and archivist by profession. As sewer or bowels, the labyrinth signifies the base materiality of existence, from whose miasma excrement is sublimated into valued objects. Hence the books to which both Bataille and this boy resigned their fates; the goal of the labyrinth is to transform that accursed waste matter into something of value, something of community. Ironically, despite his valorization of base materiality, Bataille couldn't help but write books.

The recognition of chance is the suicide of knowledge.

Night is a representation richer than being.
Chance arises from the night . . . .
Georges Bataille

Zarathustra, in his stillest hour, in his greatest solitude, dreamt a fearful dream in which his heart spoke to him without voice: "You know it, Zarathustra? You know it, Zarathustra, but you do not say it!"[12] What Zarathustra cannot bring himself to say, not even to himself, what is never directly enunciated, what is only alluded to, expressed obliquely, in dreams, whispers, feverish hallucinations, circumlocutions, silences and ellipses, is the enigma of the Eternal Return. In the deepest abyss of this nightmare, his heart no longer spoke, and he was surrounded by laughter: "Alas, how this laughter tore my entrails and slit open my heart!" Even the labyrinth of the entrails and the passions of the heart could no longer support this intensest emotion, this loftiest thought.

The Eternal Return, in an aberrant use of the conditional, is an enigma without solution; it is the fate of seeing life itself as an enigma. For Nietzsche, the Eternal Return is manifest as both the highest feeling and the highest thought.

(1) As the highest feeling, hence incommunicable, the Eternal Return bears a significative message: it can only be affirmed or denied.

(a) Denied, it is demonic, the spirit of negation, of *ressentiment*. It is the reactive sign of Being, entailing presence, limitation, determination, continuity, wholeness and identity. It is lived as the sick, neurotic body.

(b) Affirmed, it is godlike, Dionysian, the spirit of limitless affirmation, of joy. It is the active sign of Becoming, entailing chance, transgression, excess, discontinuity, fragmentation and difference. It is lived as the healthy, perverse body.

(2) As the highest thought, hence communicable, the Eternal Return presents an aporia, indicated in *The Will to Power* by contradictory characterizations. This aporia bears upon every moment of life, where the Eternal Return is the absolute floating signifier, able to bear any content. The Eternal Return is either:

> (a) "an infinite recurrence of identical cases," and as such is demonic, the desire for the continuity of presence through memory, a nostalgia for Being; *or*, it is:
> (b) a "selective principle," and as such it is Dionysian, the desire for difference through forgetting, a poetic, antimetaphysical thought.[13]

Ontologically, the difference between denial and affirmation, between the demonic and the Dionysian aspects of the Eternal Return, is the difference between a reified past and an aleatory future, between pathos and bathos, between theology and an atheological discourse. Following Nietzsche, such an atheological model was elaborated by two of the founders of *Acéphale*, Georges Bataille and Pierre Klossowski.[14]

The central theme of Klossowski's oeuvre is the loss of identity, the dissolution of the self. This is a direct result of the death of God: with the disappearance of God as the ontological guarantor of identity, the self becomes the scene of an indefinite series of identities and transformations. The soul must will other selves, traverse other identities; this can only be accomplished by means of willful, active forgetting, through which the self is willed as a fortuitous moment (and no longer as a continuous identity). This task is accomplished through the affirmation of the Eternal Return: the Eternal Return is the sign of the non-willed past rewilled as willed, which transforms self-identity by inaugurating a sovereign mastery over time and volition, precisely by willing one's own fortuitous existence. As such, it is the willing of difference, of the aleatory, which is ultimately incommunicable, since it is lived as pure intensity without intention. Communicable, meaningful enunciation is merely a reactive dissimulation of libidinal intensity. And yet, so that this Recurrence not be just one more determination of Being, the Eternal Return must be forgotten, along with the self which is lost. Thus the Eternal Return is essentially the possibility of possibility by being the forgetting of forgetting; otherwise it would be yet one more sign of the dialectical process instilled as memory.

The notions of *heterogeneity* and *sovereignty* guide Bataille's estimation and appropriation of Nietzsche's work. In order to escape the systematization and domination of rationality, the self must be fully lost in immanence in order to establish the whole man [*l'homme entier*] as a completely unsubordinated realm. As such, "the whole man is only a being where transcendence is abolished, from whom nothing is any longer separated: a bit guignol, a bit God, a bit mad . . . this is transparency."[15] The self is thus no longer subject, but sovereign. And communication is no longer a teleological activity, but rather a function of both love and evil where the relation between two beings is put entirely at risk, exposed to the vagaries of chance. (Community is thus founded upon the ruins of transcendence *and* the insufficiencies of interiority.) Such chance is the absolutely irreducible, irrational element of existence, outside of any possibly systematization or rationalization.

This distaste for systematization, apparent in the writings of both Nietzsche and Bataille, receives its most radical theoretical statement in Bataille's claim that, "My method, or rather my absence of method, is my life."[16] This sets the limit of interpretation as biographism: life itself as interpretation. Yet, insofar as all interpretation is mastery, sovereign interpretation is self-mastery. Thus Bataille criticizes Nietzsche's understanding of the will to power (which for Nietzsche is variously the essence of life, the essence of the world, and the essence of being; hence it is all-encompassing). Bataille claims that Nietzsche misunderstood the opposition between sovereignty and the will to power insofar as, "Sovereignty is rebellion, it is not the exercise of power. Authentic sovereignty refuses . . ."[17] For Bataille, the will, reduced to sovereignty and interiority, remains individual will.

This difference bears upon Bataille's rejection of the utility and appropriateness of the notion of the Eternal Return, which he feels to be totally inefficacious on the practical level: it can neither instill the sentiment of horror nor provoke the ecstasy which constitute the Eternal Return as the highest feeling. It can merely amplify such feelings if they already exist, but it cannot produce them; thus the Eternal Return is derivative of pregiven conditions. Reconsider the passage from *Sur Nietzsche* cited on page 7 of the previous chapter, stressing the manner in which the Eternal Return is a dramatic mode of demotivation, freeing each instant of life from all teleology.[18] Doesn't this indicate precisely Bataille's inability to forget the Eternal Return? Does not such a demotivation, such a giving oneself over to chance, necessitate the disruption of memory, which is the causal apparatus of the psyche? Insofar as the Eternal Return appears to Bataille in the "dramatic mode," it remains a function of representation. As such, it is transformed into a sign—into the mere simulacrum of subversive demotivation—which transfigures the subject but nevertheless asserts it as *dramatis persona.*

For Klossowski, the affirmation of the Eternal Return entails the loss of self-identity, the traversal of an indefinite number of identities. Thus, at its limit, it is a sign of madness. For Bataille, the affirmation of the Eternal Return should entail sovereignty, the inauguration of the whole man, of a pure inner experience. It is thus a sign of perversion. Klossowski demands the loss of the self; Bataille demands the self as loss. Yet in both cases, the Eternal Return signifies a unique, heterogeneous, ultimately incommunicable experience, which is an enrichment of the "here and now" through the affirmation of chance.

If I wish it, to laugh is to think, but it is a sovereign moment.

Transcendence must be ruined by laughter.
George Bataille

"Alas, how this laughter tore my entrails and slit open my heart." The tragic import of this laughter that Zarathustra heard directed at himself is that it meant that he was unable to affirm the Eternal Return. This fearful, mocking laughter would be transformed into a secret, joyful, excessive laughter only at the moment the Eternal Return is affirmed.

Psychoanalytic theory teaches us that laughter is a sudden release, a free discharge, of psychic energy which had previously been cathected but which is now unusable. The pleasure (and note that not all laughter is pleasurable) inherent in such laughter is part of a psychic economy, where the expenditure of energy released by the laugh, in partially overcoming a defense, equals the energy previously cathected to the now superfluous inhibition. Thus such laughter is a sort of waste product, an "accursed part" of the psychic organization where through a desublimatory process pleasure is once again attained from a corporeal process. Yet only the child's laughter is a laughter of pure pleasure; adult laughter is always restricted by inhibitory structures, by the exigencies of the reality principle.[19]

(Hence the importance of the child in *Zarathustra*, as the symbol of the final metamorphosis towards the overman.)

In one of his earliest works, "L'Anus solaire," Bataille claims that, "everyone is conscious of the fact that life is parodic and that the world lacks an interpretation."[20] And he later reaffirms, in his *Méthode de méditation*, that, "The essential is aberration, the greatest comedy . . ."[21] But here he no longer reduces existence solely to the comic, to laughter: meditation is both a limitless comedy and a limitless tragedy. Remember, after all, that the sight of the Acéphale causes both laughter and anguish.

Laughter is one of the modes of sovereign conduct, a moment in which rationality is exceeded by a gratuitous affirmation of life, of contingency, of the body. It effects a rupture with thought, within ideality; as Bataille exclaims in his provocations against the Surrealists, laughter is scatological even though it is a nonmaterial, and thus ideological, mode of excretion. (Scatology is equivalent to heterology: marking the elimination, dissimulation and even repression of excessive, wasteful and nonproductive elements.) As pure elimination and waste, laughter is a mode of nonknowledge, the adequate but meaningless sign of an incommunicable inner experience. As such, it defies rationality:

> From the moment that the effort of rational comprehension ends in contradiction, the practice of intellectual scatology demands the dejection of unassimilable elements, which in common sense means that a burst of laughter is the only imaginable and definitively terminal outcome, and not the means, of philosophical speculation.[22]

Such a materialism, a scatology, is thus non- or hyper-dialectical: its principle is not organization by return, exchange and logic; it is rather a mode of disorganization by means of excess, waste and irrationality. The Nietzschean *"gai savoir"* is really a *"gai non-savoir"*.

Klossowski was later to relate the idea of the world as parody directly to the Eternal Return, which is not a classical philosophical doctrine, but rather:

> a *simulacrum of a doctrine*, whose very parodic character accounts for *hilarity* as an attribute of existence, sufficing unto itself when laughter bursts forth within the depths of the full truth . . .[23]

The very affirmation of the Eternal Return as parodic, comic, as the source of laughter, indicates sovereign thought, and marks

Bataille and Klossowski as sovereign thinkers (since their affirmation of the Eternal Return is joyous, and not tragic.) As laughter eliminates excessive elements from the psychic politic, the Eternal Return as a selective process eliminates excessive, sovereign individuals from the general community, from the herd. Sovereignty is exclusion. This rupture is gauged by the rejection of transcendence, concomitant with the assumption of inner experience as the guarantor of one's own fate. If sovereignty is to be radical, it must be its own necessity; yet, because of the very insufficiency of the interior experience, because of its propensity to excess, to ecstasy (that going beyond oneself common to both the formation of community and that special community known as mysticism),[24] sovereignty is essentially groundless, without a true foundation or origin. Only by making chance its necessity can the sovereign subject escape becoming just one more moment within universal reason and history.

After all, you know that noise murders thought . . .

Friedrich Nietzsche

Sovereignty is silent or fallen.

. . . I am only silence, the universe is silence.

Georges Bataille

Speaking to Zarathustra, Life herself says, " . . . you think, O Zarathustra, I know it, of how you want to leave me soon.' 'Yes,' I answered hesitatingly, 'but you also know—and I whispered something into her ear, right through her tangled foolish tresses. 'You *know* that, O Zarathustra? Nobody knows that.'"[25] What this ellipsis, this silence, does not permit us to hear is the enunciation of the Eternal Return.

There are many modes and motives of silence: prohibitions, disavowal, secrets, foreclosure, autism, rhetoric, forgetting, death. Nietzsche's analysis of conceptuality shows how concepts entail the reduction of difference to identity, to schematic and thus calculable, controllable forms. Concepts instill a communal, collective memory in the subject. Hence for Nietzsche forgetting is a precondition of sovereign existence. But even more basic is the fact that forgetting is the very precondition of presence. While memory is necessary for thought, forgetting is necessary for existence itself; we have seen how these two contradictory conditions of life are marked out within the reactive and active modes of the Eternal Return.

The inner experience (what Klossowski will later refer to as the phantasm), being totally heterogeneous, is thus essentially incommunicable. Yet, insofar as this sovereign inner experience is insufficient unto itself, it becomes manifest in an excessive expression; it thus entails a type of communication, of community. The irony is that if such experience is to be fully heterogeneous, one must either fall into silence or else risk betraying it by communication. This is precisely the risk which is apparent in Bataille's writing, in those texts which he crafts in the most intimate form, the intellectual journal (most notably his *magnum opus, La somme athéologique,* which includes *Sur Nietzsche.*) And throughout his work he utilized a rhetorical expression operating as the solution of this paradox: the *ellipsis.*

The ellipsis is the fortuitous or intentional omission of a linguistic element. Like the labyrinth, it can signify the entire gamut of possible meanings: from that where the meaning of the suppressed term is evident, to that of the vagueness and contradiction inherent in amphibological constructions, to total agrammatism.

The role of such linguistic disruptions (as well as their relation to the enunciation of the Eternal Return) may be considered in relation to Roman Jakobson's psycho-linguistic investigation of the two principles of mental functioning, as their breakdown is expressed by the two basic forms of aphasia: similarity disorders and contiguity disorders.[26]

(1) *Similarity disorders* affect the lexical selection of linguistic units and their possible substitutions and exchanges. In such disorders, the meaning of a word is dependent upon its context, upon syntax: a word out of context has no meaning. It is thus a dependent speech, whose organizational principle is external metonymic relations. This mode of discourse is *a fortiori* determined by deictics, by the pronominal shifter "I," since the shifter determines the absolute context of the enunciation. Given this centering, such a disorder entails the impossibility of translation, tautology, metaphor and metalanguage; it ends in the failure to shift from the index or icon to a corresponding symbol. Thus sentences originate as elliptical sequals to previous sentences, permitting no interpretive function. Such is the only example of a truly private language, a pure ideolect.

(2) *Contiguity disorders* affect the syntactic rules of organizing words into sentences. In such disorders, words bear their own meanings, and syntactic order tends to disintegrate. The organizational principle of such speech is internal metaphoric relations. Thus the pronominal shifters are lost first, since they are most dependent upon syntactic

order and external relations. This disorder leads to chaotic word order, to the use of monoremes (one word sentences), to the disintegration of words into phonemes, and ultimately to its most extreme form, *aphasia universalis,* the complete loss of language, silence.

Bataille's use of the ellipsis may be considered in these terms, as expressing the paradox of the inner experience. In "La nudité," which is the third part of *Méthode de méditation*, we find:

> .. ..
>
> .. .. .. this, however, is the *instant* .. ..
>
> .. ..
>
> .. this, present, neither my absence nor me, neither death nor light—and my absence and me, death and light—a slight laugh rises within me like the sea, it prodigiously fills the absence. Whatever is—IS TOO MUCH.[27]

Here, in the total nudity of excessive erotic effusion, the narrator (in a presumedly autobiographical moment) expresses the impossibility of the present: the instant is too full, encompassing the ultimate, practically Manichean, conditions of existence. This is homologous with similarity disorders, in which the actual possibilities given by the existential context determine the impossibility of symbolic expression. This inner experience is expressed by both the silence of an ellipsis and by a heterogeneous expletive, the laugh; yet it remains unsayable. The excessive character of Being—whatever is is too much—entails the determination of expression by external existence; the self is manifest in its ambiguous, contradictory existence.

In *Madame Edwarda,* the narrator describes his experience in a brothel:

> .. ..
>
> .. ..
>
> .. ..
>
> .. ..
>
> .. ..
>
> .. ..
>
> .. ..
>
> .. ..
>
> .. ..
>
> .. ..

> .. .. the mirrors which covered the walls, and of which the ceiling itself was made, multiplied the animal image of a coupling; at the slightest motion, our shattered hearts were opened to the emptiness where our infinite reflections were lost.[28]

Here, also in a moment of erotic effusion, the instant is again too full—but not with contradiction. Rather, the determination of the self is impossible, since the "I" is lost in an endless series of specular presences which produce icons, metaphors, of the self. This is homologous with contiguity disorders, in which the deictic order disintegrates, leading to an expression of the chaos of existence, which is ultimately unsayable, thus resulting in silence. The self is multiplied, manifest in its insufficient existence.

The Eternal Return (which seems to entail a sort of *aphasia universalis* since it is ultimately inexpressible), can be understood according to this schema of language disorders and the dual function of language. (1) As "an infinite recurrence of identical cases," the Eternal Return is homologous with similarity disorders, where the external metonymic relations rule the organization of linguistic entities. This manifestation of the Eternal Return indicates the desire for the dialectical continuity of past with present, and thus entails the determination of self-identity, of the grammatical function of the "I." Hence the rule of a system whose content is determined by presence, by contiguity. (2) As a "selective process," the Eternal Return is homologous with contiguity disorders, where metaphoric systems of substitution rule the organization of linguistic entites. This manifestation of the Eternal Return indicates the desire for discontinuity, the assumption of chance, and thus entails the loss of self-identity. Hence the rule of a system whose content is governed by the excessive move towards absence.

Normal mental operations necessitate that neither the contiguity nor the similarity function breaks down. Similarly, the authentic experience of the Eternal Return necessitates the recognition of its two aspects, the repetitive and the selective, the tragic and the joyous. While it must be affirmed as joyous, the tragic is always present as its horizon. There is no adequate, unequivocal expression of the Eternal Return, of sovereign existence, of inner experience. There is no adequate metaphorization of heterogeneity, no possible rationalization of chance. Only silence and its textual correlate, the ellipsis, indicate these secret, idiosyncratic events and passions.

In the place of a "sociology," a doctrine of *formations of sovereignty.*

Friedrich Nietzsche

Nietzsche went mad. Screams, laughter, silences: these were the modes of expression which remained. Was this madness the manifestation or the contradiction of the Eternal Return? If the Eternal Return is a contestation of the reality principle, a restructuring of experience according to libidinal difference, then isn't madness the limit case of such a reconstitution?; Is this madness entailed by the Eternal Return perhaps the transvaluation of all values which Nietzsche sought? In either case, because of the very incommunicability of sovereign inner experience, its traces serve as a radical, contestatory practice, where *mathesis universalis* is disrupted by a *poesis particularis.*

For Nietzsche, thinking is an arbitrary fiction, the false sign of an equally false "inner" experience. Thought and enunciation merely indicate, abstract, a few elements from an infinitely complex set of events, which he designates either as the "will to power" or as its major manifestation, the body. "Everything that enters consciousness as 'Unity' is already tremendously complex: we always have only a semblance of unity. The phenomenon of the body is the richer, clearer, more tangible phenomenon. . ."[29] Thus in the Nietzschean body politic, the homogeneity of the ego dissimulates the heterogeneity of the body; the ego, a function of language, organizes the cathexes, manifestations and expressions of the libido.

We may chart these expressions by positing a discursive triangle, the apexes of which are speech, silence, and the interjections of screams or laughter. This schema may aid in ascertaining the forms of heterogeneity of the inner experience, as well as the manner in which this experience is dissimulated by reactive social and psychological formations. Thus each apex may designate either a reactive, repressive mode of expression, or an active, seditious mode of expression. *Speech* may be a function of Logos, where rational compositions serve as cultural appropriation, *or* speech may serve a revolutionary, contestatory role by internally rupturing the structures of Logos at the very points of its own contradicitions; *screams* and *laughter* may be reactive phenomena, resulting from the neurotic exigencies of life, *or* they may serve as rebellious eruptions of corporeal energy, heterogeneous outbursts of expropriation, where Logos is disrupted by the libido; *silence* may be the zero-degree noiselessness of death, where life itself is betrayed, *or* silence may be that moment where sovereignty is elliptically expressed as incommunicable inner experience.

The cultural production of meaning entails the sublimation of libidinal intensity into intentional signifaction, whereby intentional significations are organized within a calculable, hence controllable, system of meaning. Meaning is thus the reduction of intensity to intentionality; the shifting termini of libidinal cathexes are systematized and expressed by the stable relata of intentional experience (for example, within the classical phenomenological relation between noesis and noema.)

The Nietzschean genealogical procedure reverses this sublimatory process; its goal is to reveal the multiplicity of the body which is concealed and repressed by the ego. Such a genealogy must disclose the juncture between the singular position of the body and universal history, thus accounting for those necessities and accidents according to which the fiction of the self is formed. Thus genealogy is a mode of desublimation, whereby intentional meanings are decomposed into their libidinal components, where linguistic unity is revealed as the pretext for the regulation of the body. In each case, what must be determined is whether a given expression is the manifestation of a creative phantasm or the symptom of a psychopathological reaction.

Genealogy, for Foucault, entails "counter-memory," an active forgetting which is a movement towards unknowing, where the silent but excessive articulations of the body with other bodies are effected. All interpretation is essentially periphrastic of silence; the body is the ultimate referent of all expression, the foundation of all sublimation; the body itself is expressed by every ellipsis. But not the body of the Acéphale, a minor god already forgotten: the bodies in question are always those of our parents and lovers, our torturers and educators, and ultimately our own. The inner experience is my own, but it is an interiority which is charted on the surfaces of my body and in the the trajectories of my gestures; genealogy is the topology of those surfaces and of the manner in which they become symbolic elements within systems of communication and exchange. In the end, genealogy reconstitutes the body as chance, that richest phenomenon, to the detriment of Being, that poorest phenomenon.[30] It reinstates the possibilities of joyful expenditure, of laughter . . . or silence.

Part II

SADIAN FIGURES

3

A Logic of the Simulacrum

Are we the undesirable thoughts of you mind, then to us you oppose the muteness of a flesh to be witheld from our operations.

Pierre Klossowski

Phantasms may be considered to represent the solution of an enigma. According to psychoanalytic theory, phantasmatic fabulations reveal the origins of subjectivity: the phantasm of a *primal seduction* is at the origin of sexuality; the phantasm of *castration* is at the origin of sexual differentiation; the phantasm of the *primal scene* is at the origin of individuality.[1] These are the very "stories" of origins which are at the origin of all neurosis, as well as at the telos of psychotic discourse (where the inability to support such disquieting, external, traumatic foundations leads to a fragmentation and reconstitution of the psyche in an attempt to establish the self as its own origin.) Both subjectivity and desire (the primal form of intersubjectivity) are forms of introjected passions and laws, appetites and lacunae: the formation of psychic unity is the first mode of repression.[2] The entire cultural, ideological mechanism is already at work in the slightest laugh and the tenderest punishment; it inhabits the entire gestural posture of the body and the sensitivity of the flesh (that surface which is the very form of the ego.)

But are we to believe the postulation whereby the multitude of dream figures symbolizes one person, the self; whereby the oneiric scenario represents nothing but the unitary body? There is no doubt of the truth in dreams, but don't we find there the solution to a different enigma, or perhaps even the multiplication of enigmas? Might not the very multiplicity of the passions, with their aleatory organization, be at the origin of the dreamwork? Hence the truth of the dream is disclosed in the very chaos of its representations, a collage of broken syntax and polymorphic vocabulary, where multiple reference necessarily transgresses the limits of meaning. Psychoanalytic intervention and theorization, narrativizing and organizing the dreamwork according to the analytic field of desire, are nothing but prolongations of the secondary revision which dissimulates the chaos, the active libido, from which the dream arises. The very notion of a latent content reveals the desire to interpret, to speak for another, where the will of the analyst or theorist enters the dream enunciation as a narrative axis, and where the entire field of signifiers is rearranged according to the symptoms of another.

As Nietzsche teaches, the self is a function of the body, a "prolonged extremity of chaos,"[3] a great multiplicity of libidinal energy which is unified and codified according to gregarious values for the benefit of cultural systematization. The body is the absolute referent, the arche and telos of meaning; but it is not a simple unity of matter, nor a determinate referent (signified), nor a pure system of negation. Rather, the body is an inscribed surface (a pure, excessive signifier) which bears witness to the labyrinthine complexity of chance that accompanies all origins. Notions of psychic causality and transcendence are modes of simplification, unification, standardization and control which dissimulate chance as the origin of meaning and arbitrary will as the telos of existence.

Classical psychoanalytic theory and its aesthetic double, Surrealism, are *a fortiori* procedures of pure representation, where phantasms are manipulated as the hallucinatory realizations of desire. This is the phantasm as reactive, reformed, represented; such a scenography of the self is made manifest as neurosis, paranoia, and stereotypical forms of sublimation. But lived as productive, and not reproductive or representational, the phantasm is not the object, but the very scene of desire.[4] As such, the body is disclosed as the excessive signifier of the multiplicity of chance and libido, where phantasms are the staging of desire, the eruption of sheer chance as a perverse modification of, and revolt against, the Law. But in both cases, the psyche is simultaneously regulated by the body and constrained by systems of signification. Thus the supposed "depth" of our interior lives is but a series of fictions, "the residue of signs deposited from the exterior."[5] Or else it is sheer chaos. Either expression is falsified by the internalization of the "code of everyday signs," or else a true expression of individuality is achieved and expressed as a perverse singular sign. (Hence the famous Nietzschean opposition between the gregarious mentality of the herd and the creativity of the sovereign individual.) In either case, expression suffers a constraint: for the gregarious mentality, this is the constraint of collective censorship which is internalized as superego, ego ideal, and all forms of stereotyped and idealized sublimation; for the perverse, sovereign mentality, this is the obsessional constraint of the phantasm, manifested as monomania (the polarization of expression around certain signs or passions).[6]

Perversion permits, indeed demands, two limit modes of expression, each determined by a sign which is either unique and ultimately unintelligible *or* quotidian and exchangeable; the relation between these limits forms an aporia within which the enigma of individual existence is constituted. (1) One limit is detotalization, fragmentation, multiplicity: hence the Nietzschean perspectivism, the symbol of the labyrinth and Dionysus; hence the Sadian disarticulation of the body, within a system of thought where the formal and architectonic possibilities of the human body are revealed as the very signs of passion; hence the Klossowskian "Laws of Hospitality," which enable the prostituted spouse to provide the husband with a multiplication of views and references, thus deepening the experience and knowledge of the wife seen through the eyes and caressed by the hands of so many others. (2) The other limit is totalization, unification, essentiality: hence the Nietzschean use of style as signification, and the exigencies of Apollo; hence the Sadian fantasies of physical and textual closure, specular repetition, and the encyclopedic categorization of corporeal possibilities, which is a thought that reaches the ultimate limits of rationalism;[7] hence that aspect of the Klossowskian "Laws of Hospitality" which aims at the realization of the wife's essence through the instantiation of a series of prostitutions and voyeurisms.

Whence the paradoxical nature of the "unique sign:" as unique, the sign would be monstrous, perverse, transgressive, but as a sign, it is immediately situated within a multiplicity of semiotic systems and recuperated by the Law. Laws are only inaugurated and sustained by a perpetual movement of transgression, yet all transgression is eventually recuperated by the Law, as is evidenced by the phantasms of origins. The hyperbolic form of such transgressions is to be found in Sade's texts: (1) *sexuality and desire* (the guarantor of reproduction and the continuity of the species) are expressed in their transgressive mode by incest, whereby the public, the general, the gregarious, are overcome by a truly universal prostitution; (2) *sexual differentiation* (the guarantor of structures of exchange, ruled by a phallocracy) is expressed in its transgressive mode by sodomy (the archetype of Sadian sexual perversions) whereby a purely wasteful expenditure of passion equalizes the symbolic differences of the sexual function; (3) the *primal scene* (guarantor of psychic unity and the continuity of the self within the oedipal family structure) is expressed in its transgressive mode by murder, which, in realizing the definitive scenario of the reactive oedipal phantasm, finally effects the active disintegration of that primal scene, where wives are to be raped, children beaten and tortured, fathers murdered.

At the limits of the Sadian and Nietzschean phantasms, the symbolic is to be taken literally and interpretation is to be repudiated. But repudiated only as a special doctrine: what is revealed is the manner in which the quotidian, as well as the perverse, are but different modes of interpretation, serving different purposes, expressing different passions. Life itself is interpretation.

> Besides, if the flesh is nothing but a lure, speech is nothing but wind; it is hence of the spirit.
>
> Pierre Klossowski

In relation to pictorial and linguistic expression, Klossowski explains that, "stereotypes are only the residue of phantasmatic simulacra fallen into current usage, abandoned to common interpretation."[8] Thus truth value, as well as mercantile and aesthetic value, depends upon the extent to which a phantasm may be communicated through its simulacra. Such communication effects psychic unity, the cohesion of individuals into a group, and the cohesion between groups, thus establishing traditional structures of exchange. In mass society, expenditure and consumption (and consequently production) are functions of libidinal compulsion, not of radical individuality, as modern marketing techniques demonstrate and as Sade already established in his analyses of power as a function of value. Rationality itself is only the internalized and idealized form of such collective values, serving as a constraint upon the libido.

Thus we arrive once again at the aporia, the paradox, of the "unique sign," not, as before, on the level of expression, but on the level of exchange; language is both the simulacrum of the common external resistance *and* the simulacrum of singular phantasms; or, as Lyotard claims, the simulacrum is "simultaneously an empty passional sign and an exchangeable rational sign; simultaneously will [*vouloir*] and meaning [*vouloir dire*]."[9] The unique, the monstrous, the perverse are always recuperated within the general system of exchange by means of the simulacra through which they are expressed. Such a misappropriation may well explain the confusion of the stereotype with reality and the rational with the real, a confusion which is at the very center of Western metaphysics. The history of Western metaphysics must no longer be established in terms of the conflict between realism and nominalism (which are but two modes of a *mathesis universalis*), but between a *mathesis universalis* and the diverse possible modes of a *mathesis* or *poesis particularis*.

What is at stake in the expression of the ultimately incommunicable phantasm by its simulacra is not the establishment of identity (this being a mode of categorization, identification, idealization and essentialization), but rather the authentification of difference. The dialectical process, which is at both the origin (Socrates/Plato) and the culmination (Hegal) of the metaphysical tradition, is a conceptual mode of appropriation, an intellectual kleptomania, recuperating all signs and events within its system. (This mode of appropriation is paralleled on the ecomonic level in the mass market economy, where the structures of exchange are universalized as an abstract monetary system; even the qualitative value of work is quantifiable.) The dialectic establishes a determinate chronology, a temporal context of events: the past remains as symptom, the future is traced as desire.

Such a systematization is contested by Nietzsche, a critique signaled by the notion of the Eternal Return (also central to Klossowski's thought). The Eternal Return, postulating an excessive thought (the communicability of the unique sign) and indicating the highest emotion (the incommunicability of the unique sign), establishes a pure anachronism which authenticates individuality outside of all systems. But how can the movement of return establish difference, rather than identity? How can return avoid representation?

The origin of language is a function of repetition; but before being constatative, linguistic repetition is a matter of sheer interjection, a passionate demand, a scream of pure emotion. The cry "mama," this monoreme which entails the creation of a world, is not a referential signifier:[10] "mama" originates as pure expression and demand, as the discovery of a system, a world; subsequently, the first referential signifier, "papa," entails the entry into that world, into what becomes actualized as a system of domination. Yet in both instances, the entry into language and culture commences with the repetition of a sound: the differentiation of discrete sounds as meaningful utterances is indicated by that repetition which articulates the noises of infantile babble into the significations of a linguistic system. Repetition insists, authenticates, codifies and signifies both a language and a world. Such duplication serves a constraining function, where repetition is the sign of willful activity, at the origin of power and politics: expression, communication and control are consolidated, individuality denigrated. The tragedy is that this enunciation is immediately co-opted, systematized, placed under the additional constraint of the oedipal, symbolic, ideological dimension of the linguistic system: realization is confounded with nomination. One is taught to express oneself in stereotypes, and thus to belie and obfuscate the multiplicity of the libido, of the body, through which those very first cries occured. Already at the origins of subjectivity, we find "singularity placed in the paranoiac law of the universal," as Lyotard explains.[11] Such a process of appropriation through mnemotechnics is so well described by Nietzsche in *On the Genealogy of Morals* and Kafka in *In The Penal Colony*, where the rules of the socius are directly inscribed upon the body, under the pain of suffering and death, instilling memory as the trace of collectivity, of gregariousness. The past appears as stigma, instituting the semblance of identity. Repetition is placed under the sign of memory, and is a function of *ressentiment* against the supposed irreversibility of time. Hence the notion of a psychic causality through which the origin of the self may be traced back to the oedipal situation: what I am is the function of a past which I cannot control. Repetition is placed in the service of stability and identity: iteration is not a return of particular passions, but is rather an idealization directed at the telos of knowledge.

Conversely, the Eternal Return is repetition whereby the nonwilled past (chance) is rewilled as willed; libidinal intensity (the chaos of the Will to Power) is willed as intentionality (the meaning of the unique sign.) The Eternal Return is thus nothing but a metaphor of the Will to Power;[12] it is a mode of enduring and rejoicing in the chaos of existence, a mode of possessing that chaos as the very form, origin and telos of one's life. Thus the Eternal Return is the form of sovereignty, defined as radical discontinuity, individuality, uniqueness, rupture. The transposition from Will to Power to Eternal Return is not a function of transformation (change in morphology), but of volition: it does not trace alternative forms of existence, but seals this very same existence as mine, and marks me as perpetually alterable.

The repetition which marks our acquisition of language entails the reactive circumscription of the subject, the guarantee of identity; conversely, the repetition of the Eternal Return marks the active radical affirmation of the multiplicity of existence, where the subject is lost and identity is dissipated, fragmented. (Hence Nietzsche as The Crucified *and* Dionysus; hence the multiple identities of Dionysus himself; hence the rift between Dionysus and Apollo.) The Eternal Return is not a dialectical process instilling memory, but rather the very sign of forgetting, of a unique experience, of the *loss* of language. The Eternal Return is manifested in silence, so as not to be betrayed by nomination; in *Thus Spoke Zarathustra* the Eternal Return is never directly communicated, but only revealed obliquely, falsely, in dreams, in whispers which remain unheard by all but Nature, in hallucinations, circumlocutions, silences, ellipses. What are commonly regarded as psychopathological symptons are here the signs of the highest sovereignty.

Klossowski is correct in stressing that the Eternal Return is not a concept, but a lived experience, revealed to Nietzsche in his greatest solitude. As such, it is a simulacrum of Nietzsche's phantasms, hence the sign of something incommunicable. The Eternal Return is the idiosyncratic valorization of Nietzsche's own existence; Klossowski in turn teaches us the value of idiosyncrasy and obsession as such, and offers us his own. But if this is the case, if the Eternal Return is only the form of Nietzsche's own sovereignty, what can it be for us? As soon as it is forgotten as a lived experience, it becomes a law, a doctrine, the cohesive sign of a group; taken as lived experience, it can only be the test of one's own monomania, of one's own unique sign.[13]

And if you dislike pantomime, why the devil
do you silence the actors?
Pierre Klossowski

The lesson of the Eternal Return, according to Klossowski, is that one must accept the constraint of one's own phantasms, and subsequently, as catharsis, exorcize those incommunicable phantasms by producing the simulacra which serve as their communicable trace. Ultimately, this eliminates the constraint and inaugurates sovereignty. For Klossowski, this occurs under the sign of "*Roberte*." Roberte appears everywhere in his work: in drawings, novels, theoretical writings, photographs, films. Roberte is the icon of a body which undergoes and performs a series of perverse gestures; these perverse gestures are singular judgements,[14] obeying a situational logic. Rather than being appropriated by the law of the universal, these gestures contest that law: perversion is the assignation of the personal, passional law in opposition to and in place of the collective system of laws.

Following Nietzsche, Deleuze argues that "all true thought is an aggression,"[15] and Foucault claims that "interpretation is the violent or surreptitious appropriation of a system of rules;"[16] Roberte may thus be understood as the metaphor of a thought process, the very simulacrum of Klossowski's phantasms. She is spied upon, attacked, raped, degraded; her images are multiplied according to the voyeuristic system of the "Laws of Hospitality," yet these "laws" are always belied by Roberte's own phantasms, always contested by her own perversions. The aggressions she suffers are the signs of Klossowski's thought, the simulacrum of interpretation itself. Roberte is the sign of a monomania: there is simultaneously a deceptive multiplication of her corporeal and gestural attributes with the purpose of establishing her essence (a realist project), *and* the loss of her identity in a series of simulacra, an enigmatic admixture of identities and mistaken identities (a nominalist project.) Thus we must ask: Is Roberte the exorcism of a phantasm and hence its equivalent, or is she rather the sign of the phantasm's excessive nature, and hence, ultimately, its other?

The figurative artwork effects the transformation of an icon into a symbol; caught between the antithetical constraint of the semiotic system in which the sign ultimately resides *and* the phantasm of which the sign (simulacrum) is the trace, the artwork simultaneously contests the reality principle which organizes the semiotic system *and* belies the corporeal, libidinal origins of the phantasm. The artwork is indeed a sophistry, a fabrication in both senses of the word: something produced and something false. Hence the mistaken belief in the "identity between nature and style"[17] in traditional nude painting, where the ideal of realism (revealing a desire for truth) dissimulates the interpretive aspects of style. Conversely, the idiosyncratic, sovereign expression of the phantasm is a function of "willed error,"[18] whereby the most personal secrets (Roberte; the Eternal Return; the interiors of the Sadian chateaux and the Labyrinth; etc.) become the emblems of a worldview, of a system of transformations and metamorphoses.

For Klossowski, Roberte is such an emblem. As simulacrum, Roberte is the monomaniacal invention of a sign system which attempts to reinvent a totality from a fragment, a thing from a view, a thought from a sign, a scene from a gesture. As Klossowski learned from Nietzsche, and as we too must learn from him, "here is my discovery and my purpose: to reinvent as a single thing what is only a fragment, an enigma, horrifying chance."[19] Yet the most terrifying aspect of such a theory of the fortuitous case or of a logic of the particular, of the perverse, is the realization that it is in fact I (Nietzsche, Klossowski, etc.) who am this function of chance, this enigma.[20] Such a genealogy simultaneously reveals the origin of the subject as the dissimulation of the Will to Power, libido, chance, *and* authentic teleology as the disintegration of that subjectivity effected by the adherence to fortuity. This process of the loss of identity is the condition of sovereignty. Liberty consists in the escape from the constraints imposed on the phantasm by means of the destruction of one's works and one's self-identity.

The dream reveals a symbolic psychic unity to the interpretive psychoanalytic mechanism that wishes to recuperate the dream within a totalising significative system; yet it reveals a multiplicity of the passions and a polymorphous symbolism to the sovereign individual. Similarly, Roberte reveals herself to the reactive consciousness as the quest for essentiality, the quest for identity through the actualisation of all of her possibilities by means of universal prostitution, while for sovereign thought she is revealed as the disintegration of self-identity into a multiplicity of appearances. As with the dream and the phantasm, Roberte too is no longer the projected, hallucinated, delirious *object* of desire, but is rather the very *scene* of desire. A simulacrum of Klossowski's phantasm, Roberte reveals the scenography of *his* existence: as Flaubert claimed that "Madame Bovery, c'est moi," we must claim for Klossowski that "Roberte, c'est moi". Yet doesn't one enigma always hide another? Is there really any sign that doesn't reveal an enigma, that doesn't hide a self?

So far we have only treated a certain incommunicability of the phantasm, such as what it might be for Klossowski; but what is it to be for us? For Klossowski, the classical idea of the nude is that of "a neutralisation of a primitive and violent act, an aesthetic and social compromise".[21] This violence is clearly that of the physical appropriation of the female body by the politico-economic activity and aestheticising gaze of the West. But it is also the primal violence of interpretation (as the originary form of possession and domination.) Both physical violence and interpretation are neutralized by their sublimation into art as simulacrum. Eroticism is, of course, only that form of interpretation which arranges the scenography of the sexual body; if "stereotypes are only the residue of phantasmatic simulacra fallen into current usage and abandoned to common interpretation,"[22] then we may amend this axiom of pictorial representation with the corollary that pornography is the residue of erotic forms fallen into current usage and abandoned to common interpretation. Common usage, everyday thought, is precisely noncritical thought, which entails the very neutralization of interpretation: this is thought which succumbs to the will of the group. The pornographic imagination is where "living money" (the eroticized body itself) is transformed, through its simulacra, into "dead money" (capital),[23] thus operating at the least common denominator of phantasmatic exchange, at its most gregarious level. At this point, all that remains is the possibility of violence without any interpretive thrust whatsoever, that is, pure terrorism.

Derrida, following Nietzsche, explains that, "form fascinates when we no longer have the force to grasp the force behind the form."[24] This radical critique of the formal cause, a "cause" which explains nothing but a weakness, which causes nothing but a misunderstanding, may well explain Klossowski's distaste for modernist painting, as well as his passion for the classical academic representations of *tableaux vivants*. Modern nihilism is the loss of the power to interpret, to create new fictions, to exteriorize the phantasms as simulacra. If Roberte is the simulacrum of Klossowski's phantasms, for us she is only a spectacle for occasional perusal; Klossowski *showing* us Roberte must entail our *saying* Roberte; specularity must entail speculation, or else we fall back into the trap of Western nihilism, a reactionary silence.

Klossowski tells of a certain old demon, a madman in Provence, for whom, "the yearning now was after explosion itself, and henceforth the gaze could only be satisfied by broken objects, by images gone to pieces. . ."[25] Strange that what is denigrated in Klossowski's aesthetic (i.e. the images gone to pieces in the modernist pictorial systems) should be valorized in his epistemology (i.e. the loss of psychic identity; a disarticulation of the psyche; the rule of chance and accident.)

The incongruity between abstraction and figuration pervades the entire history of Western culture, and is apparent at its foundations. The earliest Paleolithic art, which was constituted (before the creation of any figures or images) by the contemplation of such regularly formed objects as pebbles, shells, etc., was a mode of abstract art.[26] It was an art of fascination, where chance encounter deepened self-reflection and awakened subjectivity by the shock of recognizing exterior forms (simulacra) which repeat our thoughts and passions, and which give rise to other thoughts and passions in turn. The differentiation between the narcissistic propriate field and the aleatory ambient milieu, by means of this aesthetic repetition, entailed the formation of subjectivity. And yet, as a triumph of narcissim, anthropomorphism and social organization, the formal properties of this earliest art (its rounded, bulbous, regular forms) were recuperated by figurative concerns: aesthetic fascination was focused on the stylized representation of that primal object of fascination, the female human body, as exemplified in its exceedingly erotic, excessive and mythopoeic instance, the paleolithic "Venus" figurines.

This valorization of the human body was completely reversed at the origins of Western metaphysics, where in Book X of *The Republic* Plato advances an argument that may be taken as the first theorization of abstract art. Simply, in the light of a universal rationalism, the poets who speak of human deeds and semblances necessarily lie, since their work is tainted by the realm of appearances and temporality. Only a representation of rational models avows the truth; art can only be a function of what is effectively a *mathesis universalis*.

Yet a further reversal, a recuperation of the human body's representation, occurs in the Christian Church: the debate between the iconoclasts and the iconophiles was decided, in favor of the latter, in the year 787 A.D., when the Empress Irene established the cult of icons, which permitted the representation of Christ, the Virgin Mary, and the Saints. It is perhaps not by accident that it was a woman (who blinded her son and took power from him) who offered to the world the sight of the body, by placing it at the center of theological concerns.[27] The paternal ideology of God the Father and the Holy Spirit (a severity of interdictions among which is the prohibition against representing God, hence the necessity that He remain invisible) is now countered by the regenerative and protective powers of the Holy Virgin (a transfigured "Venus"). Compassion versus law.

A recent inversion of this iconophilia is that of modernism, effected by that "old demon" of Provence. Modernism may be thought to entail the loss of the integral object, sacrificing the representation of the human body for the sake of revealing the very surface, the material substructure or "body," of the artwork. We must ask, then, whether Roberte is yet one more instance of this ongoing conflict; we must ask whether for Klossowski the goal is to escape the constraint of his phantasm by exorcizing it (and thus to become sovereign), or else to perpetually signify the obessional constraint of his phantasms (and thus to remain a philosopher, a master of thought).

Certain phantasms are not, can never be, our own: Dionysus, Loplop, Nadja, Acéphale, Roberte. These bodies are merely what we chance upon in others' reveries; they attest to the fact that it is not only the sleep of reason, but reason itself (as the simulacrum of life), that creates monsters, as well as angels and gods. Every possible trope may give rise to such creatures, hence the extreme fragility of reason. Yet in these investigations, what do we risk, other than the terror of discovering that we too can give rise to such beings, and that we too are nothing but fragments of a totality which never existed, nothing but extensions of chaos?

4

A New History of the Passions

. . . and you, madame, draw yours near that
I may handle it . . . that I may socratize it . . .
D.A.F. Sade,
Philosophy in the Bedroom

On June 30, 1986, the Supreme Court of the United States upheld a Georgia law which makes sodomy a criminal offense. In a concurring opinion, Chief Justice Burger explains that the court's decision was in part motivated by the traditional Judaeo-Christian condemnation of homosexual sodomy, which is stigmatized by quotation from Blackstone's *Commentaries*. In conformation with English common law, which became the received law of colonial Georgia, sodomy is characterized as, "'the infamous crime against nature,' as an offense of 'deeper malignity' than rape, an heinous act' the very mention of which is a disgrace to human nature,' and 'a crime not fit to be named.'"[1] Yet, if there is to be any civilization whatsoever, the cultural field must be rigorously separated from the natural domain; the term *human nature* is an oxymoron, since it is precisely the unnatural which is particularly human. Hence, according to contemporary structuralist anthropology, the incest prohibition, as the very founding structure of human community, entailed the suppression of the natural act of incest, and established society by the simultaneous inauguration and exclusion of a perverse domain. (It is the incest prohibition, rather than incest itself, that is a "crime against nature.") The discourse of transgression is the basis of legalism; as Deleuze and Guattari exclaim, "The law is inscribed in a pornographic book." We are therefore compelled to ask why, in this current judgment, an act such as sodomy is literally unspeakable, and, further, to examine the implications of its symbolic efficacy.

Sade's *Philosophy in the Bedroom*, the tale of Eugénie's initiation into libertinage—signaled by her defloration—is a *Bildungsroman* whose denouement reveals the very conditions of the possibility of narrative; it reveals the institution of that utopian autofiguration where the subject shows itself as being without origins, unnatural, acivil, sovereign.

The seventh and final dialogue of this tale begins with the arrival of Eugénie's mother, Madame de Mistival, who demands the return of her young, innocent daughter from the libertines. Eugénie is astounded by the impertinence of her mother, who dares hint that her daughter may be in bad company, insisting upon her daughter's awareness of "the rights I have over her." The rest of the narrative is a discourse on the absurdity of these "rights," and an account of their destruction. Madame de Mistival is summarily raped, sodomized, and tortured both by those libertine "monsters" who surround her and by her very own daughter, who exalts in their actions. "Here I am: at one stroke incestuous, adulteress, sodomite, and all that in a girl who lost her maidenhead only today!. . . What progress, my friends!"[2] This concludes with the torture of Eugénie's mother by having her sex sewn up; Eugénie finds this an "excellent idea! Quickly, quickly, fetch me needle and thread!. . . Spread your thighs, Mama, so I can stitch you together—so that you'll give me no more little brothers and sisters."[3] Eugénie gains her autonomy and sovereignty by excluding herself from all possible kinship relations; she rejects all responsibility to any family structure (denying her mother's rule over her) and eliminates any possibility of continuing her lineage. Her mother's womb, out of which she was delivered to life, is sewn up, and she herself learns of techniques to regain her virginity, her primal "innocence," by sewing herself up. "A pretty girl should concern herself only with *fucking* and never with engendering."

The scandalous narrative is interspersed with, and justified by, the usual Sadian treatise, here expounded by Dolmancé, one of Eugénie's libertine initiators. When asked if the aim of such acts is simultaneously to outrage nature, God, and humanity, he replies:

> I've told you a thousand times over that Nature, who for the perfect maintenance of the laws of her general equilibrium, has sometimes need of vices and sometimes of virtues, inspires now this impulse, now that one, in accordance with what she requires; hence, we do no kind of evil in surrendering ourselves to these impulses, of whatever sort you may suppose them to be.[4]

Here is the source of Sade's paradox, his central contradiction: in order to institute the human realm, each person—*in imitatio naturalis*—must aspire to the greatest destructive evil in contestation of an overbearing, suffocating nature, which at every moment thwarts one's pleasures, all the while creating desires beyond the bounds of human possibility. And yet, every possible human act is duly authorized by that very same nature, which is the one cause—efficient, material, formal, and final—of every action. Nature is that which must be transgressed in order to affirm one's humanity, one's sovereignty; yet that nature can never be transgressed, since we are part of it—an impossible dialectic.

Structuralist anthropology teaches us that myth entails the dissimulation of the contradictions of human existence, that myth is a logical model for overcoming such contradictions. In *Structural Anthropology*, Claude Lévi-Strauss shows how communication is a function of the exchange of complimentary values; what is exchanged may be objects, women, words. The originary guarantee of exchange is the negative injunction of the incest prohibition, which is the zero-degree syntax of the nature/culture, cosmic/human differentiation. This negative injunction/positive disjunction entails the fluidity of exchange in a restricted reciprocity between social systems, all the while creating an exclusionary zone of prohibitions—the family or tribe. The exogamous move, by means of the incest prohibition, from a closed to an open (yet limited) system entails the structuring of subjectivity around the overrating of blood relations, and the consequent denial of individual autonomy in favor of the exigencies of community. The central figure within such a system of exchange is the woman, who plays the paradoxical role of being the object of personal desire (the husband's) *and* the object of the other's desire. Parallel to the originary use of words, she is both a sign and a value; yet she is a very special sign, because she too speaks. She is a sign and a creator of signs. This spilt representation in the symbolic function is the paradoxical constitution of femininity; the "resolution" of this contradiction is established by the social exchange of complimentary values, whereby a certain amount of pleasure taken in women is renounced for a certain amount of family stability and tribal expansion.

Yet no reciprocity is possible in pure pleasure: nature is the absence of prohibitions. Hence, in the concluding lines of *The Elementary Structures of Kinship*, Lévi-Strauss evokes an Andaman myth which describes utopia as that situation which avoids all exchange: "The bliss of the hereafter as a heaven where women will no longer be exchanged, i.e. removing to an equally unattainable past or future the joys, eternally denied to social man, of a world in which one might *keep to oneself*."[5] Such a utopia is the total denial of alliances for the sake of the pure exertion of personal autonomy and the sexual instincts. But this would be a "misuse" of 'women as signs,' since signs are destined for communication: the origins of the symbolic are tied to the origins of legality, which find their metaphysical justification in the belief that there is no such thing as a "private language."

It is therefore perhaps not so surprising that the dissenting opinion against the Supreme Court decision, written by Justice Blackmun, was in part argued on the basis of the Fourth Amendment guarantee of the right to privacy and the integrity of the home. Extrapolated from these rights is "the right of an individual to conduct intimate relationships in the intimacy of his or her own home," and ultimately the right to be *different*. In short, this is the utopian right to *keep to oneself* in attaining one's pleasures, and thus to avoid social exchange. The difference between the majority and dissenting opinions in this case thus reveals the central aporia upon which the United States Constitution is based: the contradictions between public and private life. And it is precisely the limit of this logic which maintains the restrictions upon those very pleasures which may be sought in the privacy of the home: incest is still deemed monstrous. The Sadian libertine utopia—symbolized by the isolation of the chateau and its secret chambers—is founded on incest as a truly universalizing factor. The legalistic Constitutional utopia—symbolized by the inviolable privacy of the home—is founded, however, on the prohibition of incest as an ultimate guarantee of community and exchange, that is, as the guarantee of legalism's efficacy. Thus in the case of sodomy, the Sadian text serves as a panopticon, permitting a total expression of the deed. To the contrary, the Supreme Court is divided on this issue: the majority deems sodomy an "unspeakably heinous" crime *not fit to be named*, while the minority deems it an act *not fit to be seen*. The former would have sodomites incarcerated, while the latter would have them sequestered, hidden in the home. Curious, this severe limitation on the space of utopia.

The formation of any epistemological model will depend largely upon what mode of consciousness is taken as its paradigmatic instance (neurosis, psychosis, perversion, and so forth.) If, as is the case for Sade, perversion is taken to be an emblematic sign which organizes the discursive system, then the specificity of the perversion will determine the communicative and critical functions of the discourse.

Pierre Klossowski wrote, along with George Bataille (in protest against the Surrealists), the "dissenting opinion" on Sade, correctly seeing sodomy as the perverse phantasm at the center of Sade's work.[6] The act of sodomy is emblematic of the libertine's struggle against the natural order. While incest contests the cultural order, it nevertheless remains a natural, productive act—even though it may produce monsters, as popular tradition insists. Sodomy, on the contrary, is an unproductive act, a wasteful expenditure of energy and life whereby the species is put to death in the individual, and "natural" sexual differentiation is denied in an act of sexual indifferentiation. (For the Sadian sodomite, the vagina is merely an inferior anus.) This inmixing of life and death, of sperm and shit, denotes an amoral categorical imperative through which the differentiation between nature and culture may be effected on the eroticized body. Yet this entry into culture does not entail an implementation of, or insertion into, the symbolic; rather, the sodomite passion and phantasm create a confusion of genders which short-circuits the symbolic. It collapses the representational order by means of the very contestation of the normative system, induced by the deeds of those sovereign, libertine, "integral monstrosities" depicted by Sade.

Klossowski's analysis of the cultural realm, via Sade, depends upon the differentiation between institutional norms and libertine anomalies, as these differences are played out on the phantasmatic scenario of the body.(1) The world of institutional norms is organized by the procreative law of the species, the logical structure of language, and the universal codes of quotidian existence. It maintains a determinate system of values which governs exchange; hence the commercialization of voluptuousness, where the circulation of wealth is a pretext for the circulation of bodies in the interest of institutions.[7] (2) The closed world of the Sadian libertine is governed by the anomalies of the singular passions (though these passions are always rigorously ordered in the erotic scenarios.) This is an order characterized by the domain of the incommunicable, unexchangeable phantasms, which exclude the libertine from gregarious existence. Here, "the only authentic universal communication is through the exchange of bodies by the secret language of body signs."[8] The value of the perverse phantasm, because unique, is indeterminate: it can only be established in relation to the emotions it produces. Hence the extreme, monomaniacal claim of one Sadian hero, who would be perfectly willing, indeed thrilled, to sacrifice an entire population in exchange for a single brief pleasure.

Mediating between these two worlds is that strange oxymoron, the "unique sign." This sign—a simulacrum of the incommunicable phantasm—is structured like a myth, mediating the contradiction between autonomy and gregariousness, between libertine and "normative" modes of exchange. Within the institutional world the unique sign is empty of determinate exchange, operating in a sublimable system of communication. Within the libertine world, the unique sign is full of the passions, a mark of perverse desublimation. These dual possibilities of valorization entail the following dilemma: "either communication through the exchange of bodies, or prostitution under the sign of Money."[9] Thus what seems to be Klossowski's absurd resolution of this problem—the "postulate of a universal prostitution" and payments in "living money"—is in fact an inverted, perverse instance of Lévi-Strauss's Andaman utopia. One may keep to oneself only by eliminating all structures of exchange, and this can be accomplished only by dissolving the incest taboo, that is, by truly universalizing erotic possibility, by permitting erotic encounter within the family. For Lévi-Strauss, this universalization serves the Andamans as an ultimate contraction of the erotic world; for Sade, the incestuous universalization is, rather, an expansion of libertine possibility within the world of the sealed chateau. The body is completely devalorized for the Andaman, while it is fully valorized for the Sadian. In both cases, utopia is achieved in a closed system which contests both nature and culture, hence the "danger" of its rules and the unspeakable character of its deeds.

We are currently in the midst of a reconsideration of Sade's work, this time centered on Jean-Jacques Pauvert's republication of the *Complete Works*. The development of Sade scholarship in this century is intimately linked with the surrealist movement. The first major critical texts which treat Sade's oeuvre as a total coherent system of thought—studies by Maurice Heine and Gilbert Lély—were published in surrealist journals, and the Surrealists themselves considered Sade as one of their major precursors. But the prime import of Sade's role in this history appears around 1930, the time of the rupture in the surrealist movement, and in the ensuing polemic between Breton and Bataille, much of which was centered on Sade.[10]

Breton's tautological claim in the first *Manifesto of Surrealism*—"Sade is Surrealist in sadism"—may be understood according to the following motivations: (1) the polemical shock value of Sade's name as a weapon in the revolutionary attempt to upset given cultural values, to *"épater la bourgeoisie"*; (2) the psychoanalytically oriented attempt to develop a theory of sadism as part of the epistemological foundations of surrealist aesthetics; (3) a hyperbolic exemplification of the marvelous, the surreal. Yet this tautology is also a generality which hides a certain moralistic embarrassment; it dissimulates the specifics of the Sadian text in which sodomy, murder, coprophilia, incest, and the other perversions, play a central rhetorical role. In fact, we find a combination of moral outrage and visceral disgust in Breton's response to questions posed in a series of discussions on sexuality, "Recherches sur la sexualité," in *La révolution surréaliste* (no. 11, 1928.) Once the dicussion turned to the topic of sodomy, Breton quickly intervened: "I am absolutely opposed to pursuing the discussion on this subject. If it turns to the defense of pederasty, I'll abandon it immediately." And just afterwards, when asked what sorts of perversions he wouldn't condemn, Breton replied: "All of the perversions except those of which we have just spoken at too great length." Breton's homophobia appears to have been a central factor (though quite misplaced) in his estimation of Sade, and it might indeed provide a clue to his failure to produce any close examination of Sade's writings, despite his valorization of Sade's name. These timidities are the source of Bataille's critique of Breton and the surrealists; it was their "utopian blindness" and "utopian sentimentalism" which caused Bataille to accuse them of being mere apologists for Sade. Bataille insisted that Sade's works—rather than being appropriated by a poetic dialectic—must be accepted for what they really were: the most unbearable works ever written. These writings are a heterogeneous element rejected, excreted, from the social and literary order—as Bataille was ejected from the surrealist movement—hence the very impossibility of reading the Sadian text.

Bataille opposes a base nondialectical materialism to Breton's dialectical idealism. While surrealism established the myth of a poetic dialectic which could effect the reconciliation of opposites in a surreal domain, Bataille dealt with the fundamental contradictions of human existence by means of a heterology, through which we live the following paradox: the founding cultural act is a mythical enunciation which excludes (heterogeneous) violence; yet ultimately, violence cannot be spoken and speech cannot master violence. Hence the disquietude and frustration which results from reading Sade, and the very impossibility of reading his texts.

If, indeed, Sade's work serves as an investigation into the inaugural conditions of civilization, its discontents, its utopias, as well as to any possible protest, then we must pay careful attention to every renewal of this discourse, to every nuance, in order to examine precisely what is deemed central and what is excluded from the Sadian project.

The recent republication of Sade's *Complete Works* is prefaced by a new, book-length introduction by Annie Le Brun, *Soudain un bloc d'abîme, Sade*.[11] This text has replaced the now classic essays by Lacan, Klossowski, Blanchot, Heine, Paulhan, and Robbe-Grillet, among others, that previously prefaced Sade's works in the earlier Pauvert edition. In a sense, the differences between these prefatory texts and Le Brun's work renews the half century old Breton/Bataille polemic, later central to *Tel Quel's* valorization of Bataille and Artaud.

Le Brun—allied to the surrealist circle during the period of its expiration—devoted a chapter of a recent book, *Les châteaux de la subversion*, to Sade. Relying on a decidely surrealist epistemology, Le Brun explains that Sade had succeeded in creating "the greatest poetic machine" ever known, by means of "the rapprochement of those two distant realities which are philosophy and pornography."[12] These are manifest in the Sadian text in the intertwining of treatise and narrative, where the poetic image is created not by their simple juxtaposition, but by means of, "their brutal superposition, their unforeseeable concentration on a single object which, by offending the very order of things, by dismantling the order of representation, violently unveils the infinitude of the imaginary space."[13] The space of the surrealist imaginary manifests the marvelous, where the objectivity of the body and discourse are metamorphosed into a self-contradictory "concrete irreality." Hence the imaginary, for Le Brun, is that realm of appearances where reality is torn from the laws of value—"Derealization goes hand in hand with devalorization."[14] Do we not have here the hyperbolic instance of those very "pretentious idealist aberrations" for which Bataille castigated

Breton? Does this myth not parallel that of the Andaman utopia, whose space of the imaginary is constituted precisely by the devalorization of the body? If derealization—a function of the absolute isolation of the imagination—is characteristic of poetry, then what effect can such poetry have upon our bodies? How can poetic subversion effect anything other than a purely textual play—that very *écriture* which Le Brun will take such great pains to contest—destined to the archive?

In this same essay, Le Brun asks, "Why does Sade in effect continue to elude the most serious interpretations as well as the most brilliant commentaries?"[15] This in 1982! In her recent *Soudain un bloc d'abîme, Sade,*[16] (which, we note again, replaces all of those celebrated commentaries and prefaces whose existence Le Brun had previously ignored) the polemical exaggerations of her earlier statement give way to the critical exaggerations of her present text. Here, the fascination with Sade is attributed to an "indetermination between monstrosity and banality" (p. 157), such that the monstrous lies at the very root of the marvelous (p. 295). The discursive organization of the Sadian text is thus still understood according to the surrealist paradigm of the reconciliation of, or indetermination between, opposites. Yet curiously enough, within this poetics of ambiguity, Le Brun insists upon the necessity of reading Sade literally (p. 17), in opposition to what she sees as the reduction and neutralization of Sade's work to *éciture* by practically the entire interpretive tradition after surrealism (p. 276). Her position bespeaks a metaphysical naive realism—or rather a *naive surrealism*—in contradistinction to what she sees as the major modernist error of believing that words live independently of things and beings live independently of words (p. 28).

Le Brun claims that Sade's genius was to have achieved an "integral literalness" (p. 213) based on the materiality and singularity at the source of eroticism. Yet she also insists that the strength and strangeness of Sade's work lies in a "metaphoric excess" (p. 279) which, unlike metaphor in traditional rhetoric, is "an excess which is metaphoric of the movements of desire" (p. 279). Thus Sade is portrayed as a writer of *pure literalness,* who nevertheless institutes a *metaphoric excess;* we are to read Sade completely literally, yet we must constantly beware of any attempt to demetaphorize Sade (p. 277). What are we to make of these contradictions? What would it mean to read a metaphor literally?

The *monster* may be deemed a metaphor for metaphor—a hybrid reality where incongruous beings are combined, where irreconcilable realities are reconciled in an uncanny linguistic object, in a disquieting imaginative variation. Indeed, any trope may create monsters. Yet if, as Le Brun claims, "the imaginary is indissociable from concrete reality" (p. 290) and "only this physical excess can unleash the imaginary excess" (p. 309), then this new poetics of singularity which she proposes—a reductionist "science of the concrete"—would be nothing but an epiphenomenon, where nature cannot be escaped, and where the imagination is but a powerless doubling of monstrosities. As such, there is no violence, no excess, no poetry—just a tragic mimesis of nature within an all too lengthy text.

This reduction to materiality and textual literalness ironically produces the same devalorization/surrealization as that proposed in Le Brun's earlier text on Sade. We find ourselves once again in that utopian closure of the Sadian chateau, "as if the absolute of solitude necessitated infinite desire in order to make of freedom a desperate quest for form" (p. 129). There seems to be a confusion here of the physical enclosure of Sade's incarceration with the textual closure of his works. But the Bastille is not Silling! And ultimately, is not the libertine quest a desire for bodies rather than forms; for base materiality rather than poetic effects? We must not demand forms where there is only monstrous deformation.

The erotic or pornographic scenario depends upon a charting of discursive possibilities onto the body, which serves as a semiotic/syntactic paradigm. We cannot but be aware of the emblematic monstrosity of Sade's pun on the word "*socratize*"[17]—meaning both "philosophize" and "sodomize." This conflation of mouth and anus is a semiological nightmare and an erotic joy. Oral eroticism, which culture sublimates into discourse and textuality, and anal eroticism, which culture sublimates into sculptural production and concern with money, are both desublimated in this confusion of organs. We find a parallel conflation in the Georgia antisodomy law's definition of sodomy: "A person commits the offense of sodomy when he performs or submits to any sexual act involving the sex organ of one person and the mouth or anus of another."[18] This confusion determines what in fact constitutes a "philosophy in the bedroom," signifying the central aporia of our culture, where the intertwining of treatise and narrative entails that perpetually renewed crime so desired by one Sadian libertine, a crime which is none other than the crime of writing. This is the crime which is *a fortiori* Sade's own.

Such confusion of erotic topoi seems to lead to an antilegalistic utopia in Sade, and a legalistic dystopia in Georgia. To work through the erotic heterogeneity disclosed in this "philosophical" pun, however, is to reveal a *heterotopia*, an inconsistent spatial configuration which undermines any possible textual coherence. (This would, in fact, reveal the structural conditions of the impossibility of reading Sade.) The perfect erotic condition of such a heterotopia is perhaps that described by Ernest Jones in *On the Nightmare*:

> The minutest attention was devoted in the Middle Ages to the sexual attributes of the Devil, and particularly to the organ concerned. This was generally sinuous, pointed and snake-like, made sometimes of half-iron and half-flesh, at other times wholly of horn, and was commonly forked like a serpent's tongue; he customarily performed both coitus and pederastia at once, while sometimes a third prong reached to his leman's mouth.[19]

The Devil's monstrousness resides in a totalization of possibilities within the erotic combinatory—this is the antinatural act par excellence. The Devil is not simply the avatar of base materiality, but rather of that very erotic self-sufficiency which leaves no place for God or nature in human "life, liberty and the pursuit of happiness."

If the origin of our own narratives is the impossible fulfillment of our perverse phantasms, we must savor all the more those other tales which give rise to the incubi and succubi that trouble our sleep, and to those demons that invade our homes in a night beyond reason.

5

Structures of Exchange, Acts of Transgression

Copulation and mirrors are abominable. For one of those gnostics, the visible universe was an illusion or (more precisely) a sophism. Mirrors and fatherhood are abominable because they multiply and disseminate that universe.

Jorge Luis Borges
Tlön, Uqbar, Orbis Tertius

Numerous modes of contemporary theory hold that thought, and the structure of subjectivity itself, are functions of the dominant conditions of expressibility. This stance implies that the structure of subjectivity is not a function of psychic topology, but rather of linguistic/poetic tropology. Following Nietzsche, Foucault writes that the purpose of genealogy is,. . . "to reveal the heterogeneous systems which, masked by the self, inhibit the formation of any form of identity."[1] The self is a fiction acting as a form of identity; the heterogeneous systems are the various plays of tropes and figures that simultaneously form the fictive self and undermine its ultimate possibility as stable form. The central problem of hermeneutics thus becomes the description of the manner in which the self is formed and maintained by the figurative structures of expression. In asking, "What does that mean?" one must necessarily demand, "Who is speaking?" and in asking "Who is speaking?" one must necessarily demand, "How was it said?" One might go so far as to claim that the personal voice suffuses all texts: one must discover the tropes and figures that dissimulate it. Conversely, the subject of any text or enunciation is maintained by the figural/tropic structure of the discourse: again, we must reveal and examine these tropes and figures in order to realize the tentative, and ultimately narrative, structure of all discourse of "Truth."

I wish to investigate one such rhetorical structure: the *chiasm*. In traditional rhetoric, the chiasm (*chiasmus*) is formed by the inversion of syntactical elements in the second of two juxtaposed clauses. This AB/BA structure is thus the form of reversal, making it an exemplary figure of mimesis. The chiasm is a figure in the form of a mirror, which explains the fascination that it holds for many writers. Jean-François Lyotard, writing on Merleau-Ponty, claims that the chiasm is, ". . .the figure constitutive of the sensible, the figure constitutive of figures."[2] It is the figure of sensibility because of the reversible structure of the "flesh;" it is the figure of figures because of the exchangeable economy of signs. Yet while the privileged use of the chiasm to express the structure of subjectivity and intersubjectivity must be investigated, so too must we investigate the manner in which the placement of the chiasm within different textual systems determines different models of subjectivity. The discovery of a figure or trope as the organizational principle of a textual system (or as the constitutive aspect of a model of subjectivity) must itself be understood only as yet another figure, and not as a foundation. Deconstruction, or genealogy, does not lead to foundational structures; it only provides the means of uncovering varied series of tropes and figures. It might be said that the foundation of meaning is to be found in the sum total of the differences between all possible expressions within a system, between all possible figures, and never as any single given figure.

In *Juliette*, D.A.F. Sade presents the following phantasm of the libertine character Noirceuil:

> It is a most extraordinary fantasy I have been dwelling upon for a very long time, Juliette, and I have been awaiting your return with impatience, having in all the world nobody but you with whom I could satisfy it. I should like to marry . . . I should like to get married, not once, but twice, and upon the same day: at ten o'clock in the morning, I wish, dressed as a woman, to wed a man; at noon, in masculine attire, I wish

> to take a bardash for my wife. There is still more . . . I wish to have a woman imitate me; and what other woman but you could participate in this fantasy? You, dressed as a man, must wed a tribade at the same mass at which I, guised as a woman, become the wife of a man; next, dressed as a woman, you will wed another tribade wearing masculine clothing, at the very moment I, having resumed the attire of my sex, will marry a bardash dressed as a girl.[3]

Noirceuil's fantasy presents a complex set of chiasms, the peculiar structures of which should be examined. While the structure of marriage, as a joining of alterity, is not precisely a chiasmatic structure, Sade wishes to extirpate all possibility of a radical alterity, since alterity undermines the structures of mastery. Hence marriage is presented by Sade only in terms of the master. In these ceremonies there are only imitations of Noirceuil, i.e. a multiplication of possibilities by chiasm. The structure of these ceremonies may be schematized as follows:

	Appearance	Reality
First mass: (10 A.M.)	Two men marry two women	Noirceuil, dressed as a woman, marries a man; and Juliette, dressed as a man, marries a tribade. Thus a man marries a man and a woman marries a woman
Second mass: (Noon)	Two men marry two women	Noirceuil, dressed as a man, marries a homosexual dressed as a woman; and Juliette, dressed as a woman, marries a tribade dressed as a man. Thus a man marries a man and a woman marries a woman

The chiasms formed are as follows: (1) Noirceuil dressed as a woman is a reversal of sex roles (as is a homosexual man dressed as a woman); (2) Noirceuil marrying a man is a reversal of the classical structure of matrimony; (3) Juliette dressed as a man is a reversal of sex roles (as is a lesbian dressed as a man); (4) Juliette marrying a woman is a reversal of the classical structure of matrimony; (5) homosexuality and lesbianism are reversals of "normative" sexual identities (and tribadism, a lesbian practice of imitating heterosexual intercourse, is an ironic form of this reversal); (6) Juliette imitating Noirceuil is a reversal of roles and identities within this fantasy;

(7) the two marriages are reversals of each other; (8) there is a manifest reversal of appearance and reality. Every relation within this scene may be construed as chiasmatic. It must be stressed that in no case is a "normal" male/female marriage arranged, and the structures of the reversals are always determined according to Noirceuil's, i.e. the Master's role. Even Juliette, the "protagonist" of the story, only imitates Noirceuil, hence undoing her identity in the series of scenes through which she passes.

Such "marriages" are certainly not matters of contractual reciprocity, nor of the implied emotional reciprocity of love; they are not at all structures of exchange, but rather modes of formalizing and imitating domination through the permutation and multiplication of attributes and connections. This task, aimed at absolute mastery, is indicative of the Sadian task, and structures the entire Sadian text. As Marcel Hénaff claims, in his study, *Sade: l'invention du corps libertin*:

> . . . to extend the catalogue is to permutate all of the elements without restriction. Logic is not abandoned: it is made unlimited without reserve. The catalogue is the theater of the unlimited exchange of roles and positions.[4]

Sade aims at the closure of the system, but at a very specific closure, in which there is always a permutational center of power and mastery. Yet even so, the Master too may become victim, within a new and ultimate form of chiasm. Thus there is a complete possibility of permutation and reversal: the closure is structural, not existential. Mastery is a function, almost literally, of manipulation: to organize is to control. In any case, for Sade, totality is the extrapolation of multiplicity to closure, eliminating difference by including all possibilities. This technique of expression (and presumed action) empties symbolism of all efficacy, since all possible figurative stances become (or may become) actualized. There is no more "as if," no more latency or ambiguity. Hence the ultimate redundancy of the chiasmatic relations in the previous passage about the marriage: no more is expressed, or acted out, than Noirceuil already knows or desires. No more is symbolized than already exists for Noirceuil. There is no reciprocity at the intersubjective level between the partners of the marriages: there is only pure theatricality, the pure staging of Noirceuil's fantasy. Intersubjectivity is suppressed by pure domination, and this suppression of intersubjectivity, at its limit, inaugurates the possibility of the suppression of subjectivity itself.

This denial of the usual reciprocal implications of the chiasmatic relation is also expressed by Sade in the following quotation from *Philosophy in the Bedroom,* about the use of mirrors, which are the physical instantiations par excellence of the chiasm:

> Eugénie: Oh dear God! the delicious niche! But why all these mirrors?
>
> Mme. de Saint-Ange: By repeating our attitudes and postures in a thousand different ways, they infinitely mulitply those same pleasures for the persons seated here upon this ottoman. Thus everything is visible, no part of the body can remain hidden: everything must be seen; these images are so many groups disposed around those enchained by love, so many delicious tableaux wherewith lewdness waxes drunk and which soon drive it to its climax.[5]

This use of mirrors does not express a relation of narcissism or reciprocity, but rather mutliples effects so that all is visible and controllable. This too implies an attempt at closure by exhausting all possibilities. As Hénaff (following Gérard Genette) suggests, the mirror is no longer, as it was for the Baroque sensibility, ". . .the privileged instrument of metamorphoses of an unstable, evanescent subject, uncertain of its identity. . ."[6] Rather, for Sade the mirror becomes an instrument for the elimination of subjectivity, an elimination predicated upon a completely exterior control. For Sade, the mirror doesn't complicate the organization of subjectivity, but simply exhibits the stances, positions, and postures of the body. It assures that nothing remains hidden: for Sade this serves the same purposes of power and control as does Jeremy Bentham's functionally similar *Panopticon,* which is understood by Foucault to be the very architectural figure of control, a control founded upon the minutiae of observation and confinement.[7] The Sadian specular closure parallels the architectural enclosure of the Sadian chateau.

The Baroque mirror serves to create; the Sadian mirror serves to catalogue. The Baroque mirror creates distortions which express the interior life; the Sadian mirror empties all interiority into the catalogue of possible stances. Expression becomes no more than position. And the completion of this task is achieved by the all-seeing Master: the mirror permits not only the sight of the other, but also the sight of the entire scene, with nothing hidden, not even the Master. The Master sees everything and says everything; in the Sadian universe these are sufficient conditions for knowing everything. This anti-ontotheological stance entails the replacement of metaphysics with a mechanics, *i.e.*, with a model of manipulation. The actual "philosophy" of *Philosophy in the Bedroom* is just another form of logorrhea as ordering and staging: it is a philosophy of the imperative. What was once transcendent or taboo is now a part of the scene. Thus, as Roland Barthes claims, "We better understand upon what and toward what Sade's erotic combinatory rests and tends: its origin and its sanctions are rhetorical."[8] This claim may be extended to Sade's entire ontology.

The chiasmatic structure of the mirror operates just like the chiasmatic structure of the marriages: not as a model of intersubjective reciprocity, but as an organization of discourse which eliminates subjectivity itself by eliminating all depth, all latency, and all auto-figuration, except that of the Master. Subjectivity is replaced by subjugation.

Foucault is correct in writing that, "The precise object of 'sadism' is not the other, nor his body, nor his sovereignty: it is everything that might have been said."[9] Such sadism is precisely the control of the symbolic by means of its elimination in the literal, by denying the symbolic as openess to difference, to the Other. Hence the monotony of Sade's texts. The Sadian text is structuralist methodology become nightmare. It is subjectivity undone by the presumption of totality. The mirror, the chiasm, does not afford the foundation of subjectivity or sociability by presenting the self as a semblance of the other, as is the case for Lacan.[10] Rather, such use of the chiasm denies all structures of exchange by leaving nothing to be exchanged within a complete presentation of the scene and a complete control of language and the body. Sade reduces the diacritical relations of the chiasm to the reductionist relations of analogy (in which the first term, that of the Master, determines all subsequent relations.) The Sadian text is one of systematics, closure, and semiotic constraint, not one of rupture or transgression.

The chiasm is a central figure in Merleau-Ponty's final work, *The Visible and the Invisible*. For Merleau-Ponty, the chiasm is, as Jean-François Lyotard suggests, the figure of sensibility, and consequently the figure of subjectivity and intersubjectivity. The foundation of the chiasm (which is reversibility[11]) is the separation, the ". . .fragmentation of being. . . (two eyes, two ears: the possibility for discrimination, for the use of the diacritical), it is the advent of difference (on the ground of resemblance. . .)[12] Within this mode of fragmentation is the touching/touched phenomenon, constitutive of both subjectivity and intersubjectivity, since, ". . .each of the two beings is an archetype for the other. . ."[13] This archetypal relation of the flesh is the chiasm. For Merleau-Ponty, subjectivity is not a positivist phenomenon, but a diacritical phenomenon; the subject is not an entity, but an open field of compossibilities within the flesh. The subject is founded upon resemblances within an originary differentiation.

Sade's marriage scene is a chiasmatic model of reduction to a central structure of mastery; Merleau-Ponty's model of the chiasm as the form of intersubjectivity effects just the opposite. Merleau-Ponty writes that the chiasm,

> . . .forms its unity across incompossibilities such as that of my world and the world of the other—By reason of this mediation through reversal, this chiasm, there is not simply a for-Oneself for-the-Other antithesis, there is Being as containing all that, first as sensible Being, and then as Being without restriction. . . Chiasm, instead of the For the Other: that means that there is not only a me-other rivalry, but a co-functioning. We function as one unique body.[14]

For Merleau-Ponty, the self and the other are incompossibilties which live through different worlds (in the Heideggerian sense of the worldhood-of-the-world). Yet these incompossibilities of alterity are ultimately lived as compossibilities within the same flesh, which subtends the cultural world and sustains it. What Merleau-Ponty criticized as the "for-Oneself for-the-Other antithesis" amounts to the antithesis between Master and victim in the Sadian text, where Master and victim are not "archetypes for the other," but rather of completely different ontological orders. The Sadian Master always considers the multiplication of bodies, and aims at eliminating consideration of the "for-the-Other" by manifesting a pure "for-Oneself." Needless to say, for Sade there is no intersubjective functioning as "one unique body," and there is ultimately no incompossibility within the controlled permutations and combinations of the Sadian, sadistic scene. Even the Master/victim antithesis is not an incompossibility, since there is always the possibility of the Master becoming a victim.

In Merleau-Ponty, the being of flesh is "Being without restriction."[15] This does not imply the Sadian catalogue of permutations without restriction, what Hénaff (following Bataille) referred to as a logic without reserve. For Merleau-Ponty, the lack of restriction of the flesh implies that the flesh is a "being in latency."[16] This is precisely the latency, the ambiguity, that we have seen eliminated from the Sadian personnage and the Sadian scene, an elimination effected by destroying the symbolic function by means of manifesting an unlimited catalogue of events. Conversely, for Merleau-Ponty the latency and ambiguity of the flesh are constituted according to,

> . . . the occult trading of the metaphor—where what counts is no longer the manifest meaning of each word and of each image, but the lateral relations, the kinships that are implicated in their transfers and their exchanges.[17]

While Sadian mastery is a function of the dissolution of the symbolic function and of the manifestation of an unrestricted scopophilia, the Merleau-Pontian flesh is a function of the latencies, invisibilities, and depths of meaning implicit in polysymbolism. "Overdetermination (= circularity, chiasm)."[18] Such polysymbolism or overdetermination is the structure of the phenomenological horizon, which is the very ontological foundation of freedom. While Sade may have used Ockham's razor, Merleau-Ponty was concerned with a poetic multiplication of effects.

Merleau-Ponty describes the flesh as a "mirror phenomenon," utilizing the same metaphor as Sade to express its chiasmatic relationship.

> . . . man is the mirror for man. The mirror itself is the instrument of a universal magic that changes things into a spectacle, spectacles into things, myself into another, and another into myself. Artists have often mused upon mirrors because beneath this "mechanical trick," they recognized, just as they did in the case of the trick of perspective, the metamorphosis of seeing and seen which defines both our flesh and the painter's vocation.[19]

The chiasmatic "mirror" phenomenon entails the "fission of appearance and Being."[20] The metaphysical doubling of the chiasmatic fission has also been expressed by the doubling of appearance and reality in the Sadian marriage scene. Yet Sadian discourse ultimately reduces the metaphysical to the physical, indeed to the corporeal, with the intent of consolidating mastery. Merleau-Ponty, on the other hand, maintains the transcendent as the horizon of the corporeal, with the intent of inaugurating the very possibility of freedom.

It is true for both Sade and Merleau-Ponty that, as Merleau-Ponty writes: "Speaking subject: it is the subject of a praxis."[21] Yet for Sade such praxis is the mechanics of manipulation, of domination, within which there is a duplication of speech and scene, a mastery of the scene through speech. This duplication is possible only through absolute mastery (or infinite imagination.) But for Merleau-Ponty, praxis aims at the instantiation of freedom and the ultimate dissolution of mastery, after which not even as "Truth" can there be an absolute adequation of word and deed. The Merleau-Pontian task is a deconstruction of the alliances of power and discourse; the Sadian task is that of the consolidation of power through discourse.

Finally, it must be said that the results of Sade's and Merleau-Ponty's texts are, in an ironic sense, identical: they both achieve the deconstruction of subjectivity. In Sade's texts this is accomplished by the reduction of the subject to an infinitely interchangeable figure in a totalizing scheme of pure mastery and possession. To the contrary, Merleau-Ponty recognized the dissolution of subjectivity as the function of an originary difference where, ". . .what there is to be grasped is a dispossession."[22] Thus for Merleau-Ponty there can be no totalizing philosophy, only an indirect ontology.

Tropes and figures objectify: they simultaneously afford a measure of difference and identity, and subordinate the subject to a determination, a fixation, of attributes.

Merleau-Ponty: "Overdetermination (= circularity, chiasm) = any entity can be accentuated as an emblem of Being."[23] This claim may be amended to state that any figure can be accentuated as emblematic of the subject. Hence the polysymbolism of signs parallels the polymorphism of the flesh. This implies the efficacy of the Baroque model of subjectivity suggested by Genette and Hénaff, a model contested by Sade. Hénaff: "In short, if a baroque character exists which traverses all figures, it is quite simply the soul."[24] Here the function of hermeneutics is not to determine how the subject utilizes figures, but conversely to establish how figures organize forms of subjectivity. Lyotard suggests that, "All theory of metaphor is a theory of the soul, the subject."[25] And Foucault, following

Nietzsche, claims that: "The purpose of history, guided by genealogy, is not to discover the roots of our identity but to commit itself to its dissipation."[26]

What remains after this deconstruction, after this dissipation of subjectivity into an endless and foundationless series of tropes and figures? One possibility is a "logic of events," as Foucault and Deleuze wish to develop. Such a logic refers to a ". . .caesura which fragments the moment and disperses the subject into a plurality of possible positions and functions."[27] According to classical rhetoric, which is foundationally ontotheological, such functions of the subject endlessly attempt the expression of an absolute signified; the signifier is merely a function of the signified, where the signified is an absolute value. But in the post-Structuralist rhetoric of a logic of events, the signified is always a function of the signifier; the signified is never anything else than another signifier. All signifieds are only figures and tropes. Value is nothing more than the determination, donation, and manipulation of attributes. This is precisely what Roland Barthes claims that Sade discovered: ". . .Sade always chooses the discourse over the referent; he always sides with semiosis rather than mimesis. . ."[28]

Yet it is never enough to determine what a trope or figure reveals: one must also seek what it conceals. Lyotard is thus correct in claiming, apropos of Merleau-Ponty's notion of the body as a chiasmatic structure of the flesh, that:

> It is not the body that disturbs language, it is something else that disturbs both language and the body. To accept the body as the location of events is to endorse the defensive displacement, the vast rationalization produced by the platonic-christian tradition with the intent of concealing desire.[29]

According to Lyotard's reading, Merleau-Ponty's theory of the body dissimulates the libido. Yet it is equally true that the libido is always cathected, that is to say, always bound to figurative systems. Such figures and tropes serve equally as the blockage *and* the expression of the libido. The discovery that the subject is a function of figuration serves to dissimulate the fact that these very same figures, the figures of subjectivity itself, serve to dissimulate the libido and desire.

Philosophical systems, much less tropes and figures, always define only a dimension of the imaginary, and never Being or subjectivity in totality. Thus, in the end, our most explicit interpretations, just as our most secret thoughts, will be held suspect. Not because of what they mean, but because of what they are: figures of ourselves.

6

Demented, Deoedipalized, Deconstructed

. . . it may well be that we are talking horseshit . . . we apply the term now to describe unsoundness in an abstract conversation or, indeed, in any over-metaphysical tendency in speech.

Ernest Hemingway
Death in the Afternoon

The forms of our gods are as diverse as the aims of our passions. Or of our fears. Our strategy for eliminating deities depends upon the names that we give to these gods, as well as to the motives for suppression. I wish to investigate one such name of god, and a certain delirious motive.

. . . our personal hallucination now developed as boundlessly as perhaps the total nightmare of human society . . .

George Bataille
Story of the Eye

In "The Sexual Triangle," Jan Kott schematizes the graphic system whereby, ". . .projections of the libido can be presented as transformations of discourse."[1] This system is the schema of the sexual triangle, the apexes of which—mouth, anus, genitals—define a system of semantic relations. The triangle thus signifies the corporeal limits of a semiotic universe, where meaning is determined according to the specific reversals, exchanges, substitutions, identifications, transformations, ratios, and parallels between the terms of this system. (Thus, for example, corresponding to the opposition mouth/anus is the analogous inverse opposition eating/excreting, and the analogous parallel opposition vomiting/excreting.) All possible permutations and combinations within this triangle are meaningful, yet within any given cultural system and historical period only certain relations will be valorized, and all others stigmatized.

Insofar as *Story of the Eye* is organized by a multifarious and abundant sexual activity, the scheme of the sexual triangle may be useful as an interpretive code since "the juxtaposition of the linguistic surface and symbolic activity can define and direct the decoding of clinical and poetic delirium."[2] This method would be particularly appropriate considering Michel Leiris' postulation of the story's "three modes of excess: sexual delirium, blasphemous outbursts and murderous fury."[3] These modes of transgression correspond to the apexes of the sexual triangle: sexual delirium, blasphemy and murder correspond respectively to the genital, oral and anal modes of transgression.

And yet, as Barthes notes, "the erotic theme here is never directly phallic."[4] This pronouncement may be emended by claiming that the religious theme is never directly monotheistic, and the legalistic theme is never directly moralistic. Leiris recognizes this when he describes the erotic activity in *Story of the Eye* in terms of, "innumerable possible permutations in a universe so little hierarchized that all is interchangeable there."[5] Indeed, nearly all possible relations between the terms of the sexual triangle are manifested in this tale (kissing, cunnilingis, analingis, sodomy, coitus.) Furthermore, every term of the major metaphoric series of the story—eye, egg, testicle—is combined with each of the terms of the sexual triangle. The combinative is complete: all permutations and combinations are achieved, and none are privileged. Hence there is a semiotic closure of the system in which the genital function is never privileged, and perversion is never denigrated.

> Transgression. . .is the solar inversion of satanic denial.
>
> Michel Foucault
> "Preface to Transgression"

> . . .where all is essentially founded upon perversity: seduction of the bull by the

> shimmer of the cloth, temptation of the matador who edges closer to the fall—a sort of ripening of evil in a pointed and artful web, under a great sun of luciferian beauty. . .
>
> Michel Leiris
> *Miroir de la tauromachie*

> Goya's crucifixion is a cynically romantic, wooden oleograph that could serve as a poster for the announcement of crucifixions in the manner of bullfight posters. A crucifixion of six carefully selected Christs will take place at five o'clock in the Monumental Golgotha of Madrid, government permission having been obtained.
>
> Ernest Hemingway
> *Death in the Afternoon*

One of the central scenes of *Story of the Eye*, both in relation to the structure of the sexual triangle and to the metaphoric series eye-egg-testicle, is that Granero's death. On May 7, 1922 the great matador Manuel Granero was killed in the Madrid arena, an event witnessed by Bataille. This scene is fictionalized in the narrative of *Story of the Eye*:

> The first bull, the one whose raw balls Simone looked forward to having served on a plate, was a kind of black monster. . . In the end, the death of the solar monster was performed cleanly, with the beast blinded by the scrap of red cloth, the sword deep in the blood-smeared body.
>
> The events that followed were without transition or connection, not because they weren't actually related, but because my attention was so absent as to remain absolutely dissociated. In just a few seconds: first, Simone bit into one of the raw balls, to my dismay; then Granero advanced towards the bull, waving his scarlet cloth; finally, almost at once, Simone, with a blood-red face and a suffocating lewdness, uncovered her long white thighs up to her moist vulva, into which she slowly and surely fitted the second pale globule—Granero was thrown back by the bull and wedged against the balustrade; the horns struck the balustrade three times at full speed; at the third blow, one horn plunged into the right eye and through the head. A shriek of unmeasured horror coincided with a brief orgasm for Simone, who was lifted up from the stone seat only to be flung back with a bleeding nose, under a blinding

> sun; men instantly rushed over to haul away Granero's body, the right eye dangling from the head.[6]

The first bull, the "solar monster" (symbol of the masculine powers of a virile, fecundating sky and sun), suffered the expected and desired death in the ring, as well as a double castration: both the symbolic castration of blinding by the scrap of red cloth (the muleta) and the literal castration following the *mise-à-mort*. It was upon these castrated testicles that Simone wished to feast, as do some afficionados of the corrida. And according to the logic of the sexual triangle she did indeed feast upon them, with both her mouth and her *vagina dentata*.

But the second bull effected a reversal of events: this time it was the matador, Granero himself, who was blinded and killed by a fatal cornada. Simultaneous with this disaster, Simone was "flung back" (like Granero) with a bleeding nose as she was "blinded" by the sun, at the very moment of orgasm, *la petite mort*. Thus a symbolic equivalence is established between the bull (solar monster), Granero (matador), and Simone (libertine protagonist.)

Death and the erotic are related in the corrida. Michel Leiris explains in *Miroir de la tauromachie* that the essentially phallic figure of the bull interacts with the matador in a sort of erotic dance which approximates the movements of coitus, the swordthrust being the final moment of intromission, and the death spasm being orgasm. And as Hemingway observes in *Death in the Afternoon*:

> . . .the beauty of the moment of killing is that flash when man and bull form one figure as the sword goes all the way in, the man leaning after it, death uniting the two figures in the emotional, aesthetic and artistic climax of the fight.[7]

It may be added that this description also holds true when it is the thrust of the bull's horn into the matador's flesh that unites the two figures at the moment of death. Thus only at the moment of death, the "moment of truth," can we tell which figure, man or bull, played the masculine role: the drama is retrospectively organized by its denouement, death. Although either man or bull may die, according to the dramatic logic of the corrida it is the bull who should die, since the corrida is a drama which symbolizes the discipline, sacrifice, and effort necessary for the spirit to overcome the blood passions. Eroticism must be understood within this mode of sublimation, since the erotic cannot exist in a state of nature.

The erotic is founded upon the relation between passion as pure libido and the spirit as displacement and repression of the libido.

In the classical corrida of Spain the entire spectacle, including the matador's capework, was oriented towards the moment of death. But the modern corrida, initiated by the great Juan Belmondo, is distinguished by a primacy of the capework, in relation to which the *mise-à-mort* is a subsidiary finale. (Indeed, some non-Spanish corrida have gone so far as to eliminate the killing of the bull. And in all corrida the picadors' horses are now protected from disembowlment by protective pads. Yet the death of the horse is deemed by some to be necessary to the drama in order to prove to the bull that his efforts are not in vain, and also in order to prefigure the death of the bull.) While emphasis upon the capework seems to accentuate the dangers to the matador, some, including Hemingway, claim that it entailed the decadence of the corrida, insofar as it diverts spectatorial attention from the drama's true telos: death.

The maneuvers, among which is the all-important capework, are called *suerte*, which is variously defined as, "chance, hazard, lots, fortune, luck, good luck, haphazard; state, condition, fate, doom, destiny, kind, sort; species, manner, mode, way, skillful manoeuvre; trick, feat, juggle, and piece of ground separated by landmark."[8] Indeed, any of these may be an appropriate description of the capework, of the conditions and actions which lead to the moment of truth, the moment of death.

Yet if the moment of death is indeed the moment of truth in *Story of the Eye*, then we must ask what truth is revealed by the drama. Or is this rather some sort of comedy? To what effect is the equivalence between the bull as solar monster, the matador Granero, and the spectator Simone?

What after all are these churches now if they are not the tombs and sepulchers of God?

Do we smell nothing yet of the divine decomposition?

Friedrich Nietzsche
The Gay Science

After the event in the Madrid arena, the protagonists travel to Seville, where they enter the church of Don Juan:

> At either side of the entrance door hung two famous canvases by the painter Valdès Leal, pictures of decomposing corpses:

> interestingly, one of the eye sockets was being gnawed through by a rat.[9]

This painting is emblematic of the scenario to follow, in which a priest is murdered in a manner symbolically equivalent to the fatal scene of the corrida.

After Simone's blasphemous confession, the three portagonists repeatedly abuse the priest sexually, culminating with Simone raping him while strangling him to death, just as he achieves orgasm, another coincidence of death and *la petite mort*. At the moment of his death, his body and Simone's form one figure, just as does the bull and the matador at the moment of truth. This equivalence between the priest and the bull is established by the description wherein, "Sir Edmund nudged him with his foot; the monster leaped up and drew back, bellowing with such ludicrous fury that we burst out laughing."[10]

The priest (a "monster") is likened to the first bull (the "solar monster"), which may also be imagined leaping, bellowing and later threatening before being put to death. And it should be noted that at the moment before the *estocada* (the swordthrust) the matador's arms form the sign of the cross upon which the bull is impaled, crucified. Furthermore, after the murder, they remove the priest's eye so that Simone can play with it: thus they priest too enters into equivalence with those who are blinded: the first bull by the red mulata, Simone by the sun, and Granero by the second bull's horn. It is this other, theological, *mise-à-mort* which is the story's finale.

The lack alluded to earlier, in relation to the presumed closure of the combinatory formed by the sexual triangle and the metaphoric series eye-egg-testicle, is now revealed. During the blasphemous drama in the church, they discover the key to the tabernacle, and immediately remove the consecrated hosts.

> "Look," he explained to Simone, "the eucharistic hosts in the ciborium, and here the chalice where they put the white wine.
>
> "They smell like come," said Simone, sniffing the unleavened wafers.
>
> "Precisely," continued Sir Edmund. "The hosts, as you see, are nothing other than Christ's sperm in the form of small white biscuits. And as for the wine they put in the chalice, the ecclesiastics say it is the blood of Christ, but they are obviously mistaken. If they really thought it was blood, they

would use red wine, but since they employ only white wine, they are showing that at the bottom of their hearts they are quite aware that this is urine."[11]

Whereupon they force the priest to desecrate the hosts with his own sperm and urine.

According to Catholic dogma, through a metaphoric relation, the wine symbolizes Christ's blood and the wafer symbolizes Christ's flesh; Sir Edmund's blasphemous revision of this symbolism, with urine instead of wine and semen instead of wafer, metonymically symbolizes God as Phallus, God in the form of Priapus. The tale's anti-phallocratic theme is sustained: indeed, the phallus and God as transcendental signifiers are missing. While present in the nominalist structure of the sexual triangle, the phallus is lacking from the coordinating metaphoric series eye-egg-testicle. (The penis is only metonymically related to the testicle, as the Priapic God is metonymically related to the host as semen.)

The textual logic of *Story of the Eye* is organized by the alterations of the eye's position on the sexual triangle, and by its metaphoric and metonymic variations. Thus the signification of the tale is not dependent upon the absolute position of a transcendent God; the position and significance of such a God itself is dependent upon the relation between the sexual triangle and the symbolic series eye-egg-testicle. This *deus absconditus* becomes a signified forever lost in an infinite play of signifiers: the signified "God" operates at best through a forlorn mode of identification, where "You are what you eat" (e.g., the bull's balls or the lover's sperm instead of the Eucharistic hosts). Such a God, therefore, may serve at best a fetishistic purpose.

The irony of the equivalence between the corrida and the church scene, with their respective "moments of truth," now becomes apparent. This "moment of truth" is nothing other than the dissolution of the very foundation of truth, the death of God. This moment guarantees that there be no "truth," but rather a free circulation of attributes and qualifications sustained by a projected closure of rhetorical possibilities. Hence the reason for the polysemy of the term *"suerte," i.e.*, the maneuvers leading to the moment of death, which includes the range of meanings from chance to destiny, fortune to doom, trick to skillful maneuver. Quite simply, meaning is a function of the distribution of attributes within a system, regardless of the motives or occurances which determine that distribution. The name of God is just one more term within this system, no more privileged than any other term, and susceptible to limitless variations, positions and rhetorical substitutions. Thus while the priest's murder exemplified sexual delirium, blasphemous outbursts and murderous fury, it is no more transgressive than any other event in the story.

The priest and the bull are symbolically castrated by blinding. This ritual symbolic castration is a de-Oedipalization whereby God is satirized by Priapus and summarily despoiled. And the further irony is that according to popular tradition, Priapus is believed to avert the evil eye: the eye of the priest, after having been disorbitated, may indeed serve as such an omen:

> . . . I drew her thighs apart, and found myself facing something I imagine I had been waiting for in the same way that a guillotine waits for a neck to slice. I even felt as if my eyes were bulging from my head, erectile with horror; in Simone's hairy vagina, I saw the wan blue eye of Marcelle, gazing at me through tears of urine. Streaks of come in the steaming hair helped give that dreamy vision a disastrous sadness. I held the thighs open while Simone was convulsed by the urinary spasm, and the burning urine streamed out from under the eye down to the thighs below. . .[12]

The evil eye is that of their former compatriot, the now dead Marcelle. It is the disorbitated eye of Granero. Of the bull. Of Simone. And of course, of the priest. It is also the eye of God. It circulates within the sexual triangle; it occupies multiple subject positions; it shifts metaphorically within the series eye-egg-testicle. The *suerte* of the eye, and the various maneuvers of castration, are ambiguosly related in the mortal, climactic moment of truth. Yet ultimately this eye, the organizing metaphoric term of this text, disappears!

But what is the limit, or the meaning, of this textual circulation of the eye? To what end is the symbolic murder of God? Does not the logic of this tale imply that Priapus must avert his own evil eye? Isn't this a variation on the originary tale of Oedipus himself, the very Oedipus who cannot possibly appear as a symbolic structure of this tale?

> The law is written in a pornographic book.
>
> Gilles Deleuze
> *Rhizome*

> . . .it permits a profanation without object. . .
>
> Michel Foucault
> "Preface to Transgression"

Deleuze and Guattari, in a passage of *Anti-Oedipus* which *a fortiori* proclaims the revolutionary position of desire, argue that:

> The three errors concerning desire are called lack, law, and signifier. It is one and the same error, an idealism that forms a pious conception of the unconscious. And it is futile to interpret these notions in terms of a combinative apparatus that makes of lack an empty position and no longer a deprivation, that turns the law into a rule of the game and no longer a commandment, and the signifier into a distributor and no longer a meaning, for these notions cannot be perverted from dragging their theological cortege behind—insufficiency of being, guilt, signification.[13]

It is as if this passage were a gloss upon the text of *Story of the Eye*. The three errors of which Deleuze/Guattari write—lack, law, signifier—correspond to the three modes of transgression which Leiris claims are central to the story—sexual delirium, murderous fury, blasphemous outbursts—which in turn correspond to the organizational structures of Western metaphysics—phallocentrism, egocentrism, logocentrism. The valorization of the sexual triangle as an Oedipal structure is effected according to these systems. Yet the valorized triangle does not govern the textual structures of exchange in *Story of the Eye*, but is itself manipulated. And the very signification of God in the text is determined by the manipulation of the terms of the sexual triangle in relation to the circulation of the eye. This God never finds a proper signifier within the text. But when, after all, did God ever find a proper signifier in our ontotheological tradition? Isn't it precisely this very lack of signification which was of the textual essence of God, and of the various theological dramas within which he appeared? For this reason the ritualistic murder in the church may be considered a black mass: such a mass does not effect the renewal of the spirit through the ingestion of the consubstantiate host; rather, it effects the desecration of that host and a symbolic castration in the church as a theater of cruelty. God, erected as phallic King, becomes a totemic sacrifice.

Deleuze/Guattari protest that:

> From the moment that desire is made to depend upon the signifier, it is put back under the yoke of a despotism whose effect is castration, there where one recognizes the stroke of

> the signifier itself; but the sign of desire is never signifying, it exists in the thousands of productive break-flows that never allow themselves to be signified within the unary stroke of castration.[14]

In *Story of the Eye* desire is indeed traced along "thousands of productive break-flows," manifested by the infinite circulation of metaphoric terms within the closure of perverse possibilities. And these flows are certainly not "signified within the unary stroke of castration": rather, castration is the ironic reversal whereby desire is sublated by death. Ultimately, it is that grand castrator, God the Father, the solar monster, who receives this stroke, administered beyond the symbolic system of the sexual triangle.

> I laugh when I think that these eyes persist
> in demanding objects which don't destroy them.
>
> George Bataille
> *"La pratique de la joie devant la mort"*

In *Death in the Afternoon* Hemingway relates the tale of a bull in Valencia which killed sixteen men and wounded over sixty others in amateur events. One of those killed was a young gypsy, whose brother and sister followed the bull from town to town in the hope of assassinating it in revenge, but they didn't have the chance. Finally, the owner of the bull decided to have it slaughtered, both because of its age and because of the attempt to suppress such amateur events.

> The two gypsies were at the slaughter-house and the young man asked permission, since the bull had killed his brother, to kill the bull. This was granted and he started in by digging out both the bull's eyes while the bull was in his cage, and spitting carefully into the sockets, then after killing him by severing the spinal marrow between the neck vertebrae with a dagger, he experienced some difficulty in this, he asked permission to cut off the bull's testicles, which being granted, he and his sister built a small fire at the edge of the dusty street outside the slaughter-house and roasted the two glands on sticks and when they were done, ate them. They then turned their backs on the slaughter-house and went away along the road and out of town.[15]

Part III

A FINE MADNESS

7

The Errant Text

. . .any entity can be accentuated as an emblem
of Being (=character) . . .

Maurice Merleau-Ponty

The strictures of ideology are apparent in art, madness and philosophy; yet these varied modes of expression may serve as the most telling critiques of ideological systems. We may consider one manner in which this can be accomplished, and in doing so unravel some of the ontological implications of the problem of style, which is intricately tied to the question of ideology.

Meaning is a function of the ratio between the simultaneous determination, indetermination, and overdetermination of signs (whether these signs be linguistic, pictorial, or otherwise.)

(1) *Determination* is a function of a sign's contextualization within a coded significative system. The limit of determinacy is an *idée fixe,* which is structured in accordance with the *techné fixe* of a praxical or cognitive system. The extreme limit of determination is the reification of meaning within an ideological system of thought. Ideology is a significative system which takes a specific, limited meaning to be a universal truth, implying an absolute signified as the referent of every signifier. All thought is determinate to a great degree: the quotidian determinacy of thought and action is most often related to the practical ends of existence, and does not find itself at each point ideologically bound. But at its limit, determination as a coding function is totalizing, ideological.

(2) *Indetermination* refers to the manner in which a sign operates as a "floating signifier," which will receive new meaning according to each new context, each new system, within which it is placed. Indeterminacy permits a sign to be appropriated by any system, within any code, and consequently receive a new meaning with each new use. It maintains the horizonal openness upon which freedom is grounded. Indetermination is a decoding, detotalizing function.

(3) *Overdetermination* refers to the tropic/figural, symbolic possibilities of signs, *i.e.*, to the fact that any sign may symbolically connect any of the significative systems within which it is found with any other, hence achieving a proliferation of meanings. This aspect of overdetermination is expressed by Marc Richir:

> . . . the very world is constituted by a logological proliferation, by chiasms of chiasms, by phenomenalizing bonds which constantly subvert the apparent hierarchies in order to reverse them—which constantly topple the subordinate "into the emptiness of a new open dimension," transferring it (by metaphor) to the level of a new dimension while implicitely maintaining within it all of the chains to which it remains tied (by "metonymy.")[1]

This means that any sign (logos) proliferates meaning by entering into new systems of thought and expression, but that each sign carries over into the new system meaningful vestiges of all of the previous systems within which it occured. Signs forcefully bear their history within their use, hence any hermeneutic must take into account this historicist character of signs in relation to the production of meaning. Such a theory of signs will entail the conception of philosophy as a productive discipline, as the source of a multiplication of metaphysical entities, contrary to Ockham's famous claim against such philosophical excesses. Overdetermination is a recoding function; it is the basis of all interpretation and exegesis, including philosophy.

Codes and sign systems determine the conditions of expressibility. Yet the horizonal openness maintained by the possibility of overdetermination is the ground of interpretation and creative freedom. Conversely, ideology is the suppression of freedom achieved by closing off this horizontal openness, by an excess of determination. These issues may be clarified by consideration of the following examples.

Eugene Minkowski, the phenomenological psychologist who conducted extensive studies of the psychopathology of the lived-body, related the following details of the case history of one of his patients:

> These ideas of guilt, ruin, imminent punishment, and persecution were accompanied by interpretations of a really surprising scope. This was the "residue politics," as he called it—a political system that had been instituted especially for him. Every leftover, all residue, would be put aside to be one day stuffed into his abdomen—and this, from all over the world. Everything would be included without exception. When one smoked, there would be the burnt match, the ashes, and the cigarette butt. At meals, he was preoccupied with the crumbs, the fruit pits, the chicken bones, the wine or the water at the bottom of the glasses. The egg, he said, was his worst enemy because of the shell—it was also the expression of the great anger of his persecutors. When one sewed, there would be bits of thread and needles. All the matches, strings, bits of paper and pieces of glass that he saw while walking in the street were meant for him. After that came the nail parings and hair clippings, empty bottles, letters and envelopes, subway tickets, address-bands, the dust that one brought in on one's shoes, bath water, the garbage from the kitchen and from all the restaurants of France, etc. Then it was rotten fruit and vegetables, cadavers of animals and men, the urine and feces of horses. "Whoever speaks of a clock," he would tell us, "speaks of the hands, cogs, springs, case, pendulum, etc." And all this he would have to swallow. In sum, these interpretations were boundless; they included everything, absolutely everything that he saw or imagined. In these conditions, it is not difficult to understand that the smallest thing, the most minute act of daily life, was immediately interpreted as being hostile to him.[2]

Garbage; waste; detritus: these are the dimensions under which everything in the world, and every part of everything, is understood. But in turn, the significative dimension of "garbage" operates as a specific meaning within the more all-pervasive, but always unstated and nonreflective, system of paranoia. The paranoic system of this patient utilized garbage as a significative dimension in order to close off thought's horizons and thus deny the possibility of all free activity. As Minkowski explains, this patient built a present on a blocked future. It is, as Merleau-Ponty writes in general, ". . . the fixation of a 'character' by investment of the openness of Being in an Entity

. . ."[3] While dimensions structure and determine experience, freedom is the ability to recognize, choose, and change such dimensions; it is the ability to question the self, existence, and Being.

All creative thought is a simultaneous decoding and recoding, but there can never be a full suspension of codification. Freedom is the maintenance of significative horizons, of the possibility of thinking and acting within a multiplicity of codes and dimensions. Ideology, on the other hand, entails bondage to a given code or dimension: ideology totalizes by attempting to determine existence according to only a limited representation of its aspects. Freedom takes the whole apart; ideology takes a part for the whole.

In Minkowski's case history, the dimension of garbage signified and supported the creation of a persecutory world, a system of threat and pain. It determined the patient's worldview as disjointed from the everyday significations of the lifeworld. The tragedy of this reduction of experience to such a limiting, albeit meaningful, system of thought is not that everything becomes garbage, but rather that there is no choice in the matter, that one is bound, not free.

The same dimension, garbage, may reveal an entirely different meaning when applied to another system of thought, when used as a different style of encoding experience. To illustrate this, an example from Dadaist art may be contrasted to the above case of paranoia. Consider that the materials used by Kurt Schwitters to create his collages were assembled from all sorts of refuse, from garbage. While much of this refuse, as used by Schwitters, is formally reminiscent of that used in Cubist *papier collé* works, the crucial difference is that while Cubists subordinated those bits of detritus to the greater formal scheme of their works, Schwitters conceives of his entire artistic enterprise on the basis of such material. The Cubists subordinated the garbage to the forms of the work; Schwitters subordinated his works to the forms and textures of garbage! Furthermore, Schwitters began to conceive of an entire world according to the dimension of garbage.

> I could not, in fact, see the reason why old tickets, driftwood, cloakroom tabs, wires and parts of wheels, buttons and old rubbish found in attics and refuse dumps should not be as suitable a material for painting as the paints made in factories. This was, as it were, a social attitude, and artistically speaking, a private enjoyment, but particularly the latter. . .I called my new works utilizing such materials 'Merz.' This is the second syllable of 'Kommerz.' It originated in the 'Merzbild,' a work

> in which the word 'Merz,' cut out from an advertisement of the 'Kommerz und Privatbank' and pasted on, could be read among the abstract element . . . I looked for a collective term for his new style, since I could not fit my pictures into the older categories . . . So I called all my work as a species 'Merz' pictures, after the characteristic one. Later I extended the use of the word 'Merz,' first to my poetry . . . and finally to all my related activities. Now I call myself 'Merz.'[4]

Here, "Merz," that is, the detritus and waste and ruins of commercial products, became the category under which everything, including the artist himself, was expressed and understood. Schwitters' account of the conception of Merz is particularly interesting for the present discussion of codes and dimensions since it shows how a particular thing, or type of thing, (in this case a scrap of advertisement, a fragment of a word) can become the emblem of an entire system of thought, of a worldview. Indeed, Merz became a "collective term," a dimension, for a "new style." (Merz is an all-inclusive attitude which may be paralleled by John Cage's accomplishment in musical theory and practice of considering all sounds as possible components of music, within the rubrics of an "indeterminacy theory.") But Merz goes beyond the artistic realm, since Schwitters realized that he himself was also Merz. Merz is thus the emblem of a world-system; it is the encoding of all experience under a specific term. Such a term loses its facticity in order to become a dimension, in order to ground all other facticity.

On the surface, there is a distinct similarity between Merz and the "residue politics" of Minkowski's patient, since both of them utilize garbage as the unique dimension to circumscribe and codify their experience, to form their worlds. But there are crucial, and ironic, differences between these two worldviews. Schwitters describes Merz as a social attitude that engenders a private enjoyment. (This is of course one of the functions of art. But while Merz is life as art, Minkowski's patient is absolutely incapable of aesthetic appreciation.) Inversely, Minkowski's patient describes his "residue politics" as engendering pain ("guilt, ruin, imminent punishment and persecution"), an attitude in which objects and other people are experienced as persecutory things, *i.e.*, as sources of his torture. Yet this residue politics is certainly not a true political organization, since politics is necessarily a social, civic function, whereas the residue politics was "instituted especially for him."

Merz is a productive system of expression, which leads to the ultimate limits of what Lévi-Strauss called "*bricolage*," (*i.e.*, the ability to fix or construct anything with the materials at hand), while the residue politics leads to the ultimate limits of paranoia and destruction. Merz is a metaphor that generates an entire system of thought: this is the indication of a free, productive, dominat*ing* activity. (Merz is not a mannerism since it is not bound to a previous form of expression.) Inversely, the residue politics is a metaphor that was generated by a paranoic system: this is the indication of a totalizing, totalitarian, ideological thought (*i.e.*, a personal, pathological ideology in conformity with the "politics" of the lived-body, and not a civil, demotic politics.) It is a dominat*ed* activity, a reactive reproductive thought.

But the examples of Merz and the residue politics go far beyond a simple description of horizonal dimensions, of particular (even if unusual) codes. They illustrate the extreme limits of thought. The residue politics expresses the limit of thought's totalizing function: everything becomes emblematic of a particular system, and thus all significative horizons are closed. Merz expresses the opposite aspect of thought, the limit of its differentiating function: the system becomes emblematic of everything, and thus the significative horizons remain open since nothing is bound to the system, but everything is informed by it. Merz is detotalizing thought and practice, as is in principle all Dada. Residue politics turns the world into garbage; Merz turns garbage into a (artistic) world. Yet neither stance is a holistic account of everyday experience, since thought is never completely bound nor completely free. The origin of thought is the intertwining of contingency and freedom. This is to say that thought is always a function of situatedness, and that freedom cannot be grasped in an abstract mode, but can only be lived through in a situation, through concrete relations in the world.

Signs are polysemic and polyvalent: any sign may be bound simultaneously to numerous significative systems, hence the possibility of overdetermination, hence the need for hermeneutics. The valence of a sign, its combinative power, is ultimately determined by the existential situatedness of the sign-user (*i.e.*, speaker, writer, painter, etc.; and listener, reader, observer, etc.) Situatedness is the guarantee of the differences between the uses (and consequently the meanings) of any given sign. This is why, in value theory as well as in hermeneutics, one must know, following Nietzsche, not only *what* was said, but also *who* was speaking. The personal voice suffuses *all* texts (and indeed all sign-systems): it is just a matter of learning how to locate that voice and deconstruct the tropes and figures that dissimulate it. The considerations of situatedness, the lifeworld, and history, imply that the hermeneutic process cannot achieve an ideal, essential meaning. Ideality is shattered by the existential considerations of meaning, and both the arche and telos of meaning shift with each enunciator, with each hermeneutic or creative attempt.

Codes, dimensions, are the architectonic structures that determine the possible uses of signs. But they are historical models, and not eternally valid structures. So, as the codes determine the uses of signs, so too do the uses of signs eventually, continually, restructure the codes. As the signs simultaneously condense and separate meaning, sediment and differentiate structures, an interplay of equivalences and differences develops as the originary structure of thought.

If meaning is the codified relation between the equivalences and differences of the signs within a system, then significative change occurs according to what André Malraux aptly terms "coherent deformation." Characterized by Merleau-Ponty:

> It is just this 'coherent deformation' of available significations which arranges them in a new sense and takes not only the hearers but the speaking subject as well through a decisive step.[5]

Coherent deformation is the process whereby the form, the facticity of the world is shattered by praxis, with the result that a new meaning ensues. The "coherence" maintains the equivalences between signs; the "deformation" achieves the differences between signs.

Style is the form of coherent deformation. It is the form of all meaning as facticity. As Merleau-Ponty explains: "All style is giving form to the elements of the world which permits the orientation of the world to one of its essential parts."[6] In terms of philosophy, this means that, ". . .the ontological capacity (=capacity to take a being as representative of Being)."[7] While such "essential parts," such dimensions (*e.g.*, garbage), may be instituted by either contingent or aleatory aspects of the situation, each dimension, as it "stylizes" thought, guarantees that whatever enters the given significative system may be emblematic of that system. For example, Malraux wrote that Van Gogh's famous painting of a chair, ". . . seemed to me an ideogram of the name Van Gogh and also the ideogram of a chair."[8] Thus we may no longer speak of possession, signatures, or essences. An author's or painter's name signifies a style, a system of signifiers, and a signifying system which indicates not the person of the artist, but rather performs the presentation of a world; such is a coherent deformation of our common, everyday world, and of our cultural heritage.

Malraux suggests that, "God is a great creator of forms, although he has no style."[9] As a corollary to this idea, consider Emmanuelle Arsan's claim that, "The most perfect artistic creation is that which moves farthest from the image of God."[10] This implies that style is a function of praxis, of facticity and situatedness. The all-encompassing ideal of God's thought, a pure *pensée de survol*, would be styleless because it would eliminate the possibility of variation, of the interplay between differences and equivalences within a system that is necessary for the advent of style. Thus while style is established through coherent deformation, the term "deformation" implies the existence of some formation. Such a formation is constituted by the cultural world, which is the field of our facticity.

Yet stylization is not mannerism, since style sustains the horizonal openness of significative systems. Stylistic equivalences operate not merely as identificatory presence, but also as differential exchange. The systems of equivalences are structures of exchange. And style is the form of that exchange. Style informs the conditions of expressibility and exchangeability which structure all possibilities of thought. But as differentiating, style guarantees that the closure of any significative system is not absolute. Such a lack of closure denies the efficacy of a classical notion of univocal truth and eternal essences. There is no longer an absolute cosmos: meaning is now dependent upon the contingent and aleatory combinatory of signs. The "cosmos" is the facticity of the cultural/historical system. Because of the structures of exchange between signs, there is no absolutely privileged signifier. Privilege is only relative, only meaningful within particular systems. Ideology is the attempt to institute such privileged signifiers, and privilege is a function of the role a sign plays within a system, not the function of any value intrinsic to a sign. No such value exists.

We find within the modern tradition certain signifiers which work in direct opposition to such traditional totalizing, privileged signifiers as "God," "Beauty," "The One," "Phallus," "Evil," etc. There are signs which create a locus where all signification and symbolism is decentered, signs which detotalize and disorder, such as the "Flesh" for Merleau-Ponty, the "Eternal Return" and the "Earth" for

Nietzsche, and "Sodomy" for Sade. Such signifiers shift the locus of thought from taxonomy to tropology, from ordering and classification to production and creation.

But what then becomes of philosophy? In a story entitled, "Tlön, Uqbar, Orbis Tertius," Jorge Luis Borges writes:

> The metaphysicians of Tlön do not seek for the truth or even for verisimilitude, but rather for the astounding. They judge that metaphysics is a branch of fantastic literature. They know that a system is nothing more than the subordination of all aspects of the universe to any one such aspect.[11]

Jean-François Lyotard recognizes this relationship between philosophy and fantasy; "Reality is never anything but a sector of the imaginary field in which we have accepted the renunciation, the decathexis, of our fantasms of desire."[12] This seems to hold true *a fortiori* for classical Western metaphysics. Freud states it even more forcefully:

> . . . it was obvious that the forms assumed by the different neuroses echoed the most highly admired productions of our culture. Thus hysterics are undoubtedly our imaginative artists, even if they express their phantasies mimetically in the main and without considering their intelligibility to other people; the ceremonials and prohibitions of obsessional neurotics drive us to suppose that they have created a private religion of their own; and *the delusions of paranoiacs have an unpalatable external similarity and internal kinship to the systems of our philosophers*. It is impossible to escape the conclusion that these patients are, in an asocial fashion, making the very attempts at solving their conflicts and appeasing their pressing needs, which, when they are carried out in a fashion that has binding force for the majority, go by the names of poetry, religion, and philosophy.[13]

Do the manifestations of such phantasms as philosophical thought find their locus not merely *in*, but rather *as*, the transcendental, as an attempt to dissimulate desire and finitude in the phastasm of totality? Is Mythos always a function of Logos? Need this always be the case?

Consider Jeanne Tripier, an artist who was institutionalized as mentally ill and diagnosed as having, ". . . chronic hallucinatory psychosis; psychic excitement; Loghorrea, megalomania." We find in her diary:

> Xbdqgxatuvmaytiviskitos alsaqualificatifsogo bibiscoloyatel domiconilosiskibitos; alleuiyabisloyosicos urwisky yoyodelsicomatocciscoyatismoyos; Jagocesissa Jgdcovryiscovoyaviscotismayomatisstos; viviscos J. d'Arc! pipisiscotoyomaticcosyovadismoloyadelmos prépare, de très grandes surprises, à tous les peuples nomades.[14]

This is seemingly an instantiation of the metaphysics of Tlön: the astounding, *i.e.*, "the very great surprises" for which we must prepare, are not only those words which which we slowly discover in the text: qualificatif, con, alleuiya, wisky (*i.e.*, "Urwisky," the primal waters of life!), coma, viviscos, pipi. These "surprises" are also what we are to become: they are our future. For Tripier, "all the nomadic people," signifies herself, since she identified variously with Jeanne d'Arc, Josephine de Beauharnais, Zibodandez I, Lucifier I, Mercure, Sainte Thérèse, Ponce Pilate, Morphée des Catacombes, l'Orang-Outan, Sophie la sorcière moderne, and many others. One must prepare for what one may become. One must prepare for alterity. The horizon of the future remains open, even if fantastic. This is the Deleuzean "nomad thought," the Derridean "dissemination;" it is philosophy as logorrhea, as a productive textual discipline.

We have indeed, in our philosophy, a parallel example. Nietzsche, speaking under the detotalizing signs of the Eternal Return, Dionysus, and the Earth, claimed that, "I am every name in history." It must be stressed that this list includes Dionysus, who himself bears several names. This is a recognition that the self, the "who" of the text, is also a fiction. The horizon of existence remains open: this is the Nietzschean affirmation, the authentic "yea-saying," which is also indicated by Tripier in the chant of "alleuiya." Such an "alleuiya" is never just affirmation as an "amen," which as Roland Barthes points out is at the limit of language.[15] The "alleuiya" reaches beyond the limit.

Such an insidious listing destroys all taxonomic schemes.[16] It aims at a purely open horizon. It leads us from the text to the existential textures of existence. As Geoffrey Hartman claims, "Exemplification is always serial, subversive, plural."[17] Such listing refers to the "stigma" of the "here and now," and is thus a principle of indeterminacy. It too decenters and detotalizes the text, as well as the subject. The list is the text as errant, erratic, and endless. Hence all interpretive logic must be a logic of events, of occasions, and never merely of structures and systems.

Meaning originates through the double movement of the uprooting and inscription of signs: the decontextualization, decoding, and detotalizing simultaneous with the contextualization, coding, and totalizing operations of thought. Vacillating between the poetic forms of nonsense and the stereotypes of everyday speech, all forms of the lifeworld are but preludes to history and prolegomena to all future metaphysics.

8

L'Amour Fou, L'Amour Unique*

No other woman will ever have access to this room where you are thousands, until all of the gestures which I have seen you make are decomposed.

Reciprocal love, as I envisage it, is an apparatus of mirrors which, by the thousands of angles through which the unknown can appear, returns to me the faithful image of she whom I love, a divination of my own desire ever more surprising and gilded with life.

André Breton
L'Amour fou

On the cover of the Surrealist journal *Minotaure* #3-4 (1933) are displayed four Tarot cards, among which is *Le fou*, the madman, or the jester who simulates madness. This card is a passive symbol, denoting carelessness, impulsiveness, madness and the submission to external influences. As a lunar symbol, it also denotes the intuitive, the unconscious, and possession. This card (from which the modern Joker is derived) is either numbered XXII as the final card in the series, or it is numbered 0 as the first card, or else it remains unnumbered; it is thus the zero-degree signifier of the Tarot, an absolute floating signifier which can assume any value. It is the enigma of engimas. The madman of the Tarot is in fact emblematic of the Surrealist project, insofar as it is a transformative articulation whereby the entirety of reality can be modified, disrupted and transformed. Such transformations of desire arrive from the exterior, from chance encounters which we must comprehend as a mode of the irrational, and which we must await as our fate.[1] But what is this madness, what is this mad love?

The third issue of *La Révolution Surréaliste* contains Michel Leiris' Surrealist glossary, "Glossaire: J'y serre mes glosses," which offers the definition of the word "define": "To define is to disperse. The dilemma of madness." The Surrealists' fascination with madness is partially due to the fact that madness is a *de facto* transformation of reality, an escape from the confines of rationality. Hence the central aspect of Surrealist methodology, thematized in the first *Manifesto of Surrealism* (1924) as a "pure psychic automatism," "the absence of any control exercised by reason, exempt from any aesthetic or moral concern," already describes the textual and pictorial production of the insane, which is consequently appropriated by the Surrealists. This valorization of the primary process of the unconscious is aimed at creating a world in which the marvellous is manifested, opposites are reconciled, and desire is given free reign: such a disruption, contestation and transmutation of everyday reality was to create the world of the surreal.[2] And the method of such Surrealist production was analogous to that of the seer: by a sort of absolute aesthetic availability (*disponibilité*), the Surrealist would confront the world as a scene of "objective chance," the "found objects" of which would become the signs of one's own desire. Once discovered, such objects would manifest that "convulsive beauty" which Breton saw as the central mode of Surrealist aesthetic production, and a mark of Surrealist Eros.

In another entry of his glossary, Leiris wrote: "Revolution—the solution to every dream." But how did such a solution manifest itself? What were the aims of this revolution? 1929-1930 was a pivotal moment in the Surrealist movement: with the publication of the *Second Manifesto of Surrealism* Breton "officially" expelled from the movement the dissident Surrealists (Masson, Desnos, Boiffard, Artaud, Leiris, Queneau), most notably Georges Bataille, then editor of the review *Documents*. In this manifesto, Breton criticizes Bataille insofar as, "Monsieur Bataille professes to consider in the world that which is vilest, most discouraging, and most corrupted. . ." Hence, "It is to be noted that Monsieur Bataille misuses adjectives with a passion: befouled, senile, rank, sordid, lewd, doddering. . ." Bataille responds to Breton in an article entitled, "La 'vielle taupe' et le préfixe *sur* dans les mots *surhomme* et *surréaliste*," which opens with an epigram from Marx: "In history as in nature, the rotten is the laboratory of life." Bataille accuses the Surrealists of "pretentious idealist aberrations," and claims that without such baseness, "there can be no revolutionaries, there is only nauseating utopian sentimentality." He opposes Breton's orthodoxy with a sort of heterodoxy, with what he terms a *heterology*, a scatological, parodic view of existence derived from Nietzsche and mythopoeic-sociological analysis. For Breton, the goal of Surrealism (on both the psychic and material levels) was the reconciliation of opposites in a surreality. Surrealism is thus a mode of *dialectical idealism*, despite the suggestion implied by the title of the journal to succeed *La révolution Surréaliste*, which was *Le Surréalisme au Service de la Révolution* (with the revolution in question being the Marxist Russian revolution.) For Bataille, to the contrary, despite the revolutionary impetus of his work, the goal of heterology is the transgression of norms by means of a pure, wasteful expenditure; this is a mode of *non-dialectical materialism*, where the primary goal is not collective social revolution, but individual sovereignty. Thus the differences between Breton and Bataille can be summed up as the differences between a passive idealist dialectics and an active material heterology; between a sublimatory and a desublimatory aesthetics; between metaphysics and a sort of pataphysics.[3]

It is within the context of this rupture in the Surrealist movement that *L'Amour fou*, the first major exhibition of Surrealist photography, must be placed. Bataille's position serves as the central hermeneutic scheme for the rereading of Surrealist photography, and the history of Surrealism in general, that is initiated by the catalogue articles, especially the texts of Rosalind Krauss.[4] Such a reinterpretation involves a major revision not only of the histories of Surrealism and photography, but also of the entirety of modern French intellectual thought:[5] by interpreting Surrealism from the perspective of the dissidents, those excluded from the movement, we are presented with what Foucault wrote of as a suppressed knowledge, what Bataille himself wrote of as heterogeneous thought.

In the first of her two catalogue essays, "Photography in the Service of Surrealism" (a revision of her "The Photographic Conditions of Surrealism" which appeared in *October* #19, Winter 1981, and which was a study at the origin of the exhibition) Rosalind Krauss is concerned with circumscribing the apparent heterogeneity of Surrealist photography not in terms of formal or stylistic properties, but rather in terms of the semiological functions of the

Surrealist photograph. We are thus primarily involved with the constitution of the photograph as a sign, which, because of the iconic function of the photograph, leads to the apparent paradox of the constitution of reality as sign. In the photograph, presence is transformed into representation by the disruption of the very unity of presence. The entire world is, as Breton claimed, a "forest of signs," but this forest is constituted precisely by Surrealist praxis, according to specific semiological functions. The sign is not a pregiven existential structure, but an aesthetic construct.

How does photography achieve this mode of mediation, this manifestation and determination of "convulsive beauty?" Two determinant factors of Surrealist photography which fulfill this function are located. First, *doubling* is recognized as one of the central tropes of Surrealist photography, variously achieved by the techniques of double-exposure, superimposition, mirror images, photomontage and collage. Informed by the structural anthropology of Claude Lévi-Strauss, the psycho-linguistics of Roman Jakobson, and the deconstructive theory of Jacques Derrida, we discover how the repetition involved in doubling is the very basis of meaning, of intentionality, and the very inauguration of signification itself within a chaotic field of events. Doubling is the origin of meaning; it thus serves as a "signifier of signification." Hence doubling establishes a syntax within which the meaning of all other signs is established. Secondly, the limit of the photographic field is, *a fortiori*, the *frame* of the photograph. While the photographic frame always institutes a rupture in the continuity of the visual field of everyday reality, an abstraction from the perceptual field, a mediation of experience, Surrealist photography structurally encourages the viewer to read the frame itself as a sign, an empty sign which determines the meaning of the photograph itself as a sign or sign-system. Thus framing serves as yet another "signifier of signification." What is essentially at stake here are the conditions according to which the photograph as an index and icon is transformed into a symbol. And yet, can not *any* technique produce an effect which can be incorporated as a semiological trope, and can't *any* trope be taken as central by a hermeneutic system?[6]

In Rosalind Krauss' second catalogue essay, "Corpus Delicti," (a version of which appeared in *October* #33, Summer 1985), the central trope of Surrealist photography is relocated from *doubling* (as a *formation* of meaning), to that of the *informe* (informed; formless—as a *deformation* of meaning), a concept which in Bataille's thought is that by means of which all categories can be unthought, subverted.

Here the Surrealist utilization of the photographic techniques of anamorphosis, solarization, brûlage, rayographs, negative printing, time-exposures and close-ups creates representations of objects, especially female bodies, which are integrally deformed, whose very boundaries are lost within the photographic scene. The human body is distorted, deformed, transformed by the implosion of an alien, exterior space. And we might add that this mode of deformation is not determined by that "coherent deformation" which Malraux understood as the essential feature determinant of style, and which Merleau-Ponty later understood as the very mode of continuity of experience. Rather, what is entailed here is a sort of *incoherent* deformation, whereby the very determination of everyday experience is contested, transgressed. Yet we must ask whether such formlessness implied the impossibility of any semiotic determination whatsoever, contrary to what is suggested in the earlier article.

Given the new context of the *informe,* the notion of doubling is reworked. Utilizing Roger Caillois' analysis of mimesis and Lacan's theory of the mirror stage, doubling is now seen as the sign of the subject's loss of individuation, a derealization, dispossession, schizophrenization, where the difference between the real and the imaginary is collapsed. The subject is thus mastered from without; we are led to yet another model of "objective chance" or possession, through which the marvellous, the uncanny, may manifest itself. Only here the subject, and not merely its representation, is at stake in these material, and no longer ideal, excursions into Surreal existence. While in the earlier text doubling functions as the very institution of signification by the disruption of presence, according to the later text doubling functions as the disintegration of the subject's self-presence, the very dissolution of signification. Emblematic of this process is the Surrealists' fascination with fetishism (the symbolic substitution of the perpetually absent female phallus) where the sexual difference that founds human identity is dissolved, and where gender is lost in the unformed or transformed object. As the photograph is a reconstruction of "nature as sign," the fetish is the reconstitution of "woman as sign," the indication of a fabricated sexuality.

Thus it is entirely appropriate, as Jane Livingston shows in her catalogue essay, "Man Ray and Surrealist Photography," that the female body is the privileged object for Man Ray, the archetypal Surrealist photographer. His aesthetic voyeurism was fully congruent with Breton's dialectic of the marvellous, in an attempt to reconcile ego and libido. Man Ray achieved this not by the chance juxtaposition of objects within a Surreal scenario, but rather by means of presenting the self-transformation of given objects, especially the female body. Thus his creation of photographic metamorphoses entailed not the transformation of one object into another, but rather the production of multiple versions of the self. His concern was one of the redepiction, and not the reembodiment, of figures. Thus Livingston's aesthetic is informed by the more "classical" Surrealist position elaborated by Breton, and not by Krauss' appropriation of Bataille: for Livingston, there is an ultimate analogical integrity between the terms of the photographic series of transformations; for Krauss, transformation is precisely the sign of the loss of bodily and egological integrity within the unformed. We might further note that such a valorization of Man Ray over, for example, the works of Hans Bellmer, would indeed promote a dialectical theory of articulation and transformation rather than a nondialectical theory of disarticulation and transgression. Bellmer's photographic work foregrounds especially the sadistic component of scopophilia, where the sculptural and photographic effects disarticulate the female body into a sign of violence, possession, and masochistic pleasure.

Yet there seem to be certain key photographic conditions of Surrealism which are barely touched upon by this exhibition. For example, yet another crucial rendition of multiple versions of the self, invested with "demoniacal" possession, is presented in *La Révolution Surréaliste* #11 (1928) in the article, "Le cinquantenaire de l'hystérie (1878-1928)" which is illustrated with six photographs of that most famous, most beautiful hysteric, Augustine, culled from the *Iconographie Photographique de la Salpêtrière*. Due to their presence in this Surrealist journal, these photos, marking the fiftieth anniversary of Charcot's studies of hysteria, form an integral part of the photographic incunabula of Surrealism. The accompanying article by Aragon and Breton celebrates hysteria as the greatest poetic discovery of the nineteenth century, and they propose a new definition of hysteria which, as a supreme form of expression, "is founded on the need for reciprocal seduction." Years later, in the very issue of *Minotaure* marked by the sign of the Tarot's madman, Salvador Dali, in a brief text accompanying his photo-collage *Le phénomène de l'extase,* also celebrates the hysteric, ecstatic condition of Surrealist phenomena as exemplary of critical thought, and writes: "I ask the art critic: what would you think of such a work in the very moment of your ecstasy?" This is indeed the question which we must continually ask ourselves in relation to the pleasures, the seductions, the fascinations afforded by the artwork. Dali, in fact, offers an observation which may serve as a central consideration in the relation between aesthetic structures and psychological symptomatology: "Certain images provoke ecstasy, which in turn provokes certain images." Rather than attempting to choose between two theories of hysteria—one where desire gives rise to the image, the other where the image gives rise to desire; one of hysteria as mimesis which leads to self-possession, the other of hysteria as mimesis which leads to dispossession—Dali posits the hysteric condition as a vicious libidinal and hermeneutic circle, one of a truly reciprocal seduction.[7] Thus the iconography of hysteria, much like the photographic iconography of Surrealism, is not merely a scenario of women possessed by demons, but also (and perhaps above all) of men possessed by the phantasms and images of the women they love, desire or imagine. The Surrealist image is not simply that of the body *deformed* by desire; it is also the sign of desire *informed* by the body.

Charcot's psychiatric iconography of hysteria serves as a photographic panopticon purporting to reveal a total view of hysteric attitudes; to this we may contrast the fact that Breton's two great "love stories," *Nadja* and *L'Amour fou*, while containing photographic illustrations, do not include photographs of the beloved women. Is this because, as Barthes claims in *La chambre claire* as an excuse for not including that photograph of his mother upon which his entire discourse on photography is based, such a photo can only have an emotional, idiosyncratic meaning for a person who was part of its history, and never for a detached observer? Or is it to be understood according to the principle set forth by Bruno Bettelheim in *The Uses of Enchantment*, who finds nonillustrated books of childrens' fairy-tales preferable to illustrated ones, since the illustration of the characters would prevent the child from forming an ideal, imaginary image of the protagonists, and thus prevent the auditors from incorporating the tales protagonists into their own unique, secret, phantasmatic existence? Are these two factors indeed mutually exclusive, or do they in tandem form the motivational scheme of the poetry and imagery of the marvellous? Do we not find, in this conflict of possible motivations, the central conflict that ruptured the Surrealist movement?[8]

Perhaps what we are unable to see can serve as a conclusion, to illustrate the antipodal expressions of that convulsive/hysterical art of Surrealism. Consider, first, that Breton's Nadja adores her little daughter because she resembles other little children, "with their mania for taking out their dolls' eyes to see *what's there* behind them." In harsh contrast, Bataille, in the very last lines of his journal *Acéphale*, exclaims that, "I laugh when I think that these eyes persist in demanding objects which don't destroy them." Is it a hysterical blindness which permits us to discover our mad love, our unique love, or is there another sort of blindness which is necessary for us to pursue our phantasms?

9

The Other as Muse

They will set a house on fire, and it were but to roast their eggs.

Francis Bacon

Is freedom, as Daniel Paul Schreber insists in his *Memoirs of My Nervous Illness,* ultimately "freedom to think about nothing"? Or does the very order of the universe depend upon a "forced play of thought", thoughts which are always imposed from without? It would seem as if this compulsion to think—a libidinal necessity before being a semiological activity—is what binds the individual to communal systems of signification and exchange. Thought: what breaks the libidinal circuit of autoeroticism. Thinking of nothing: what breaks the hermeneutic circle of culturally imposed meaning. Signification is determined within this dialectic of the thought and unthought, where perhaps madness—the eruption of unthought thoughts, of the unconscious—is the only path to a truly universal rationality. In offering his *Memoirs* to the world, Daniel Paul Schreber presents a religious epiphany, a heretical apocalypse, where the theological drama of his paranoia is symbolically played out on his own body, through the greatest torments and the greatest joys. His paranoia, resulting in those "miracles" whereby his words, deeds and bodily functions were completely controlled by God, is precisely what allows him the most intimate, erotic contact with God. But it also engenders that megalomania which transforms him into a martyr, God's whore, and which allows him the offense of suggesting that, "such a relation as that which I have with the divine rays would permit one to believe oneself capable of shitting on the entire world." It is precisely between this narcissistic scatology and this universalizing eschatology—between this body and these words—that we might situate our own predicament, our own humanity.

In the year 213 B.C. the Emperor of China, Shih Huang Ti, ordered "the burning of the books;" the destruction of all books dealing with history. This attempt to destroy the past was balanced by an equally grandoise attempt to protect the present: Shih Huang Ti was also the Emperor who completed the construction of the Great Wall.[1] He called himself The First Emperor, ordained that history begin with him, and claimed that he was God. This megalomaniacal attempt to control space and time and others, to create one's self and one's world, was effected to the least detail: Shih Huang Ti claimed that during his reign all things would bear their proper names. His passion was universalized as cosmos and logos, in the extreme world-historical manifestation of narcissism.[2] This is the ultimate limit of *ressentiment*, what Nietzsche has shown to be the wrath and contempt against the irreversibility of time.

Jorge Luis Borges surmises that the Emperor Shih Huang Ti might have undertaken these two immense tasks, the burning of the books and the completion of the Great Wall, as a reaction against the immensity and uselessness of the past, and against the futility of worshipping the past. Perhaps, according to Borges, the Emperor thought: "Men love the past and neither I nor my executioners can do anything against that love, but some day there will be a man who feels as I do and he will efface my memory and be my shadow and my mirror and not know it." This supposition is a simulacrum of the manner in which our Shih Huang Ti was the shadow of that legendary first Emperor whose name he took, who presumedly invented writing and the compass, and whose name undoubtedly perished many times in the vast configuration of the burning of the books. Borges was indeed correct in his assumption: among the earliest known Chinese statues are twelve bronze colossi which were erected by Shih Huang Ti—these statues were subsequently melted down by a Han ruler in order to make small coins. And yet, just as in the First Emperor's lifetime the attempt to obliterate the past by the burning of the books was counterbalanced by the attempt to preserve the present by the completion of the Great Wall, so too at a later date was the attempt to destroy the memory of the works of Shih Huang Ti by melting down the statues to make filthy lucre counterbalanced by the continuation of another act in his memory: we are told that for centuries people befoulded his grave. Yet, even in the light of the immensity and perhaps greatness of his works, we should not reproach those who befouled his grave, since we should note what Freud wrote in a letter to Karl Abraham about excrement: "After all, these are productions just as well as thoughts and desires." We should not forget that the immediateness of expression, while dissimulated by the objectivity of the world-historical, is also its source.

In the beginning was the word.
The Divine Logos

All nonsense is abolished.
Daniel Paul Schreber

We are reminded, by Elias Canetti, that formerly in China,

> . . . when the emperor laughs the mandarins in attendance laugh too; when he stops laughing, they stop. When he is sad their faces fall. One would think that their faces were on springs which the emperor could touch and set in motion at his pleasure.
>
> This taking the king as model is universal. Sometimes it results only in admiration and veneration: nothing he does is unimportant or meaningless. But sometimes it goes further than this and people regard his every movement and utterance as a command: for him to sneeze means "Sneeze!"; for him to fall off his horse means "Fall off your horses!" He is so full of the force of command that everything he does must be an expression of it. Abandoning words, commands become actions again; in this case actions compelling imitation.[3]

We find that this imperative function of language obtains not only at the extreme limits of political power, where oedipal memory is instilled in language as proscription and imitation, just as it is instilled in the flesh as the pain of punishment. Such an imperative language operates at the very origins of speech, where for the infant the earliest "language" is not constatative, but expressive and performative. The initial interjection of the cry, the scream, marks the epiphany of subjectivity within a world of pain, but soon serves as an imperative, a command. The consequent glossolalia of babble as imitation marks the differentiation inherent in language, and constitutes the entry into systems. And the repetitions of echolalia mark the ephiphany of intersubjectivity, the entry into ethics and the social. Yet these repetitions of echolalia do not repeat presence, but found it. Different places, different bodies, different words are a function of the loss of the mother, of her becoming invisible, and of the consequent attempts at a magical conjuring of her presence, an attempt at recovery. And yet this magic, this desire made word, this summons, is already ambivalent in its emotional force: it expresses the pain and anger of the loss, as well as the desire for the pleasure of presence. Thus the instauration of the world through the word, the differentiation of the self and the other, is marked by the differentiation of thanatos and eros. Such a world, soon to be ordered and categorized within the domain of Oedipus, is founded upon *ressentiment*. *Ressentiment* entails the entry into temporality; temporality is the separation of the invisible (mother) from the visible (self); and language supports the invisible, which prolongs my world into transcendence.

Yet the infant does not create itself, nor its world. Its language is already the language of the other, and it is impelled to speak, to repeat. Thus not only is the unconscious, still to be formed, "the discourse of the Other;" consciousness too is founded upon the repetition of the other's speech. The world that the infant "creates" is a world already created, and recreated, for (by) it; that self which the child discovers is a self which is, ". . . the advent of difference on the ground of resemblance . . ."[4] The paradigms of such echolalia are a function of power, of the parents' omnipotence; an omnipotence which is projected upon the infant and introjected as its own megalomania. The narcissism of the infant is the projected narcissism of the parents, and is thus already a function of oedipalization. It should be noted, though, that it is ironically because of the lack of omnipresence that the parents are discovered to be omnipotent.

We see this clearly in the infantile game of *fort/da*, as analyzed by Freud in *Beyond the Pleasure Principle*. The infant represents the mother's disappearance by making a spool disappear, accompanied by the enunciation *"o-o-o-o"* (*fort*: gone); then her reappearance is represented by making the spool reappear, accompanied by the enunciation *"da"* (here or there.) We find that the mimetic here serves two functions, and expresses the emotional ambivalence of these events. The reappearance (*"da"*) is obviously pleasureable because it entails the return of the desired object, the mother. But the disappearance (*"fort"*) is also pleasurable, not only because it is a passive condition for her return, but even more so because it is an active response to her absence, because it is the infant's interpretation of her disappearance as one of its own acts, as a function of its own power, its own omnipotence, its casting off of the mother. It is the infant's attempt to create its origin by changing its own past. Thus the mother is symbolically murdered before the oedipalized murder of the father. These acts simultaneously signify love and *ressentiment*; it is a victory and a loss, where as Julia Kristeva explains, the entry into syntax is a victory over the mother as distancing, and yet this is a partial victory, since all naming is but a never completed replacement of the archaic mother.[5] If, as Kristeva claims, space causes laughter, it must be added that time causes anguish. Thus the infantile imperative is equally supplication.

The functions of echolalia, of mimesis, are twofold: there is the continuation of the performative function of language as a cry of distress, a call for aid; and there is the constatative function within which the world is inaugurated as a scene of passion and action. Echolalia is productive and reproductive, an egocentric enunciation which simultaneously breaks out of narcissism, since this imitation is based upon the identification with, and the need for, the parents.

Fort/da; o-o-o-o/a: the separation of linguistic differences supports the foundation of theory as *pragma*. Theory is the confrontation of spectacle with invisibility and loss, with time. The paradigms of thought, as both Freud and Merleau-Ponty teach us, are both possession and dispossession, in an eternal confusion of reversibility. The desire to know is a sublimation of the desire to grasp. The separations of self/other, self/world, inside/outside, are maintained and refined within language, and the subtleties of theory are always a function of power.

Childhood innocence is a parental fantasy serving as a dissimulation of their own primal guilt. Innocence is not at the beginning: it is created as a screen to dissimulate the terror of the primal *ressentiment*. The *"o-o-o-o/a"* of the infant is as full of malice as it is of love. We find one such phantasm of innocence in Dadaist art. Consider the following stanza from the score of Kurt Schwitters' phonetic poem, the *Ursonate* (1924-1925):

Oooooooooooooooooooooooooooooooo
Bee bee bee bee bee . . . .
Oooooooooooooooooooooooooooooooo
Zee zee zee zee zee . . . .
Oooooooooooooooooooooooooooooooo
Rinnzekete . . . bee . . . bee . . .

Oooooooooooooooooooooooooooooooo
änn ze . . . . änn ze . . . .
Oooooooooooooooooooooooooooooooo

Aaaaaaaaaaaaaaaaaaaaaaaaaaaaaaaa
Bee bee bee bee bee . . . .
Aaaaaaaaaaaaaaaaaaaaaaaaaaaaaaaa
Zee zee zee zee zee . . . .
Aaaaaaaaaaaaaaaaaaaaaaaaaaaaaaaa
Rinnzekete . . . bee . . . bee . . .
Aaaaaaaaaaaaaaaaaaaaaaaaaaaaaaaa
enn ze . . . . enn ze . . . .
Aaaaaaaaaaaaaaaaaaaaaaaaaaaaaaaa

Oooooooooooooooooooooooooooooooo
Bee bee bee bee bee . . . .
Oooooooooooooooooooooooooooooooo
Zee zee zee zee zee . . . .
Oooooooooooooooooooooooooooooooo
Rinnzekete . . . bee . . . bee . . .
Oooooooooooooooooooooooooooooooo
änn ze . . . . änn ze . . . .
Oooooooooooooooooooooooooooooooo

The primal opposition o/a (*fort/da*) is amplified and repeated amidst numerous glossalia and echolalia in this *Ursonate,* this primal sonata. Yet while the seriousness, the tragedy, of the infantile enunciation and symbolic act is dissimulated by the parents within the nomination of "play," conversely the playfulness of Schwitters' poem is dissimulated within culture under the rubric of the seriousness of "art." Yet, despite the superficial structural similarities of the two works (the infant's "*fort/da*" and Schwitters' *Ursonate*), their signification is diametrically opposed. For the infant, the signification of the *fort/da* inaugurates re-representation, where ultimately tropes and *typos* dissimulate *topos* (*corpus.*) Conversely, for Schwitters in his *Ursonate* and in all of *Merz,* we find an antirepresentational, iconoclastic art which forces upon the spectator the recognition of the very materiality, the body, of the artwork. And it may be noted that in this stanza of the *Ursonate* the syllable which most directly approximates a word is "*Rinn,*" the German word for gutter ("*Rinne.*") This is emblematic of Schwitters' entire oeuvre, *Merz,* since for Schwitters the gutter was the topos of discovery and creation.[6]

In Chapter XVI of his *Memoirs,* Daniel Paul Schreber also recounts an incident bordering on glossolalia, where the very scatological materiality of his body becomes the symbolic element through which the miraculous, destructive powers of the other—the Divinity—is manifest. "W-a-a-a-r-r-u-m sch-ei-ei-ei-s-e-e-n Sie d-e-e-e-e-n-n n-i-i-i-icht?" "Why don't you shit?" insist, over and over again, those voices which torment him. Since all of Schreber's physical and mental processes—defecation as well as speech—are controlled by "divine miracles," his diarrhea is no less significant than his loghorrea: both aim at the destruction of his rationality. Schreber's strategy to battle these malevolent symptoms leads us through sheer repetition: he attempts to silence the voices that torment him, as well as his compulsion to speak, by reciting poems consigned to memory; and he tries to control the terrible pains of the need to defecate by simply giving in to that need—which (perhaps hyperbolically stated) results in a state of extreme "soul-voluptuousness." He fights a repetition imposed from "without" with a repetition imposed from "within." Hyperbolic paranoia is conquered by ironic reversals and repetitions; a counterfeit thought is used to battle ideas. Schreber invents a sophistic theology to evoke, and struggle with, the torments caused by an overbearing system of guilt and repression. He reinvents heresy to purify his soul, as a means of catharsis, as a means of mitigating the power of the discourse of others.

If others are divergences of my speech, it is only because I have already been constituted as a divergence of theirs. We can think and communicate only because, as Merleau-Ponty claims, the universal is unthought, because ideality "has a future in me. . . with the others, and finally, having become writing, has a future in every possible reader. . ."[7] And yet this future of my speech is a discourse of power, since its origin is a past founded upon *ressentiment,* a *ressentiment* against the invisible, against the inauguration of the world as loss. Our euphemisms for this loss are transcendence, essence, ideality. Yet these terms dissimulate the dual functions of rhetoric (even the rhetoric of the monoremes "*fort*" and "*da*" which inaugurate a world.) For the infant, as well as within the Socratic tradition, genuine *logos* is *dialogos,* with the discovery of a unique, monolithic truth as its goal. Conversely, but simultaneously, for the infant as well as within the Sophistic tradition, genuine *logos* is also *dialogos,* yet within a pluralism which maintains power and influencing the listener as its goal. Thus rhetoric is simultaneously constatative and performative, reproductive and productive. And this is always true within the chiasm of self and other, where the only source of truth is the divergences, the differences, between discourses.

I cannot be caught in immanance.

Paul Klee

If he never know himself.

Ovid

Our identity is always a case of mistaken identity.

Melanie Klein

The drama of *fort/da* with the spool was paralleled by another: "*Baby/o-o-o-o.*" Having discovered a mirror that did not quite reach the ground, the infant found that by crouching he could make himself disappear. His ultimate ontological possibility, that of invisibility, is no different than that of his mother, and he can now begin to work, or play, upon himself the transcendence which will make him a subject.

As is usually the case with mirror phenomena, we find a paradox: here, it leads to the optical/ontological difference which is the foundation of subjectivity and the world. Merleau-Ponty's analysis of this mirror phenomenon is exemplary in its explanation of the manner in which the self is always a self through confusion and narcissism:

> The flesh is a mirror phenomenon and the mirror is an extension of my relation with my body. Mirror = realization of a *Bild* of the thing, and I-my shadow relation + realization of a (verbal) *Wesen*: extraction of the essence of the thing, of a pellicle of Being or of its "appearance"—To touch oneself, to see oneself, is to obtain such a specular extract of oneself. *I.e.*, fission of appearance and Being—a fission that already takes place in the touch (duality of the touching and the touched) and which, with the mirror (Narcissus) is only a more profound adhesion to Self. The visual projection of the world in me to be understood not as intra-objective things-my body relation. But as a shadow-body relation, a community of verbal *Wesen* and hence finally a "resemblance" phenomenon, transcendence.[8]

To touch oneself and to see oneself is exactly the auto-erotic activity of the infant, an activity which engenders no impossibility, no paradox, but pleasure. If anything, it is the manifestation of the desire for totalization, for the self-sufficiency of primary narcissism. The "enigma of the body" commences with the loss of the illusory self-sufficiency: that is, with the simultaneous advent of the other through dispossession, and the advent of the self through a new mode of possession, possession at a distance through vision, in the mirror. And this is intensified through the mirroring phenomenon of mimesis of the other, with its circular plays of actions/reactions.

Symbolic activity is the appropriation of the invisible within language. And yet, though the origin of the invisible was the loss of a body (the mother's), this symbolic system is not divorced from the body. The ego is, as Freud explains, "a bodily ego: it is not merely a surface entity, but is itself the projection of a surface."[9] The body thus serves as a visible archetype, according to which the ego is "an extension of the surface-differentiation" between ego and id, self and other, self and world. The narcissistic structure of appearance obtains from the fact that the ego is based upon object libido invested in the body: the worldhood-of-the-world is always projected upon the body, even though normally the relation between *corpus* and *topos* is dissimulated within the very linguistic structures which made possible the eruption of the self in the world. Appearance is a simulacrum of origins, origins always lacking (a lack as origin) because these origins are transcendent within the visible (within the future of our words as *telos*). Appearance is the perpetual dissimulation of the body as *archē* by language. The hermeneutic circle is always a narcissistic circle.

Because the ego has its origin in the event of the loss of the other (a loss which is simultaneous with its very constitution), there can never be a cohesion of the self with itself, even at the extreme limits of narcissism. This is evident in the mirror stage, in which the narcissistic reflection is precisely the lack of cohesion with the self. The mirror stage is, according to Lacan, ". . .the transformation that takes place in the subject when he assumes an image."[10] This transformation is the production of the primal form of the "I," the "Ideal-I," which is a fictionalized origin disparate with the real "I," and a source of later identifications. If the subject is the discordance between the real "I" and the ideal "I," and the history of the subject is the attempt at reconciliation, it must be noted that this is a futile task, since the reconciliation can only be effected within language. Thus for Schreber, the discordance between the real "I" and the ideal "I"—between the human and the divine—is a discordance articulated by the very signs of corporeal transformation into a woman, into the whore of God. These signs, the prelude to an impossible martyrdom, reveal precisely the attempt to work through the contradictions of his condition: male/female, human/divine, self/other. Yet language already bears the trace of the other, which is yet a further source of identification and difference. *Fort/da*: mother's body: anaclisis = Baby/o-o-o-o: own body: narcissism. Whether narcissistic or anaclitic, the choice of love object is always a rupture of the subject. The body is always simultaneously a body-for-the-self and a body-for-the-other, whether in the realm of erotics or politics.

It is at the stage of narcissism that the socialization of the infant occurs, not only because it enters into the symbolic matrix of language, but also because it is at this stage of development that the sexual instincts are unified in order to gain a love-object.[11] Just as the subject and the instincts are unified in order to be readily incorporated within culture, so too is sexuality unified from the polymorphous perversity of infantile auto-erotism to the genitality of adulthood. This genitality (indeed phallocentrism) is the limit of the body's dissimulation, and it serves as a primary paradigm within the symbolic. And yet, as we shall see, there are psychic strategies against this domination and reduction of the instinctual life.

God. . .must have commerce only with cadavers.

Daniel Paul Schreber

Narcissus . . . shall have commerce only with shadows.

Plotinus

Certainly it is an interesting event we are dealing with: the putrescence of the absolute spirit.

Karl Marx

In March 1894, Daniel Paul Schreber began his relation with God.[12] Senatspräsident Dr. Daniel Paul Schreber, Margrave of Tuscany and of Tasmania, The Seer, Prince of Hell, The Hyperborean, a Jesuit novice at Osseg, Bourgmeister of Klattau, a young Alsatian girl defending her honor against a victorious French officer, a Mongol Prince, Miss Schreber. These were among the multiple identities within Schreber's psychotic drama, which began with a reverie in which he believed that it would be wonderful to be a woman submitting to sexual intercourse, and which culminated with the belief that he would be emasculated, changed into a woman, so that he could be impregnated by God and become the redeemer who would restore the world to a lost state of bliss by creating "a new race of men made in the spirit of Schreber." Almost every aspect of his quotidian existence was effected by "divine miracles," and his direct relation with God was effected by "Divine rays," which were also recognized by him to be nerves, semen, voices, miraculous birds (the dove of the Holy Spirit, perhaps?), which he gave girls' names. Yet in his role as redeemer he suffered: he was plagued by a ceaseless cacophony of voices in his head from which he could only gain respite by a "miracle of howling" by which his screams drowned out the voices. He was also to suffer numerous sexual abuses. And before he could redeem the world, not only would he have to die, but also the world would have to end. He read reports of his own death; believed that "soul murder" was being committed upon him; believed that God was trying to render him insane or kill him: for example, his head was full of miniscule speaking scorpions, resembling crabs or spiders, which plagued him, as did the miracled up "little men," cursory contraptions a few mm. tall, which were placed on his head to devestate him. And as for the catastrophies which would signal the end of the world, they would appear in numerous forms: deluge, earthquakes, glaciation due to the diminution of solar heat, and epidemics of various sorts, some of the symptoms of which were visible on his own body: blue plague, brown plague, white plague, black plague, oriental leprosy, indian leprosy, hebrew leprosy, egyptian leprosy.

In paranoia, libido is withdrawn from the world as a defense mechanism (in the Schreber case, Freud claims, as a regression to the narcissistic stage in defense against sublimated homosexuality.) This withdrawal is symbolized by the catastrophes which mark the end of the world, and is counterbalanced by the utopia to follow, the cure. Concurrent with this withdrawal, the libido is fixated upon the ego, hence the megalomania; the internal significations which are suppressed reenter consciousness in the form of external perceptions, that is, as delusions.

For the First Emperor Shih Huang Ti the world was a system of *pragma* to be modified as an expression of his megalomania; for Senatspräsident Schreber the delusional world was a sign of himself, an attempt at recovery, at a reordering of the psychic mechanism. Both cases are extreme: the First Emperor took himself for God in his vast megalomania; Schreber externalized his megalomania *as* God, a God who would torture, castrate and murder him, but who would also simultaneously offer him the greatest sensual pleasure ("voluptuousness") and the highest position in society—Redeemer. The lack of the Name-of-the-Father, (according to Lacan the cause of psychosis), is replaced by the Name-of-God in what we call a delusional, influencing system.

If, as Nietzsche claimed in *Thus Spoke Zarathustra*, the world is a cerebral fiction of God, we are compelled to ask, "What could one create if Gods existed?" Nothing, of course, hence one must kill God in order to create: ". . .if there were gods, how could I endure not to be a god! Hence there are no gods." And yet, we must note that according to the logic of the unconscious, which permits the cohabitation of contradictory significations, Nietzsche's realization is not a foregone conclusion. There are two possible solutions to this problem: one could either *kill* God or one could *become* God!

While Nietzsche heralded the problematic "death of God," Antonin Artaud lived this problem. He too recognized that "It was still necessary to kill God in order to live." (*OC*XVI;160) If for Western theology God was the supreme Being within a rationally ordered universe, in the modernist epoch God is, as Artaud recognized and suffered, the "monomaniac of the unconscious" (*OC*XV;315), where "immanence is a depot of God." (*OC*XVII;153) God, dethroned as absolute ruler of the cosmos, is reduced to the tormentor of that microcosm, the unconscious. The theological is subsumed within the pathological, but is no less real for that shift of topos. Indeed, his *Cahiers de Rodez* are among the most poignant, and in a sense the most typically modernist, examples of the attempt to exorcize God from His parasitic encrustation in the unconscious. The tragedy of Artaud's life was that during the period of his "madness" he couldn't simply purge himself of the God that tormented him. Rather, before Artaud could forget Him, he first had to become Him. As Nietzsche entered his madness through the identities of Dionysus and the Crucified, so too did Artaud enter through the multiple identities of God and Satan, Christ and Anti-Christ. In a sense, the asylum at Rodez was the ultimate scene of Artaud's "Theater of Cruelty," an antimetaphysical and antitheological theater which proferred an art of difference, transgression and forgetting. If metaphysics functions as the science of the return of Being as memory and representation, then modernism, to the extent that it disrupts the classical *Logos*, entails an art of production and active forgetting. Thus the prolegomena to any "theater of cruelty," as well as its greatest work, is the exorcism of God from His last domain, the unconscious.

If the Rodez aslyum was the stage for Artaud's "Theater of Cruelty," then the sanatorium at Sonnenstein was the scene of Schreber's interior passion play. Man and woman, living and dead, Messiah and man: Schreber too lived out a multiplicity of identities, which illuminate the general problems of sexual identity and difference, self-identity and origins, sovereignty and dependence.

What is evident in both cases, Artaud and Schreber, is not only the extreme interiorization of a God in a world where there is no longer a rational place for Him, but also the return of the repressed as a demoniacal God. The abstract, infinitely alien, mathematized God of Nicolas of Cusa and Leibniz is transformed into a personal, malicious, violent, lecherous and foul God. What in previous centuries would have resulted either in condemnation as heresy or valorization as sainthood, is now no longer esteemed as prophesy, but as symptom. The modern epistemē no longer has a place for the miracles which governed Schreber's existence, so they are classified as psychopathological symptoms.

After Nietzsche, the productions of metaphysics and theology are recognized as totalizing, systematizing theorization, and are thus the sign of the domination of *Logos* and the logic of domination; they can either be replaced by productive texts, signs of sovereignty and rebellion, or else they may be replaced by their own simulacra. In either case, the modernist text is a poesis particularis, and not a mathesis universalis. The texts of Schreber and Artaud delineate the breakdown of ontotheology in its final theatrical representation. Yet this representation is already dispersed by the multiplicity of subject positions which it engenders, by the differential of desire which it constitutes, and within the heterogeneity of the discourse which it makes manifest.

In Western culture, God is the classical influencing machine in His role as the guarantor of cosmic conjunction and personal identity. In mysticism God collects all libidinal cathexes; in the narcissistic megalomania of paranoia the self, the ego, collects all libidinal cathexes, only to project this aggrandizement as a personal God (a heresy!) But while the Eros of the cultural world strives to maintain the connections between the self, the other and the world, the Eros of the paranoiac mechanism strives to assume the greatest possibility of disjunctions and recombinations. Hence the multiplicity of Schreber's identities, the numerous catastrophies which will destroy the world, the many names of God, the multiplicity of meanings of the Divine rays. Schreber was self and other, man and woman, dead and alive. He could not "resolve as 'I' his discordance with his own reality," so he lived the discordance. Hence the Schreberian God functions in precisely the inverse manner of the classical Western God: as Deleuze-Guattari explain in *Anti-Oedipus,* one can only believe in God as master of the disjunctive syllogism. While oedipalization and phallocentrism are manifestations of a conjunctive apparatus, defining the origin of the self as the other, schizophrenia and polymorphous perversity (auto-erotism) are manifestations of a disjunctive apparatus, defining the autofiguration of the self. It is precisely the opposition between autofiguration and the influence of the other that structures the psychic destiny of the subject: this destiny is prefigured by the difference between the dramas of Baby/o-o-o-o and *fort/da,* making manifest the primal emotional ambivalence.

One such disjunction was made manifest to Schreber on the linguistic level by the "miraculated birds." Certain of the Divine rays appeared as birds which held the nerves of souls that had previously gained beatitude. These birds spoke to Schreber in the *Grundsprache,* the primal language (an archaic form of German full of ironic, hyperbolic euphemisms), and they spoke in homophonies, without knowing the meaning of what they said. An example of their speech:[13]

Santiago/Carthago
Chinesenthum/Jesus-Christum
Abendroth/Athemnoth
Ariman/Ackerman
Briefbeschewerer/Herr Prüfer schwört

This internal dialogue (monologue) of discrete differences between sounds indeed manifests the structure of the *Grundsprache.* In this primal language, the differences between sounds achieved in glossolalia and echolalia evoke a self and a world. The meaning isn't known, but is established in the very act of enunciation: the meanings of these homophonous disjunctions are explications of Schreber's condition and invoke his attempt at recovery. Simultaneously, these disjunctions signify the primal ambivalence of pleasure and pain. Thus, "Herr Prüfer schwört" ("Mr. Examiner swears") invokes the paranoiac mechanisms of delusions of observation, where God is continually watching Schreber and calling him a "slut." The "Briefbeschwerer" (paperweight) actually symbolizes the origins of his cure, since such a paperweight would be that which secured the papers on which Schreber wrote his autobiogrpahy: this autobiography opposes Schreber's discourse to the discourse of the God which curses him. God as Ariman; Schreber as laborer, writer, and Redeemer (Jesus Christ), awaiting the "twilight" of the impending apocalypse, which will smother him too.

We find a similar homophonic structure in the writings of the proto-Surrealist poet and linguist, Jean-Pierre Brisset:[14]

Les dents, la bouche.
Les dents la bouchent
L'aidant la bouche.
L'aide en la bouche.
Laides en la bouches.
Laid dans la bouche.
Lait dans la bouche.
L'est dam le à bouche.
Les dents-là bouche.

Here the homophony plays out the oppositions of possession/dispossession, incorporation/exclusion, acceptance/refusal, infant/adult. The very scene of language becomes the place of its exclusion: the infantile mouth is filled with milk, or the adult mouth closed, plugged, by the teeth. But when milk is lacking there is pain, and the cry. Later, the teeth, which aid the mouth in speaking and eating, become ugly and painful within an ugly mouth because of the milk upon which it depended and choked, for which there is *ressentiment*. Finally, the teeth must be hidden, the mouth must be closed: this entails a rejection of language, of the "mother tongue." What was an overture to the other ends as a radical refusal, as silence. Indeed, if with Schreber we take the parts of the body and the bodily functions as cosmic metaphors, then we may agree with Antonin Artaud that, "Being has teeth."

The Talmud warns against reading Scripture by so inclined a light that the text reveals chiefly the shape of your own countenance.
Harold Bloom

. . . this imminence of a revelation which does not occur is, perhaps, the aesthetic phenomenon.
Jorge Luis Borges

We are all children of Schreber: Schreber, screaming at the sun, hoping for silence; Schreber in drag, trying to seduce God.

All this as desire for beatitude, for "the grandiose triumph of the order of the universe" where "all legitimate interests end in harmony." But it is precisely this harmony of origins and ends which must always escape us: the unity of Schreber's beatitude as the spectacle of "the Perspective-that-God-be-with-us" entails the impossibility of a "*pensée de survol*." In fact, we are always caught between Narcissus and Oedipus, between autofiguration and the figurations of repression. The self is, as Merleau-Ponty claims, a "unity by transgression." But this is a dialectic of transgression, of possession and dispossession, between the self and the other. Always incomplete, always lacking.

In his parable, "The Great Wall and the Tower of Babel,"[15] Kafka explains:

> . . .the Great Wall alone would provide for the first time in the history of mankind a secure foundation for a new Tower of Babel.

And yet, he asks:

> How could the wall, which did not form even a circle, but only a sort of quarter or half-circle, provide the foundation for a tower?

How indeed! Just as the First Emperor, Shih Huang Ti, walled in his empire and destroyed all the books of the past in order to establish and maintain his grandiose narcissistic unity, calling himself God; just as Schreber walled himself in an insane asylum and ceaselessly screamed to silence the voices that plagued him, in order to recover the beatitude that was due him within the order of the universe, within the order of the self; so too must the Great Wall as closure provide the foundation for the new Tower of Babel, the tower which would permit humankind the "*pensée de survol*" of God. And yet that tower was never built, not due to a lack of technical efficiency, not due to a theoretical ineptitude, but due to the lack of closure of the Wall. So too with the self: there is no complete self as center because there is no definable periphery of the self: the periphery of the self is the other.

The Tower of Babel reaching towards God; the First Emperor as God; Schreber having sexual intercourse with God: the entire sense of our culture reduced to the incantation, the interjection, "God!" Philipp Wegener[16] explains that such exclamations, while being emotional outbursts, are simultaneously "clauses not meant to be heard," hence a form of monologue, and "forms of prayer" which, since they address a deity, originate in "purposeful dialogic speaking." Simultaneously monologue and dialogue, simultaneously addressed to the self and to the other, simultaneously referring to the self and the other. And this is ultimately true of every enunciation. Even of the scream as an expression of pain, or of joy. As Schreber teaches us, "All nonsense is abolished," precisely because, as Wegener explains, there is,

> . . .a double transfer of monologic speech and dialogue. The purposeless utterances become purposeful utterances because of the effect they have; on the other hand, through the mechanization of movement, the meaningful utterances may change themselves into purposeless monologic outbursts of noise again.[17]

As the reproductive, mimetic enunciations of infantile echolalia engender the outbursts which produce subjectivity, so do the private, repetitive enunciations of prayer aid in engendering the vast mechanisms of history. There is no nonsense, just a disquieting strangeness which we often encounter in art, in utterances, in situations. This strangeness is the Other, our muse.

10

Psychopompomania

God is the monomaniac of the Unconscious.
Antonin Artaud

The Temptation of Saint Anthony

The iconoclasts warn us that the desire to behold God or the angels entails the risk of madness. The sight of demons offers a delirium hardly less threatening. It is thus not surprising that texts on exorcism such as the *Malleus Maleficarum* (*The Witches' Hammer*, 1486) aided at least one poor soul to be rid of over 100,000 demons. We might, perhaps, consider the origins and persistence of these fears and visions if we are to appreciate the discrete differences which separate a desirable aesthetic iconolatry from a much disparaged religious idolatry. This will permit us to approach the sacred iconography ubiquitous in the productions of Art Brut, in order to reveal its seditious relations to classical Christian iconography as well as to a certain modernist iconoclasm.

The apocalyptic Paleo-Christian ethos reached both a culmination and a critical turning point in 4th century Coptic Egypt.[1] The eschatological presentiment of imminent apocalypse engendered a completely new ontology: a new relation to time in which each event is judged and teleologically understood according to the cataclysmic exigencies of an impending Last Judgement; and a new relation to the world in which each object, person and event bears a symbolic value overdetermined by the search for daily signs of annihilation and redemption. In their most extreme instance, these hopes and fears engendered an ascetic refusal of this world, a flight—both physical and spiritual—from society towards a purer region. Such purity was guaranteed by a morbid, often masochistic asceticism, by revelling in the putrid, sordid, macabre, and unbearable limits of life. Denial of the "corrupt" physical body entailed the creation of a miraculated body—halfway between man and angel—ruled by pure *apatheia*.

This ascetic flight from society led to an extreme isolation and interiorization of spiritual values, and the quest for a complete abolition of personality—a death to this world. In this search for a place without man, a place occupied only by angels and demons, numerous anchorites exiled themselves into the vast, empty, forbidding deserts of Egypt. Most famous among them is Saint Anthony, whose temptations provided one of the most powerful iconographic representations of the demonic realm. Appropriately, Saint Anthony chose as his abode a dark, silent tomb, where he practised both lengthy fasts and sleeplessness (since sleep is, after all, the devil's realm) as part of his ascetic ritual. This primitive "sensory deprivation experiment," experienced in the spiritual context of an immanent apocalypse and Last Judgement, resulted in hallucinatory visions of those famed demons which tempted and tortured him—demons sometimes beautiful and seductive, sometimes ugly and terrifying.

As the history of early Christianity is the tale of a vast syncretism aiming at an orthodox iconography and hegemony, so too was Saint Anthony's isolated delirium the result of a synthesis of the particular material conditions of his religious existence. Ascetic withdrawal in a tomb was already an aspect of ancient pagan Egyptian religious ritual, practised by the *catochos* (priests attached to the Seraphic Temple at Memphis) in a quest for eternal life and the continuity of the soul's existence in the afterworld. The Egyptian tradition of funerary art, exemplified by the *Book of the Dead*, attests to one of the world's great endeavors in this domain. Saint Anthony's desert abode was probably such a *hypogeum*, a tomb, whose walls were covered with frescoes describing and hieroglyphically depicting the Realm of the Dead. Not surprisingly, through an inverted syncretism, Saint Anthony's delirium transformed the Egyptian Gods into Christian Demons.

In *Les hommes ivres de Dieu*, Jacques Lacarrière suggests that the historical situation which gave rise to these visionay ascetic saints resulted from the consolidation and ultimate legalization of Christianity in the fourth century, where formerly external persecutions, now overcome, were interiorized and spiritualized.[2] As the legalization and institutionalization of Christianity progressed in that century, the first monastic orders—those communities modelled on a divine city—were created in Egypt. The battle with the Devil, enacted in its hyperbolic instance by the ascetic saints of the Egyptian desert, was at least for the moment believed to have been won with the foundation of the first monasteries, from which the Devil had been excluded (except, of course, for the return of the repressed.)

The monastic orders were founded upon the very sites of the most extreme demonic phantasms. The monastic institution guaranteed its very hegemony by surpressing these demons, which is to say by eliminating the existence of those visionary saints whose fears and passions gave rise to such demonic forces. For the order of a political Church could not support the anarchy of those demonic forces that are God's counterpart. While the apocalyptic imagination saw in every aspect of daily life signs of an apocalypse to come, monasticism revealed a literal lack of imagination, by controlling the smallest gestures and acts of everyday life—the apocalypse and its phantasms were indefinitely deferred for the sake of worldly order. One mode of asceticism and incarceration was exchanged for another. Now, as then, we need only ask how the material conditions of religious existence give rise to, or suppress, the demonic or angelic visions of those who seek another world. Conversely, we must reveal how the specific modes of expression disclose the exigencies of those material conditions. Now, as then, we might consider those who speak in the "language of angels" or the "tongues of God" in order to reveal a certain structure of the unconscious, as well as a certain means of suppression.

The Passion of Sainte Jeanne Tripier Jeanne d'Arc

> I believe that mythomania is at the base of all language, grammatically organized and entering into history.
>
> Antonin Artaud

Jeanne Tripier was a spiritualist medium incarcerated in a psychiatric asylum near Paris in 1934, well after the beginnings of her mediumistic revelations, which continued through the many years of confinement. She was diagnosed as having:

> Chronic hallucinatory psychosis. Psychic excitation. Logorrhea. Probably initial megalomania. In 1915, the belief in a large

inheritance, litigiousness . . . Speech initially enigmatic, then informative. Doubling of the voice by the work of writing; she need only begin writing for her spirit to become inert in order to receive ideas and information. Multiple spirits are lodged in her brain, leaving only to return. Active and passive telepathy. She is Joan of Arc's missionary. She is the medium of the prime necessity, chief justiciary, planetary, etc. Succinct symbolic drawings with extremely varied and unsuitable captions, what she calls passive drawings.[3]

Jeanne Tripier's enunciations manifestated a vast network of "interplanetary" communications, through which she spoke the words of, or identified with, innumerable beings, including Jean de Lumière I, Sophie la sorcière moderne, Zed Zed Zibodandez (Universal Dictator), Xionne (King of the Lunar Body), Morphée des Catacombes, L'Orang-Outan, Jésus des Miracles, Josephine de Beauharnais, Judas, Espéranto, Sa Majesté Jupon, le Colimaçon Borgne, le Mouton du Nivernais, Ponce Pilat, Médecins des Morts, Béglose (King of Modern Chemistry), Jupiter I, Lucifer I, Mercure, Sainte Thérèse, Fort Turc, Coco l'Haricot, etc. But her central and most persistant identification and communication was with Sainte Jeanne d'Arc (Joan of Arc)—Mme. J.T.J. d'Arc.

From the very moment that she entered the asylum of Maison-Blanche, at 4:30 P.M. on October 4, 1934—doubtless administered by the Médecins des Morts, the Doctors of the Dead—Jeanne Tripier considered herself dead, in a scenario expressed as that of Joan of Arc burnt at the stake. Henceforth she deemed herself an apocalyptic revoluntionary, whose role was to serve as spiritual missionary announcing the end of the world and preparing the just for the Last Judgement (at which point, not coincidentally, those imprisioned in the asylums were to be freed). This new era will be ushered in by the onslaught of barbaric hordes, led by Lucifer, Satan, Hitler, leading to a general examination of conscience and a consequent purification of souls. Such is her desperate staging of catastrophe, a modern Babylon inspired by Joan of Arc.

Jeanne Tripier's writings, those records of the spiritualist messages she transmitted and the warnings of impending disaster, were scattered with unintelligible, partially unutterable texts, communicated from the afterworld.

Xbdqgxa tuvmaytiviskitos alsaqualificatifsogo bibiscoloyatel domiconilosiskibitos; alleuiyabisloyosicos urwisky yoyodelsico-

> matocciscoyatismoyos; Jagocessisa Jgdcovryiscovoyaviscotismayomatisstos; viviscos J. d'Arc! pipisiscotoyomaticcosyovadismoloyadelmos prépare, de très grandes surprises, à tous les peuples nomades.[4]

In anticipation of the Barbaric invasions, we must decode these messages by considering the interplay of certain key terms which appear: *qualificatif, con, coma, viviscos, pipi, wisky* (*i.e.*, the *Urwisky*, the primal waters of life,) and perhaps especially the *alleuiya*, that sign of ultimate affirmation which reaches beyond the limits of language, just as do her glossolalic texts.

Glossolalia, or *speaking in tongues*, has been a constant if usually marginal phenomenon of the Christian tradition, finding its theological justification in the Pentacostal events of the first Whitsun, where on the seventh day after Easter (Resurrection) the Holy Spirit descended upon the apostles in a form of baptism. This ecstatic possession by the Holy Spirit, this *enthusiasmos* of the worshipper filled with God, was manifested in cries of jubilation and in a variety of cacophonous, unintelligible speech—a rhapsody of divine inspiration.

Glossolalia—a type of speech characteristic of children, poets, schizophrenics, mediums, the religiously possessed, charismatics—is an absolute religious enunciation which is the inverse of prophesy. While both are charismatic, prophesy is the sign of divine presence insofar as it proffers a specific message and program, while glossolalia is the pure, unmediated expression of divine presence through inspiration; prophesy communicates knowledge, glossolalia presents passion. As such, glossolalia is the very image of language inscribed in its excess, the complete disjunction of signifier and signified—the quest for a pure use of the signifier, untained by any referential function whatsoever, other than the manifestation of an unattainable divinity. Consider a different glossolalic text, from contemporary Pentacostalist services, the major modern source of speaking in tongues:

> kolama siándo, laboka tohoriămasí, lamo siándo, laboka tahandoria, lamo siando kolămasi, labo siándo, lakatándori, lamo siambăbă kătándo, láma fia, lama fiandoriăkó, lobokan doriasandó, lamo siandoriako, labo siá, lamo siandó, labăkan doria, lama fiá, lama fiandolokolămăbăbăsí, lăbo siandó, lama fiatándoria, lamokáyămasi, labo siandó.[5]

Unlike Tripier's texts, which might be more accurately described as *glossographia* since they were directly written down without having been pronounced, this Pentacostalist text is true glossolalia, not intended for written transcription.

Linguistic analysis of glossolalia reveals that it is the contrary of everyday speech.[6] This analysis depends upon three primary structural properties of language: (1) the segmentation of the syntagmatic chain of words; (2) the constitution of paradigmatic classes of words; (3) the distinction between contiguity and similarity. All three functions break down in the glossolalic text. (1) The distinction between discrete linguistic segments (phonemes, words) is disrupted within the continuity of sounds; thus all possible segmentation is strictly undecidable, and there is only a pure random articulation of the sound sequence; (2) the form/substance distinction within language is abolished, insofar as no paradigmatic classes of linguistic untis may be established, since there are no defined limits within the enunciatory field; (3) consequently, the distinction between paradigm and syntagm is abolished. Similarity now becomes a function of contiguity, of the instantiation of homophony (an imperfect form of repetition.)

In short, glossolalia is language where the relation between sound and meaning breaks down; it is the realm of pure sound, the manifestation of language in the realm of its pure materiality. But this is not to say that glossolalic pronunciations are meaningless; rather, their meaning is a result on nonlinguistic functions, of performative, dramatic, contextual usage. The role of the speaker or writer determines whatever significance may be attributed to such speech acts, be they acts of jubilant praise or atrocious denunciation. As such, they are manifestations of pure expression, language made body and gesture, and must be understood within the typical context of the kinetic behavior associated with such enunciations. As one glossolalist, quoted by William J. Samarin, explains:

> I didn't want [God] to control my entire being. He could work through my hands or my feet, flatten my ears or make my nostrils flare, but I didn't want God to tamper with my tongue.

This fear of being totally possessed, of completely losing control, may be considered a central motivation within any understanding of ecstatic pneumatology; it is an index of the purity of the glossolaliating spirit. This will be seen as a sign of the greatest fear that the spirit can produce—the lack of differentiation between man and woman, living and dead, self and God.

Also crucial to the investigation of glossolalic phenomena is the fact that while ordinary discourse is repeatable, glossolalia essentially is not, for all of the structural reasons stated above. Thus it approaches the ideal of a private language. All ordinary language entails the determination of the speaking subject, by means of deictics, as a central feature of discourse (*i.e.*, by using the linguistic shifters whose reference changes with every change of speaking subject; *e.g.*, *I, you, here, there, now*, etc.) Glossolalic utterances, to the contrary, permit no differentiation between the subject of the utterance and the subject of the statement, no real determination of the subject. It is for this very reason that such speech acts may be deemed of divine inspiration: if the subject cannot be located as a function of the enunciation, then the origin of the enunciation cannot be linguistically determined. The speaker escapes the "circuit of discourse" by giving voice to an absolute statement.

This reveals the potentially revolutionary impact of such language. Organized religion owes its power in great part to the fact that it controls the symbolic mediation with death and the dead, by controlling the hermeneutic of sacred texts and the liturgical system through which such mediation occurs. The importance of the spiritualist phenomenon is to be seen in the manner in which it circumvents the role of the institutional priesthood in effecting relations with the afterworld; in a sense, it democratizes the psychopompic process.[7] Hence Jeanne Tripier's abomination of the clergy. And hence the importance of the glossolalic phenomenon, where the relation between sacred enunciation and any possible interpretation is necessarily equivocal and without final appeal, since it is, after all, deemed to be the language of the angels, or of God. There is no appeal to institutional interpretation, and consequently no submission to institutional power and coercion.

The Condemnation of Saint Antonin, Insurgent Flame

The denaturization, the unconscious translation of a principle which makes our entire volition exist, is what we must count on in order to commence the great war which will save our identity. We believe that we are ourselves, yet we no longer are because we do not perceive that what made our selves was enraptured in the stars by the very one who was chosen within us and whom we took to be our own summum, whereas it is within this summum of ourselves, in this ineffable energetic of the self which petrifies us by its imprescriptibility, by the flash of its shocks, where this denaturization, this translation of which I speak, takes place, but with a rapidity so subtle, a legerdemain so swift, that the conjurer succeeds in hiding within us, to become us and to think for us . . .

Antonin Artaud

Artaud insisted that, "I will not abandon the souls found last evening on Charon's bark." (XX,364)[8] Indeed, not only wouldn't he abandon them, but he would soon join their ranks. Almost immediately upon his release from the asylum at Rodez, following a total of nine years of incarceration, Artaud wrote a poem/text, *Artaud le Mômo*, which may serve retrospectively as an introduction to the 7 volumes which constitute the notebooks kept at Rodez, the *Cahiers de Rodez*. In *Artaud le Mômo* he explains how the therapeutic techniques utilized in such asylums constitute a mode of black magic, which entails the institutional dissimulation of death itself: "Those who live, live on the dead. And it is also necessary that the dead live." (XII,57) The therapeutic technique in question is electroshock therapy, which Artaud suffered during the years of his incarceration, and which inflicted upon him both real and symbolic wounds.[9] The "artificial death" (XII,60) created by electroshock caused him to, "encounter dead people whom I would never have wanted to see." (XII,65) And as he reiterated time and again in the *Cahiers de Rodez*, "I am dead." (XV,142; XVI,301; XVII,139)

> Scientific electroshock does not seek new forces in the unconscious to replace the lost being; it releases evil spirits which were hidden because condemned, and invites them to live in the place of the patient's self. (XX,53)

Thus when we are told that, "Antonin the Holy Spirit permitted himself to be confined, anaesthetized and placed in a coffin. . ." (XVI,239) we must realize that Artaud's incarceration/death permits the most extreme manifestation of an *active forgetting*, where self-identity is abolished for the sake of a multiple identificatory presence. We thus find Artaud variously identified with God, Satan, the Anti-Christ, Lucifer, Cain, Saint Antonin, King Antonin, Antonin of the Redemption, and Saint Antonin of Florence, among many others. He was a vampire, man and woman, living and dead, father-mother, man-woman, pure libido. But he was also quite specifically *not* Lucifer, *not* God, *neither* Saint Antonin *nor* Antonin Artaud, etc. Thus his identifications are both singular and multiple, positive and negative, conjunctive and disjunctive (utilizing both inclusive and exclusive disjunctions).

Artaud was caught within a web of conflicting identities, and bound within a quasi-theological, schizophrenic megalomania. The ultimate dispossession of the self coincided with the acme of sacred countercathexes: he was divested of any single possible ideality of the self, while being bound to a divine, anxiety producing influencing machine. His selfhood consisted of the divergences between other selves—both sacred and profane—and between other discourses, always heretical.[10] Through these torments he escapes the symbolic by materializing the invisible sacred beings as the very pains, the very stigmata, of his own body.

In his earlier work, *Le théâtre et son double*, Artaud outlined his project for a new theater which would be religious, mystical, hieratic, and where theatrical events would no longer be subordinate to a written text, as was the case in Western theater to that time. At Rodez, this new theater is played out on the scenario of his very own body, where cosmic force becomes libidinal production, where the symbolic is reduced to human rhythms marked by the "divine," and lived in enthusiasm and passion. As Artaud claims, again in an ambiguous divine identification: "I am not the bread but the fever" (XV,86)—he who, in an excessive moment of religious exuberance, swalled 152 hosts!

Saint Antonin was a martyr: "He is the contradictory Angel of the entire Unconscious of things." (XV,40) It is indeed a negative, inverted soteriology which marks both his experience at Rodez and our own attention while reading the *Cahiers*. Crucified and bearing a crown of thorns, Artaud screams out Christ's last words on the cross as his own: *"lama lama sabachi-tani"* (XX, 118; XXI,272), awaiting the horrors of the apocalyptic wars, where the hordes of Gog and Magog are led by the Anti-Christ, while Satan himself is all the while ready to seduce humankind. (XX,44) Yet in doing so he is simultaneously enacting the greatest of Modernist tragedies—signalled by Nietzsche but lived through by Artaud—for amidst his most profound sufferings *he knows that God is already dead*:

> What we are doing is to traverse the body of whole eternities in the midst of all the souls of God's dead; and this unclean body, which nevertheless does not entirely want to sin,

doubtlessly represents the resistance of the dead God to an eternal being. (XVI,39)

In leading us through the realm of the dead, contrary to Virgil in Dante's *Divine Comedy*, Artaud reveals to us that God Himself is now among the ranks of Death's multitudes. The dead Artaud introduces us to the dead God, and we are on an equal narrative footing with the absolute. Perhaps God was punished because, as Artaud suggests, He is "the unconscious in revolt against love." (XVIII,131) Artaud's loss of love, paralleled by the horror of his own sexuality—sexuality being the desublimation of a most sacred love—explains his martyrdom, the sufferings of which may be plotted out in the following play of words from *Artaud le Mômo* (XII,186 and note):

cupidité libidinaire
copulosité liminaire
libido capitulaire

Libidinary cupidity: an excessive lustfulness. *Liminary copulosity*: the originary copulation, or the primal interconnectedness between events. *Capitulary libido*: the intimate relation between ecclesiastical ordinances and desire. The quest undertaken at Rodez was one of discovering the origins of the self: either in the *Other* (the originary copulation of the parents in the primal scene); or in *God* (as the mystical end of all libidinal cathexes, as is so often the case in paranoic systems); or in the *Self* (as hyperbolic lust precluding the intervention of God, Nature or the Other).

The *Cahiers* reveal the struggle between these three possibilities of origin and domination, yet Artaud clearly opted for the latter solution, regardless of the psychological and theological struggles which this entailed. Consider his claims in *Ci-Gît* (*Here-Lies*), a text contemporary with *Artaud le Mômo*, whose very title indicates the final, morbid, funerary context of these words, where the search for origins can only be concluded at the very endpoint of life, from the viewpoint of death. This text begins,

I, Antonin Artaud, I am my son, my father,
my mother,
and me. . .

and concludes in further contradiction,

I believe in neither father,
nor mother,
I have no
papa-mama,
nature,
spirit
or god,
satan
or body
or being,
life
or nothing . . .
nothing that is outside or inside
and especially not the mouth of being,
a sewer-hole pierced with teeth
through which the man who sucks his substance
from me
always looks through at me,
taking me for a papa-mama,
and securing an existence
free from me,
upon my corpse . . . (XII,99-100)

This quest to create the self as its own origin, to free the self from the vampirism of alterity, is achieved retrospectively from his own coffin, through the impossible enunciation of his own death. The self-as-origin is already inscribed in Artaud's "scriptural" attempt to change his own name, to name himself, to rewrite his identity. In the *Cahiers* we find the following glossolalia, based on the syllabic disjunction of Artaud's own name, and followed by a homophonous declension of these syllables (XX,174):

AR - TAU
AN - THRO - PAU
de POU - PAU
AU PAU
PA POU
TA POU TAI - MAU

This amalgam of syllables creates a homophonic verbal portrait of Artaud in his suffering: Artaud appears as *anthropos*, as primal man, whose existence is threatened by parasitic, vampiric beings

(POU/*poux;* lice, or parasites in general—here confused with the primitive Papuan and the Papal, as well as the father, PA.) He exists between his own creations (AR/*art*) and the evils or diseases of existence (MAU/*maux*).

In a text written just after his release from Rodez, *Suppôts et Supplications,* we find again the syllabic disjunction of his name, here presented with an explanatory gloss consistent with our previous observations on the *Cahiers*:

> AR - TAU
> where they always wanted to see the designation of a dark force but never that of an individual.
> Well I am this individual. I am, me, this dark force. (XIV**,14)

In short, he himself was what he feared, what he struggled against.

Yet furthermore, we must pay careful attention to the specific significance of the name AR-TAU. While the most general meaning of AR/art would define the status of his very body as text, as artwork, it is rather in the significance of TAU that we find the theological genealogy of his work and his deliria. In blasonry or heraldry—the study of identificatory insignia—*tau* is a figure in the form of a "T", also called the *crux commissa* or *Cross of Saint Anthony.* This device symbolizes both the cross of the Crucifixion and the pastoral staff derived from it, certainly identified by Artaud with the staff that he took on his mystical quest to Ireland, and which he believed to be Christ's or Saint Patrick's—this voyage culminated in the loss of his staff and his fall into madness.

Artaud believed that his own body was created in the 4th century A.D.,[11] which would make its origin contemporary with that of the cross. The symbol of the Latin cross is not found in Christian iconography until the mid-fourth century (ca. 320-330 A.D.) and there is no representation of the Passion or the Crucifixion before 350 A.D.[12] Furthermore, the transformation of Artaud's name into an insignia parallels yet another 4th century event, Constantine's transformation of Christ's monogram, CHI-RHO, into the very insignia which was initially to serve as an apotropaic emblem for his army, then as a general sign of his own institution which was to become that of the Christian Empire in 325 A.D., when Christianity became the state religion with the Edict of Milan. The emblem CHI-RHO reveals the sign of the cross, as does the sign AR-TAU.

Thus Artaud, by transforming his name into a sign of the cross, places his delusional/theological date of origin as contemporaneous with that of the institutionalization and legalization of the Christian religion. It is not perhaps coincidental that this paralleled his own situation of institutionalization in the asylums, which resulted in a violent, extreme countercathexis onto the theological realm.

Just as he transforms his own name into a sign of the cross, he inversely transforms Christ's name into a sign of his own condition. "*Ji et cri, contracté en jiji-cricri.*" (XII, 250) The disarticulation of Christ's name becomes a sign of Artaud's own passion, of his libidinal intensity, where his screams (*cri*) contract his words and contort his body in a gnostic system of contradictions and suffering, in what is the very simulacrum of religious consciousness—a paranoid syncretism that entails theology as allegory, as a sign of psychology or egology. The entirety of the religious system functions for Artaud as a sign, in a desperate quest for his own origins. Reiterating this point: "*Ils ont dieu dans leur cri-me.*" (XVIII, 15) ("They have god in their crime," where *cri-me* also signifies his own screams, as the result of such theological crimes.)

This inscription of origins in one's own name also pertains to the title that Artaud gave himself: *Artaud le Mômo. Mômo*, a Provencal word for madman, is structurally congruous with those other words found at the very origin of language in the child's speech—*papa, mama, pipi, caca*—words also scattered throughout Artaud's later writings. In the language of the infant, these minimal syllabic vocal repetitions and oppositions indicate the origin of signification within the transition from the meaningless sounds of babble to the articulated sounds of speech. Lévi-Strauss explains:

> Even at the babbling stage the phoneme group /pa/ can be heard. But the difference between /pa/ and /papa/ does not reside simply in reduplication: /pa/ is a noise, /papa/ is a word. The reduplication indicates intent on the part of the speaker; it endows the second syllable with a function different from that which would have been performed by the first seperately, or in the form of a potentially limitless series of identical sounds /papapapapa/ produced by mere babbling. Therefore the second /pa/ is not a repetition of the first, nor has it the same signification. It is a sign that, like itself, the first /pa/ too was a sign, and that as a pair they fall into the category of signifiers, not of things signified.[13]

But while the child "creates" language from amidst the glossolalic and echolalic babbles of its prelinguistic expression, Artaud conversely creates his texts, his art, his identifications, by transforming the structures of language into glossolalic pronunciations. Thus for Artaud, the primal words—*papa, mama, pipi, caca, momo, jiji-cricri*—do not indicate a reversion to the origins of language, but rather signify the creation of a sophisticated modernist text in which the elementary forms of discourse reveal the very disarticulations of the modernist artwork as well as of the schizophrenic body. As a model for his creation of glossolalic texts, consider the lexical disarticulation and the homophonic, alliterative syntactic rearticulation in the following phrase: "*soi, quoi, loi, moi, roi, toi, zut et Ça*" (XII,58) (self, what, law, me, king, you, dash! *and* It.) This would be to invert the famed Freudian dictum, which would now proclaim: "Where ego was, there shall id be." Here, through the desublimation of the self (*soi*) to the libido (*Ça*), the major themes of the *Cahiers* and Artaud's subsequent works are disclosed in the primal relations between sound and sense, revealed in the libidinal sources of phonetic articulations.

The presentation and use of such glossolalia must be understood in the context of Artaud's project for a new theater, announced in *Le théâtre et son double,* one of the century's major tracts on theater/antitheater. Artaud, comparing the theater to the plague, insists that, ". . .the theater is a disease because it is the supreme equilibrium which cannot be achieved without destruction. It invites the mind to share a delirium which exalts its energies . . ." (IV,39) Here, "language in the form of *Incantation*" (IV,56) leads the spectator to recover the religious, mystical, hieratic essence of an anti-psychological theater long lost in the West. In such a theater, the scenario is no longer subordinate to the written word, and speech itself is manipulated like an object. (IV,87) Screams, cries, groans and the sundry, dissonant sounds of the body itself replace meaningful language.

This desublimation of the voice will create a sort of "*musique pauvre*" ("poor music")[14] in contrast to the traditional sublimation of sounds into music.

> Musical instruments are only a means to replace the work of the voice and the body with tricks discovered by an ungifted race.
>
> I am not particularly astute, but I ought to know how to play music in a certain fashion with my voice, my hands

> and my feet, *on the earth* and not in the clouds, never, though that can be heard from very far away. (XXI,72)

Artaud wishes to rectify the error of an ethereal music by means of his desublimation of music to the corporeal, earthly realm, where "the abyss of music is at the body's core." (XIX,19) Thus a central trope in Artaud's writings, in his ontology of the spirit, would be *musication*, whereby the sonorous quality of words takes precedence over their meaning. This is the case in glossolalia as one of the limits of language on the verge of nonsense. It is the exact inverse of the *nominalism* of everyday speech, whereby words are unremittantly endowed with meaning and referential expliciteness.

> Thus, if I am only cacophony, which is the voice of my diseased [*mal*] being, it is time to make my being exist, let it arrive in its element, the evil [*mal*] which is the disease [*mal*] of my very being because being wills no evil [*mal*], because it does not understand evil [*mal*]. For words are cacophony and grammar suits them poorly [*mal*], that grammar which fears evil [*mal*] because it always seeks the good, well-being, while evil [*mal*] is at the core of being, a painful plague of cacophony, a dreadful fever of disharmony, the scabrous pustule of a polyphony where being is good only in being's disease [*mal*], the syphilis of its infinity. (XVIII,115)

In this explanation of Artaud's own relation to language as cacophony—where the polysemy and ambiguity of the word *mal* (evil, disease, poorly) creates the conflation of theological, medical, and poetic discourse—we realize that his glossolalia cannot simply be taken for the inarticulate "word-salad" typical of much schizophrenic speech, nor as an example of purely religious charismatic glossolalia, nor as a modernist poetic device. It is rather through the confluence of these diverse functions, through a polyvalent, "polyphonic" mode of enunciation, that the meaning of his glossolalia is established. Artaud's glossolalia must thus be understood according to several interwined registers: (1) within the differences of the theological, medical, and poetic discourses in which it is situated; (2) through the varied languages which appear in it, such as French, English, Latin, Greek, etc.; (3) in relation to the theoretical and poetic/theatrical statements of his earlier texts; (4) and within the immediate context of the texts of the *Cahiers* in which they appear. Thus his glossolalic cacophony is to be located between supreme meaning and nonsense, between the beautiful sounds of music and the silence of *aphasia universalis;* between the very limits of "*Euphonie, aphonie.*" (XIX,209)[15]

Connecting this musicality with theology, Artaud explains that, "Redemption involves restoring the consciousness of being's despair of Eternal Rest to the Music of Eternal Rest" (XV,192). Such music would thus take part, however obliquely, in the broad function of music in the liturgy of the Christian Church. As the fourth century theologian St. John Chrysostom declared: "Music was invented in heaven, which resounds with the song of the Heavenly Hosts; our singing is nought but an echo, an imitation of the songs the angels sing."[16] Perhaps the Gergorian Chant (Pope Gregory's codification of 4th century chants during the period of vast institutionalization of the Christian Church in the late sixth century) is the supreme instantiation of such music, which simultaneously provides a materialization of the voices of Angels and the disarticulation of the speech of man. As one scholar of medieval music postulates:

> Both the theory and the subsequent notation show signs of grace notes, trills, shakes, melting vowels and a thousand and one embellishments which would scandalize present-day apostles of tradition.[17]

The structure of Gregorian chants provides an opportunity for the distention and disarticulation of speech on three levels of complexity; the relation between words and musical notes is distinguished as either: (1) syllabic—one note per syllable; (2) neumatic—several notes per syllable; (3) melismatic—an extended melody per syllable. The most extreme example of this musication, this breaking up of the word to create musical sound, is to be found in the *Alleluia* of the Mass. At the first occurance of the word "alleluia" the final syllable /a/ is set to a long melisma; in its final occurance at the end of the piece it was often extended still further—this extension was termed a *tropus* (literally a turn, thus conflating the functions of *figure of speech* and *melody.*) It is not all surprising that this musical excess should occur in the *Alleluia,* which serves as a musical *jubilus,* defined by Saint Augustin:

> He who sings a jubilus uses no words; he expresses his joy in inarticulate sound. His heart is overwhelmed with joy and mere words no longer suffice. He lets himself go in a cry of happiness too great for words.[18]

The extreme, unbounded affirmation of the *Alleluia* is never just the closure of a musical text, its "amen," but rather exists beyond the limits of language. It is the corporeal, meaningless expression of infinite joy, or rather of joy before an infinite God.

This sacred expression of the jubilant *alleluia* persists in contemporary music. Consider Maurice Ohana's description of the use of the human voice in his 1977 *Messe* (Mass):

> The composer calls for *a sound that is restored to its natural form.* By this he means that it should be obtained by a voice production that, prior to all notions of standardized technique and far from bel canto, rediscovers naturalism and the ability to change: open or nasal, clear or raucous, the sound is transformed, trembles, oscillates, grows or is extinguished, obeying, as if in improvisation, the impulses of a spontaneous and deepseated corporeal urge. The text, split up into phonemes of variegated colour, then becomes nothing more than the canvas for the spiritual reality that the word previously hid, rather as if its expression as music released the energy with which it was secretly charged: a meaning behind meaning, exposing the nakedness of rapport between believer and his God, as he invokes, acclaims or implores Him. As the key-stone of the Mass, the *Trope,* which was dropped from the liturgy eight centuries ago, takes up the Gregorian practice of grafting into a piece a text in which faith finds a more familiar expression.[19]

Artaud's "music," his glossolalia, like his psychological identifications, vacillate between the sacred and the profane. Yet while the Gregorian chant presents a euphonic, harmonic, melodic disarticulation of the voice, Artaud's glossolalia entail a cacophonic, disharmonic, atonal vocalization.

It is not only the Christian tradition that provides the context of Artaud's glossolalia (permitting, for example, his own enunciation of Christ's "lama lama sabach-tani" to serve as an incipient glossolalic chant.) Another central incantation in the *Cahiers de Rodez* is the Vedic mantra *Aum* (*om*). Utilized in Buddhist and Hindu religious practice, *Om* is the purest expression of the living breath itself, and thus represents the production of all other sounds, which are contained within it. This sound serves Artaud as an archetype, a paradigmatic instance, of the disruption of everyday language and the creation of glossolalia. In the first volume of the *Cahiers,* the term *Aum* is juxtaposed with its homophonic double *homme* (man) (XV,99). The declension of this homophonic relation is obtained through a syllabic, melodic, and metaphoric slippage: *"Avant l'espirt il y a l'aum, l'am, l'âme, c'est à dire le corps de l'homme que je suis, et c'est toute ma conscience"* (XVII, 22) ("Before the spirit is the om, the am, the soul, this is to say the body of the man I am, which is my entire consciousness.")

Homophony (based on alliteration and consonance) is a form of difference in similarity, and is thus emblematic of the function of tropes in general. The slippage of sound also entails a slippage of sense, of identity, Artaud, *l'homme des Aums,* (XVI, 316) vanquishes his own painful, hideous body by transforming it into a state of sexual *indifferentiation*: *"Je suis homme femme"* ("I am man woman.") (XVIII,93) This is indicated through a curious combination of homophony, rhyme, and dissimulation through erasure. At one point in the *Cahiers* he specifies that, *"L'âme est aum, l'aum est âme."* ("The soul is om, om is the soul.") (XVII,130). But a note to this phrase reveals that in the manuscript the original phrase was rather, *"L'âme est aum, l'aum est femme."* ("The soul is om, om is woman.") (XVII,292). Thus *Aum,* a primal incantatory chant giving rise to all sorts of glossolalia and echolalia, indicates both the masculine and the feminine, which define in their very incommensurability Artaud's own mode of identification. Sexual identification is abolished, and all beings are conflated into a primal, cloacal magma of which Being is comprised.

> The soul is om,
> om is the soul,
> everything is shit, cunt, prick, whore, sperm, ass,
> crud, pus, illness, urges, salad, macaroni, opium,
> nicotine, crap, wretchedness. (XVII, 130)

In the Tantric chant, the incantation of *om* serves to simultaneously reveal the full presence of the totality of Being and the illusory nature of the corporeal world—the two are ultimately one and the same, symbolized by the spiritual body. It is within this existential/theological contradicition that Artaud locates himself. The narrative of the *Cahiers* reveals the impossible, gnostic desire to escape from the loathed body, that source of the basest, vilest, most horrendous aspects of a hybrid Being—which is none other than Artaud himself. Thus his inscription of his own name into the Christian and Vedic liturgy reveals the libidinal binds from which he could not liberate himself, and entails the impossible iconoclasm of his glossolaliating poetics. "The cross of the impossible and not of the possible." (XVI,70)

In Artaud's trans- or meta-theological dramaturgy and musicalization, glossolalia often verges on the completely unintelligible: *"Khanda Khantur Khenarbila"* (XV,210), to give just one early example from among many others. But the final volume of the *Cahiers* reveals many more everyday words within the glossolalic texts: besides the everpresent syllabic doublings of the "primal" words *papa, mama, caca, pipi, zizi, toto,* etc. we also find *pax, couper, fugue, pique, kali, yen, puta, cher, feu, kama çutra, gloria in excelsis,* and many others. We even find the most stereotypical expression of musicality, when one glossolalic text ends with the phrase, *"tra la la la la, misère"* (XXI,390), while another goes:

> *yor kiki*
> *e koko rikera*
> *yor rikera*
> *e coco roko* (XXI, 227).

Yet rather than indicating the onset of a banalization of language through a "cure," it in fact reveals that poetic production is in part a function of stereotyping: tropes are based on *typos,* as a *clinamen,* turning away from words' stereotypicality. Glossolalia is an effect, and not a cause, of Artaud's poetic production, which is a turning away from ordinary language towards the most sacred and the most profane realms of expression and existence.

Yet Artaud's glossolalia hardly entail a theogony: "And I don't engender beings like glossolaliating turds, doubles arising from what?" (XVI, 32). Even if glossolalia is at the origins of language (as the linguists teach us) and even if excrement is at the origins of art (as the psychoanalysts teach us), it would be a serious category mistake to confuse the two domains within a unitary, theological realm of creativity. To insist upon the theological, nosological or aesthetic aspects of such glossolalia would be to deny its major function in Artaud: the pure expression of the body, always at odds with the spirit. Anything more would be metaphysics, which is precisely what the Theater of Cruelty was designed to avoid, and which was precisely what Artaud suffered during those tortured but productive months of incarceration at Rodez.

The Trial of Gilles de Rais

> The science of Satan is always only that of our own *surplus.*
>
> Antonin Artaud

In the very first pages of the *Cahiers de Rodez*, entitled, "Le retour de la France aux principes sacrés" ("The Return of France to Sacred Principles"), Artaud submits certain observations about the theater of the Middle Ages, specifically the Mystery Plays, which are consistent with his position on the new theatricality outlined earlier in *Le théâtre et son double.* In this theater of dramatic trance and curative magic (XV,14), there is manifest a,

> . . .crucial point of mental explosion where the words of the Word are not yet spoken nor already born, but where the soul burns like a country where the Barbaric invaders are everywhere scattered, and these Barbarians are the desires-passions, internal psychic states, the effluvia and odors of the self at the moment when what will become tragic force and thought in the Manifest will take form in unconscious being. (XV,11).

Here, the most flamboyant manifestation of such a theater, "Has nature as its decor, and torchlight and the flames of the stake as its lighting." (XV,10).

On the very last page of the *Cahiers*, written just hours before his release, Artaud returns to the same theme. The last words written at Rodez were: "I will martyrize the people of Orléans." (XXI, 481). This is certainly an allusion to the story of Joan of Arc, the Maid of Orléans, who herself was burned at the stake. It is the same Jeanne d'Arc with whom Jeanne Tripier identified (in a time and place quite similar to that of Artaud), and of whom Artaud wrote: "A man is needed to support Joan of Arc's heaven and her visions, or else all the powers will perish." (XVI, 40).

Such a man existed: he was Gilles de Rais. Gilles de Rais was the legendary general who led Joan of Arc's army and who, after Joan's martyrdom, secluded himself in his castles and proceeded to sadistically murder numerous young boys, thrilling in cutting off their heads and relishing in the sight of the gushing streams of blood and their final, dying expressions.[20] Gilles de Rais transformed himself into the demonic inversion of Joan of Arc's saintliness in an antinomian scenario of radical evil and ultimate self-sacrifice. It is not altogether strange that Gilles de Rais is never mentioned by Jeanne Tripier or by Artaud; yet a return of the repressed nevertheless occurs.[21]

The scenario at Rodez was Artaud's own passion of the soul, which was, as we have seen of a decidedly antinomian nature, and most certainly a form of self-sacrifice. Artaud refers to himself as a martyr, which is equally the case of Jeanne d'Arc (XV, 247)—but his martyrdom is more specifically understood in terms of totemism. "I will never finish with this history of the TOTEM that I am. . ." (XII, 145). By regarding himself as a totem, (XVIII, 147; XXI, 246) a "strangled totem," (XII,24), he reinforces his identification with the Christian God, in that religion based upon totemic sacrifice *par excellence*. Artaud offers himself as a heretical substitute for Christ on the cross.

For Artaud, the theater is a form of communication through sacrifice, just as for Maurice Blanchot writing is a form of self-sacrifice. As Artaud insists in *Le théâtre et son double*, the new theater of cruelty must be like the plague in its function of purification, and it must benefit from certain temptations (modelled on the Temptations of Saint Anthony) from which life has all to lose and the mind all to gain. Indeed, Artaud speaks of himself in terms of a "painful plague of cacophony," (XVIII, 115) as an expression of the ultimate Temptation:

> The temptation to represent the unrepresentable was a temptation resisted but which wanted to live, and it must be destroyed since it was the crime of Manifestation. (XVI, 28).

This statement perhaps more than any other describes the intertwining program of Artaud's Theater of Cruelty and the *Cahiers de Rodez*. This is a critique of the sublime, the metaphysical, the ideal and the infinite—to which the sacred must not be reduced, and in which the holy must not be lost. Hence the locus of "passion" in Artaud's own body. Through his critique of representation, Artaud creates a theatricality and an aesthetic where art is a function of production (and not reproduction); where choreography is transposed onto the body; where music is transposed solely onto the voice. The body is no longer dissimulated by the theatrical scenario; it produces and reveals its libidinal existence. No longer caught within the symbolic web, the self becomes a creator of signs, a machine of the imaginary, its own temptation, its own incarnation. But to accomplish this, it must also be its own sacrifice, a sacrifice which will bring down with it entire ontotheological systems.

Considering the numerous contradictions, inconsistencies and incommensurabilities expressed in the *Cahiers of Rodez*, we might propose as an allegory an event recounted by Lacarrière in *Les hommes ivres de Dieu*. He writes of two sixth century stylites (ascetic holy men who spent years atop huge columns)—one orthodox and the other a heretical monophysite—who lived on adjacent columns and spent their time hurling insults at each other.[22] Taken separately, each of these theological systems may be conceived of as competing *metaphysical* systems; considered together, as part of the same tale—a truly universal history of Christianity—their incommensurability can only entail the institution of a sort of *pataphysics*. We will remember Alfred Jarry's definition of *pataphysics* in *Gestes et opinions de Docteur Faustroll, Pataphysicien*: it is the science of the particular, which studies the laws of exceptions and accidents. It is the "science of imaginary solutions, which symbolically accords with the lineaments of the properties of objects described in their virtuality."[23]

Such a pataphysics accurately describes Artaud's own situation, as he himself suggests in the *Cahiers*:

> This unconscious caused me so much pain that I ended by having the time to know myself, but where was I therefore so as not to know where I was, I who am the will and the non-moral but *pataphysical* inner knowledge of necessity . . . (XVI, 326).

We must also remember that Artaud's earliest theatrical productions and theorizations went under the sign of *Le théâtre Alfred Jarry*.

Pataphysically examined, heterodoxy would be the history of exceptions, and orthodoxy itself would be nothing other than a particularly successful heresy. Caught between the fear of the metaphysical and the hatred of the physical, the return of the repressed manifest in Artaud's life is really that of our own—the incunabula of a new self.

Part IV

CINEMATIC TRANSGRESSIONS

11

Cartesian Simulacra

WINDOW: By analogy. An empty space left in an act or manuscript, to be subsequently filled in.

Le Petit Robert: Dictionnaire de la langue française

When the Baal Shem had a difficult task before him, he would go to a certain place in the woods, light a fire and meditate in prayer—and what he had set out to perform was done. When a generation later the "Maggid" of Meseritz was faced with the same task, he would go to the same place in the woods and say: We can no longer light the fire, but we can still speak the prayers—and what he wanted done became reality. Again a generation later Rabbi Moshe Leib of Sassov had to perform this task. And he too went into the woods and said: We can no longer light a fire, nor do we know the secret meditations belonging to the prayer, but we do know the place in the woods to which it all belongs—and that must be sufficient; and sufficient it was. But when another generation had passed and Rabbi Israel of Rishin was called upon to perform the task, he sat down on his golden chair in his castle and said: We cannot light the fire, we cannot speak the prayers, we do not know the place, but we can tell the story of how it was done. And, the story-teller adds, the story which he told had the same effect as the actions of the other three.[1]

The camera obscura, as a model of representation, is to be found at the heart of modern rationality. In his *Second Meditation* (1648) Descartes, attempting to found rationality on the sovereignty of the spirit, postulates the limits of doubt as a precondition for the very possibility of truth:

> If I chance to look out of a window on to men passing in the street, I do not fail to say, on seeing them, that I see men, just as I say that I see the wax; and yet, what do I see from this window, other than hats and cloaks, which can cover ghosts or dummies who move only by means of springs? But I judge them to be really men, and thus I understand, by the sole power of judgement which resides in my mind, what I believed I saw with my eyes.[2]

Isolated within his room, a vast camera obscura, the world appears as pure spectacle, where other men may be but mere simulacra upon that stage created by the framing of the window. This metaphor of the camera obscura is already prefigured in Descartes' *Dioptrique*, Book V (1637), where the structure of vision is modelled on the camera obscura; and in his earlier work, *Règles pour la direction de l'esprit*, Book III (1628), the mind itself is metaphorized as a camera obscura, where intelligence is a function of the "light of reason" seen by "the mind's eye." Thus the scenario of the *Second Meditation* affords a palimpsest of these three modes of camera obscura: the "mind's eye" is behind the physical eye that finds itself looking out of the window.

Cartesian sovereignty derives from the reduction of transcendence to immanence; the truth of what lies beyond the window is determined by judgement, not by perception, so that the veracity of perception is ultimately a function of intuition. The self is caught in immanence; while judgement transforms *doxa* into a presumed certainty, the idea is a representation raised to thought.

In the *Dioptrique* Book V, Descartes claims that sight itself is modelled after touch, likening sight to the palpations of the world by a blind man's cane, thus eliminating the essential feature of sight, *i.e.*, action at a distance, the very incarnation of transcendence itself. He ultimately wishes to ground, or replace, the function and effects of sight by the work of judgement, and to admit no visual supplement to thought.

This foreclosure of the sensual—closing the window, closing our eyes, blindness—is a necessary precondition of thought;

Descartes wishes to effect this sensory deprivation experiment to the utmost; as he writes at the beginning of the *Third Meditation*:

> I shall now close my eyes, stop up my ears, turn away all my senses, even efface from my thought all images of corporeal things, or at least, because this can hardly be done, I shall consider them as being vain and false. . .[3]

And yet, "because this can hardly be done," doesn't the very impossibility of accomplishing such a blindness, such an unrestricted judgement, point to a paradox in the Cartesian system: if the reduction of the sensual world to thought cannot be fully accomplished, if there is always a perceptual supplement which cannot be suppressed and which thus maintains its hold on consciousness, isn't there always an influx of *doxa*, of uncertainty, into the clear and distinct thoughts which for Descartes are the very guarantee of truth? Wouldn't the attempt to transform the *doxa* of sensation into the *orthodoxy* of rationality entail the *reductio ad absurdum* of a worldless *res cogitans*, where the "sum" of the *cognito ergo sum* would be an empty signified, and thus the *cogito ergo sum* merely a tautology?

Indeed, the Cartesian camera obscura(s), while being the central metaphor of a rationalist epistemology, is also one moment of a larger representational tradition. Might we not consider Cartesian metaphysics as an epiphenomenon of that history, an impasse in the quest for an impossible blindness, within a camera obscura still all too lucid?

In 1826 Nicéphore Niépce took the first photograph, an 8 hour exposure through a window of his house in Châlon-sur-Saône. It is a blurred, grainy, somewhat cubist view of buildings, of almost no representational value; on the back of it is written in French in another's hand, "The heliograph. The first results spontaneously obtained by the action of light." This is a quite curious claim, given that the entire Neo-Platonic tradition proffered an ontology/theology of light where the Divine light was the active cause of all existence. It is no doubt due to an empiricist prejudice, one of the results of the Cartesian tradition whose scientifism made possible the discovery of this heliographic process, that the role of light in the metaphysical tradition is forgotten.

If, as Derrida claims, " . . . the entire history of our philosophy is a photology . . . "[4] within which, as we have seen, Cartesian metaphysics plays a central if somewhat paradoxical role, it is apparent that the event of the first photograph is a privileged moment in that history; both insofar as every technological innovation creates a global shift in our ontology and our sensorium, and also insofar as every artwork or aesthetics already implies a new metaphysics.

Within the superimposition of three camera obscuras in Descartes' system—mind, eye, room—the same metaphor is used to delineate the incompatible realms of sensation and knowledge. But where this equivocation is suppressed by creating a third term of the metaphor, a literal one—the room itself as camera obscura—Niépce interposes yet a fourth, the camera obscura of the photographic apparatus. Yet the peculiarity of this new mode of camera obscura is that, unlike all previous ones which created only fleeting simulacra, the photographic apparatus fixes the image. The Cartesian "idea," privately projected in the camera obscura of the "mental box," developes that generality which grounds our sovereignty by interiorizing transcendence; the photograph, a public object created within but seen outside of a camera obscura, realizes a derangement of the world and of ourselves, creating the simulacra of objects within a world of objects, and multiplying our nostalgia for objects lost and objects never possessed, for worlds gone and worlds never even seen. Rather than merely *doubling* the world in our phantasms, as does the traditonal camera obscura of the mind, the photographic apparatus *multiplies* these simulacra to infinity. The Cartesian transformation of *doxa* into a rational *orthodoxy* is superceded by the creation of a vast material *heterodoxy* of images and perspectives.

If *imitation* is par excellence the rhetorical figure of construction by revolution,[5] then photography (heliography) leads this revolution to its limits by establishing the possibility of an infinite, aleatory, decontextualized multiplication of visibility. If for the Cartesian mentality blindness is a precondition of knowledge, then this vortex of visibility created by photography doubtlessly leads to a vertigo of anguish in the face of this multiplication of simulacra.

According to Roland Barthes, the photograph proffers, ". . .a 'fundamental belief,' an 'Urdoxa,' which nothing can undo, unless it is proved to me that this image *is not* a photograph . . . "[6] For Descartes, knowledge was the result of the suppression of *doxa*, of the elimination of simulacra within a "clear and distinct" intuition; for Barthes, certitude is a function of imaging, of the photographic multiplication of simulacra which are more than symbols of the visible, which are actually *indexes* and *icons* of past visions and visibility.

The Cartesian paradox is that knowledge is modelled on the camera obscura, yet necessitates blindness to the visual world; the Barthesian paradox is that in the photograph we have a past which is present, and a presence that will insinuate itself into every future.

> . . .Photography is undialectical; it is a denatured theater where death cannot be "contemplated," reflected and interiorized; furthermore, it is the dead theater of Death, the foreclosure of the Tragic; it excludes all purification, all catharsis.[7]

By excluding time, photography marks the tragedy of temporality; if, as Nietzsche claims, *ressentiment* is the ill will against time itself, against the irreversibility of time with its "once-and-for-all" character, then photography is the hypostatization of such *ressentiment*, its very aestheticized epitome. Not permitting the incorporation and transformation of the lost object through mourning, photography is a perpetual sign of an "asymbolic Death" which nevertheless perpetually dissimulates our mortality.

In the photograph, the past is already marked by that transcendence which is but the empirical telos of our flight from ourselves, *i.e.*, it is marked by death. Yet it is always another's death which is seen; by not instantiating that temporality which is our lives, photography is a false theater of society, a shadow theater where the shadows, all too frighteningly, often resemble ourselves.

Kafka found it particularly appropriate that one of the cinema theaters in Prague was called the *Cinema of the Blind*. Upon hearing of this cinema, he proclaimed to his friend Gustave Janouch, "*Cinema of the Blind*! Every cinema should be called that. Their flickering images blind people to reality." In this particularly Cartesian moment (Descartes, in the *Third Meditation* claimed that he was, "blinded by the images of sensible things") Kafka, believing that photography, "concentrates one's eyes on the superficial," epitomized the classical foundations of a supremely iconoclastic modernism.

It is the rare film indeed that meets the stringent conditions of a "Cinema of the Blind." Yet such films exist, perhaps the foremost among them being Hollis Frampton's *Poetic Justice* (1970), a central film of the American avant garde. This film is a prime instantiation of paratext as text: it consists simply of images of a written screenplay; each shot of *Poetic Justice* is the image of a different page of a filmscript placed upon a growing pile of pages situated between a cactus plant and a cup of coffee upon a coffee table. As the pile grows, a palimpsest is formed, and the narrative of the projected (*i.e.*, future) film unfolds. All this time, the narrative of *Poetic Justice* itself is nothing other than the turning of the pages.

Thus Frampton attempts the impossible sublimation of the figural into the textual within cinema.[8] The script of the film-to-be within the film *Poetic Justice* describes events taking place within a room, where the characters consist of "I," "You," and "Your Lover." Thus through the use of the linguistic shifter, any possible attempt at figuration is necessarily inadequate to the textual openness. The film-to-be is an impossible film, where the specificity of the image is effaced in the generality of words. One of the scenes is specified as:

> #5. (*CLOSE-UP*)
> MY HAND PLACES A BLACK-AND-WHITE PHOTOGRAPH OF YOUR FACE ON A TABLE.

Here, the "photograph" offers no more information than the linguistic shifter: the "real" and the "figural" are doubled, conflated, as they can only be within the written text, creating further paradoxes, further impossibilities; we are no more certain of the referent, of the characters' identities, then we were before. They may be us, they should be, but they most certainly are not.

As the "narrative" unfolds, we arrive at the following shots:

> #123. (*MIDDLE SHOT*)
> BEDROOM. YOU AND YOUR LOVER EMBRACE, NAKED, ON THE BED. OUTSIDE THE WINDOW ARE SPRUCES AND JUNIPERS UNDER SNOW.
> (*DISSOLVE TO . . .*)
>
> #124. (*MIDDLE SHOT*)
> BEDROOM. YOU MAKE LOVE. OUTSIDE THE WINDOW ARE PEACOCKS STRUTTING ON A TURF GREEN.
> (*DISSOLVE TO . . .*)

What follows is a list of 57 different things and events that are seen through this bedroom window. For example (in order):

> AN AUTOMATIC TURRET LATHE IN OPERATION
> A CALM INLAND SEA

A SQUADRON OF PIPERS
RINGS OF SATURN, LOOMING
LITTLE GIRLS SKIPPING ROPE
TUMBLED STACKS OF CORDWOOD
A DISPLAY OF OPHTHALMOSCOPES
(Etc.)

The arbitrary, disjunctive, apparently aleatory disposition of objects and events cannot be contained within any taxonomic scheme. It is, in a sense, a synecdoche for the totality of photographs in the world, an endless multiplication of images which can only decenter and detotalize knowledge, insofar as such a technē, in replicating every object, in creating simulacra of everything, reveals no stylistic, iconic or quantitative limits. It thus escapes the symbolic by eluding any unitary style, by extrapolating multiplicity to closure, eliminating difference by including all possibilities. The figurative is eliminated by actualizing every possibility as literal: the symbolic is subsumed by the imaginary.

Frampton claims that, "A still photograph is simply an isolated frame taken out of the infinite cinema."[9] If we take this filmaker's statement seriously, then Niépce's photograph bears an interesting, even if not totally privileged, place within such an infinite cinema. It becomes the metaphor, the synecdoche, indeed the existential a priori, of an infinitely multiplied visibility, where all is to be seen, where all is to be transformed by the photographic endeavor into an infinite series of simulacra. *Imitation* can no longer be considered as the figurative construction by revolution, but rather as the figural *deconstruction by convolution,* a baroque process where not only is all made visible, where not only is the visible multiplied, but also where visibility itself finally escapes the grip of ontology as photology and becomes, by means of its infinitized function, a parallel real, escaping the symbolic.

Poetic Justice is indeed a cinema of the blind, where the text may be read to the spectator rather then seen, without loss, transforming an unheard silent film into an unseen talkie—hence the "poetic justice," the irony, which determines the scenario. It is only under the condition of invisibility of the referent of the film's *écriture* that the adequation of the film's signifier and signified may be met, *i.e.,* the impossibility of referential determination due to the shifters. It is a film for all and for none, but especially for the blind.

But it is also a text in which the presentation of the camera obscura is once again augmented: now the conditions of observing these simulacra demand that we sit within a camera obscura, the cinema hall. Do these projected images described a symptomatology, where the interiorization of objects and events creates those phantasms which are the stuff of our immanence? Or do they rather describe a metaphysics, where our phantasms are exteriorized and projected as that transcendence which grounds our presumed sovereignty? In either case, the universalized eroticism of *Poetic Justice*, described by an ambivalent scenario, takes place within a camera obscura (bedroom) which opens out onto the multiplicity of possible images of the world; the scopophilic desire is desublimated into pure sexual desire, and perhaps, enchanted or exhausted by phantasms of the lover's body, one no longer bothers to gaze out of the window . . .

Ironically, *camera obscura* and *camera lucida* are essentially the same thing: they both create representations by filling a space with light, images, simulacra. Yet whether the arbiter of truth be the depths of our souls' immanence or the clear (and distinct) spaces of the infinite universe, each remains the horizon of, the referent of, the other. If any entity can serve as the emblem of Being, if anything whatsoever can metaphorize the soul, then, in a sense, Being and the soul are *nothing*. The history of metaphysics is thus an attempt to circumscribe that nothingness; and the history of philosophy as photology is the attempt to illuminate that nothingness. A futile task, one which would make all of our previous observations superfluous, especially if we consider Merleau-Ponty's claim, following Leibniz, that, "Our soul has no windows . . ."[10] or Kafka's complaint that, "Films are iron shutters."

12

On the Art of Fascination

When you lose your mind, it's great to have a body to fall back on.

Shari (Calvin Klein jeans advertisement)

The creation of our world as a habitable milieu is contemporaneous with the celebration of the self as a joyful being. Joy, in it numerous figurations, is a condition of habitability. The origins of art indicate both the continual domestication of the world and the dawn of subjectivity via the celebration of the self as a dualistic creature: technocratic and mystical, domestic and erotic, social and individual. These relationships were codified in the earliest artworks, and remain dominant thematic and structural aspects of art.

The body . . . is a visible archetype.

Maurice Merleau-Ponty

In *Le geste et la parole,* André Leroi-Gourhan, the French archaeologist, shows how the origins of art stem from a fascination with regularity within an overbearingly irregular, chaotic world.

> . . . figurative art as such was preceded by something more obscure or more general which corresponds to the deliberate [*réfléchie*] vision of forms. The unusual within forms, a powerful

> incentive towards figurative concern, existed only from the time at which the subject confronted an organized image of his universe in relation to the objects which enter into his field of perception. . . These concretions directly touch the depths of man's reflective thought. It is mysterious and even disquieting to discover in nature a sort of congealed reflection of thought of which the unusual is the incentive.[1]

Art, contemporaneous with technology, commenced the formation of a cosmos from chaos. This earliest art was not simply aesthetic "*bricolage*," but as Leroi-Gourhan implies it was rather a primitive version of the Surrealist *object-trouvé* (found object), which in its primal version included the contemplation of such regularly formed objects as shells, polished pebbles, and so forth. As Roland Barthes claims, art is a conquest of chance. It was thus through the technique of chance encounter and discovery that art had its origins. This was an art of fascination, and the contemplation of these objects was a form of self-reflection. Such art was at the origins of subjectivity, a subjectivity founded on narcissism but which entails the structural differentiation of the propriate field, the self, from its milieu. Art began as neither culturally superficial nor mimetic, but rather as an active institutor of change, formation, and criticism. Art commenced as formation, not formalization; as a product of expression and mystery, not as representation.

In terms of both formal and psychological/sociological considerations, this earliest found art led directly to the first instances of figurative art, the Paleolithic "Venus" figurines, such as the famed Willendorf Venus. Formal analysis of this figurine reveals the repetition of bulbous, rounded, regular forms, such as pervaded the earlier found art, but which now conform to a figurative, stylized presentation of a fertility symbol. Indeed, the formal constitution of this figurine accentuates its erotic, fertile, sexual aspects. Consider the exaggerated sexual and maternal organs, the overabundant flesh, its pregnancy, and especially the manner in which the salient formal lines converge upon, and accentuate, the sexual organs. Futhermore, this figurine is faceless, emphasizing the anonymity and universality of its erotic functions.

Psychologically, the origin of such figurines follows directly from the origin of art as fascinating found objects. The infant is fascinated by the mother's body: the formation of the infant's world is a function of the separation of the child from its mother. This separation achieves the creation of the world as a field of objects and a scene of independent actions and desires. Indeed, the mother is the first "thing" thus constituted and objectified (through her absence and the child's desire for her return.) Thus a profound homology exists between the ontogenetic creation of the infant's world and the phylogenetic creation of the artwork. Art has its origin in, and remains, a matter of fascination. The first figurative "aesthetic" objects, the Venus figurines, were also representations of mothers, *i.e.*, the Great Earth Mother, a symbol of cosmic (and by extension social) cohesion and regeneration. It is entirely appropriate that the first figurative artworks should be the creative figure par excellence, the mother.

This creative, regenerative aspect of art is strongly indicated, in all its self-reflective intent, in a bas-relief found at Laussel, which depicts a Venus figurine holding a horn in the form of a cornucopia (goat's horn): a fertility symbol (the Venus) holding a fertility symbol (the cornucopia, an androgynous symbol of fecundity and regeneraton). This is a perfect symbolization of artistic creativity as exteriorization, transformation, objectification, and ultimately as narcissistic activity. This is art as separation from the mother: the creation of the world in a form other than the maternal, while still maintaining formal, symbolic, and libidinal connections to the maternal body. While figurative concerns developed from the originary "abstract" art of the found objects, symbolic concern was in turn engendered by a parturition from the first figurative art, that is, from the "Venus" figurines. Hence the Laussel Venus is a presentation of the difference between figuration and abstraction, between representation and symbolism. It is perhaps the earliest example of art about art, in which the figure (Venus) confronts its own symbol (cornucopia.) The difference between the literal and the trope is manifested according to the erotic *topos* of the body.

Oh bliss of tiny creatures
    that remain
for ever in the womb that
    brought them forth!

Rainer Maria Rilke

In "Camera Lucida/Camera Obscura," Annette Michelson correctly claims that the cinematic art of Stan Brakhage is an art of fascination. Indeed, in his film *Window Water Baby Moving*, the very structure of fascination and symbolization is parallel to that of the Laussel bas-relief. This film, about the birth of the first child of Jane and Stan Brakhage, begins with a montage in which we find

Jane, in an advanced stage of pregnancy, shown nude, bathing in water. Her swelled womb is accentuated by framing, lighting, and by the caresses of both her husband and herself. We see here, figuratively, Venus arising from the waters: the birth of Venus. Yet in the second half of the film there is a literal birth, straightforwardly depicted in a montage which intersperses earlier shots of Jane in the water with shots of the birth itself, establishing a metaphoric identification of the film's two sections, of the two births: birth is presented both literally and symbolically. Finally, as if to accentuate the creativity of the mother figure, beyond being the donor of life and the muse of the artist, she literally becomes creative of the film itself when, immediately after the birth, it is Jane who films Stan, the proud father. Indeed "By Brakhage" implies "By Stan *and Jane* Brakhage."

In his later epic film, *Dog Star Man*, which is also partially about the birth of a child and eroticism, the *Prelude* reveals a vast metaphoric sequence which unites the human and cosmic levels of existence. The central images of this prelude are masculine: the Dog Star Man himself, and the sun, seen from astronomic footage as a close-up with solar flares. Yet a metaphoric equivalence is established: through formal similarity the sun is created by burns, flares and painted frames in the film, and is metaphorized by the tip of a penis. Thus there is an equivalence, an interchangeability, between the cosmic, abstract, and corporeal dimensions; existence is structured as a series of metaphoric exchanges establishing the relations of microcosmos/macrocosmos/macroanthropos through the filmic montage. Brakhage is certainly aware of this mode of relationships; witness his aphorism from "The Stars are Beautiful": "The sky is the dead decaying body of God; the stars are glittering maggots."[2]

This confusion of genre (gender) is manifested in the androgynous fusions of male and female anatomy in Part III of the film, described by Brakhage:

> Part Three has a "His, Her, and Heart" roll . . . . Female images are trying to become male and have not succeeded and the males are trying to become female and have not succeeded . . . In the "Her" roll you see mounds of moving flesh that separate distinguishably into a woman's image, but then become very tortured by attempts to transform into male. It's very Breugelesque in a way; penises replace breasts in flashes of images; then a penis will jut through the eyes; or male hair will suddenly move across the whole scape of the female body. . .

> At some point this ceases and the flesh becomes definitely woman. Then on the "His" roll. . . you have the opposite occurring: a male mound of flesh which keeps being tortured by a proclivity to female imagery; so that, for instance, the lips are suddenly transformed into a vagina. Finally the male form becomes distinct. Then, of course, these two dance together as they are superimposed on each other; you get this mound of male-female flesh which pulls apart variously and superimposes upon itself in these mixtures of Breugelesque discoveries, so to speak, or distortions.[3]

Here, the biomorphism, indeed, anthropomosphism, suggests both sexual union and androgyny as ultimate union (as does the cornucopia in the Laussel Venus.) Yet this union is a precondition for the birth depicted in Part IV of the film, where the female body takes thematic precedence as the source of creation (as it does once again in yet another of Brakhage's birth films, *Thigh Line Lyre Triangular*.) Through montage, superimposition, and anamorphic distortion, Brakhage reestablishes the foundational erotic mythopoeia in a cinema of fascination, in which metaphor is created by distortion and confusion, and is the source of wonder.

> Art, therefore, also can and should upset reality, take it apart into elements, build illogical new worlds of it and in this arbitrariness is a hidden law, which in disturbing sense has it, so that the madness that destroys our external sense leads us into our internal meaning.
>
> Witold Gombrowicz

Brakhage first utilized an anamorphic lens in filming *Dog Star Man* between 1960 and 1964, in order to create those distortions which were foundational for his mythopoeic system. Yet the use of anamorphosis was already well established in modernist art, especially in the work of Salvador Dali. In such works as *Crânes mous et harpe crânienne* (1935), *Bureaucrate moyen atmosphérocéphale dans l'attitude de traire du lait d'une harpe cranienne* (1933), and *Jeune fille au crâne* (1934) (which is a novel addition to the iconography of "Death and the Young Girl," since the young girl depicted here is lasciviously fondling an anamorphic projection of a skull), Dali appropriates Holbein's use of an anamorphic skull (*The Ambassadors*, 1533) to delineate a fantasy world of the perverse imagination, of the unconscious, as was a central task of the Surrealists. Dali utilized anamporhoses to the limits of distortion: his famous fetishistic crutches support extreme reifications of anamorphic projections. These projections are usually anatomical, and result in the creation of some of the most monstrously distorted human figures in art history. For example, in his series of engravings which illustrate a 1933-1934 edition of Lautréamont's *Les chants de Maldoror*, the anamorphic skull is the central iconic figure organizing the distortions and metamorphoses of the other figures in the work. While Brakhage uses anamorphosis to create the metaphors of a new mythopoeia, Dali uses anamorphoses to create the integral monstrosities of the Surrealist dream world.

In, "Objects psycho-atmosphériques-anamorphiques," Dali offers a theoretical account of the significance of anamorphosis: such anamorphic objects are fetishes par excellence, which bring to light the depths of the human psyche.

> Obscure feelings become classifiable, calculable entities, regulated by the light according to the cognitive order of the hardest and most precise anatomies and, in comparison, the finest articulations of crustaceans and armor take on the vague, dubious and amoeboid contours of the most deliquescent medusas and soft watches.[4]

Anamorphosis is the origin of metamorphosis and reversal into the opposite (two Freudian dream functions) which bring the unconscious to light. And appropriate to their fetishistic function, the forms taken on by these anamorphic objects are those of the Medusa and the famous Dalinian soft watches of *The Persistance of Memory* (1931), both detumescent phallic objects.

The mythical Medusa, whose hair is in the form of writhing phallic snakes, is the symbol of fetishistic fascination and dread: nobody can look directly at Medusa, Queen of the underworld, and live. Note that amulets of the Medusa were used to ward off the evil eye: the Medusa is that which cannot be looked at. Hence it is the anathema of spectatorship, and the antithesis of art objects, which demand the gaze. The fetish, like the Medusa, represents the object that remains invisible, that must be represented by something other than itself. The fetish object is a substitute for that ever-absent oxymoron, the female phallus, and for the dreadful mutilation which its absence implies. Yet the fetish may be observed.

(For Dali, the ultimate fetish object was his own wife, Gala, who exhibits a "gaze that can pierce through walls.")

Thus, in terms of the psychological structure of fascination, the interdependence of masculine and feminine functions, of presence and absence, can only be unified in the mythical, utopian corpus of the androgyne. Consider that the Latin root of the word fascination, *"fascinum,"* is defined according to the *Oxford Latin Dictionary* as: 1. An evil spell, bewitchment. 2. The penis. b. a phallic emblem (worn round the neck as a charm). c. a kind of seashell. Indeed, the archetypal charm used by the witch to cast an evil spell, to fascinate, is that of the phallus, which is also a form of shell, revealing again the androgynous ambiguity of forms. The Laussel Venus held a cornucopia which was a goat's horn, or perhaps a shell, but which was in any case a bisexual symbol; the etymology of the word "fascinate" reveals a connection between penis and shell, an antithetical sense of a primal word disclosing the antithetical origins of Eros.

Objects of fascination are primally anthropomorphic; the human body is the general archetype of symbolism. The metamorphosis of the body into symbols was the result of Brakhage's use of anamorphoses. Yet Dali's goal was different:

> Yes! once the symbolic stage is transgressed, the object becomes and is "verified" by its own "real constitution" and no longer by the associative evocations of its constitution.

Brakhage transforms the literal, material, the real, into the symbolic; Dali transforms the symbolic into the imaginative reality of a sur-realism.

> The real constitution of things is accustomed
> to hide itself.
>
> Heraclitus

Salvador Dali and Jacques Lacan were both contributors to the Surrealist journal *Minotaure.* In fact, André Breton arranged a meeting between Dali and Lacan after the publication of Dali's "L'Ane pourri" in the first volume of *Surréalisme au service de la Révolution* (July 1930), an article in which Dali sketched out his theory of the paranoic-critical method in painting. This was of concern to Lacan, then working on his thesis, *De la psychose paranoïaque dans ses rapports avec la personnalité*. Thus it is not surprising to find in Book XI of Lacan's

Seminaire, The Four Fundamental Concepts of Psychoanalysis, a section on anamorphosis in which he writes:

> Distortion may lend itself[. . .] to all the paranoiac ambiguities, and every possible use has been made of it, from Arcimboldi to Salvador Dali. I will go so far as to say that this fascination complements what geometrical researches into perspective allow to escape from vision.
>
> How is it that nobody has ever thought of connecting this with . . . the effect of an erection? Imagine a tatoo traced on the sexual organ ad hoc in the state of repose and assuming its, if I may say so, developed form in another state.
>
> How can we not see here, immanent in the geometral dimension—a partial dimension in the field of the gaze, a dimension that has nothing to do with vision as such—something symbolic of the function of the lack, of the appearance of the phallic ghosts?[5]

Precisely because of this invisibility of the phallus, the picture is a "trap for the gaze," and not a phallic amulet which averts the gaze. In a sense, the telos of the gaze is always the self within the dialectic of existence whereby the fictional, ideal "I" is in discordance with the real "I." The topological ideal of the ego is the constitution of the body Gestalt, the overcoming of the fragmented body: this is achieved (as yet another fiction) in the mirror stage, when the infant sees its own reflection and recognizes it, for the first time, as that of a unified self. The self is unified from without; it is constituted by a doubling, a false reflection which marks the vectors of desire rather than the structure of the real.

> This fragmented body [. . .] usually manifests itself in dreams when the movement of the analysis encounters a certain level of aggressive disintegration in the individual. It then appears in the form of disjointed limbs, or of those organs represented in exoscopy, growing wings and taking up arms for intestinal persecutions—the very same that the visionary Hieronymous Bosch has fixed, for all time, in painting. . .[6]

The fragmented body is highly evident in Dali's work. Consider, for example, *Construction molle avec des haricots bouillis, Prémonition de la guerre civile* (1936), or the severed hand in *Un Chien andalou,* both of which have aggression and death as their central themes. As Lacan found this vision of the fragmented body in Bosch, so too did Brakhage find this vision in Breughel. But he saw it in Breughel as a sign of his own work, in which the body is variously distorted and fragmented. And indeed, if taken as the autobiographical statements that Brakhage partially intended them to be, the films of this period were manifestations of profound internal agression, and it was through their creation that he achieved a rapprochement with his wife and a reduction of self destructive impulses. The films thus serve a cathartic function, in which the representation of the fragmented body permits the integration of the self.

The difference between perspectival projection and anamorphic projection parallels and symbolizes the difference between the gestalt of the whole body and the distorted, fragmented body. As the corporeal aesthetics of both the Venus figurines and of Brakhage's films implies a cosmology, so does the Lacanian psychology of anamorphosis imply an ontology.

The mind as bearer of this Being is what is
nowhere, what envelops every where.
Maurice Merleau-Ponty

Merleau-Ponty, in developing a phenomenological ontology, investigated the manner in which the body, "is that strange object which uses its own parts as a general system of symbols for the world."[7] The structural organization of this symbolic system is determined by the fact that:

> My body is a Gestalt and is co-present in every Gestalt . . .It is a principle of distribution, the pivot of a system of equivalencies, it is the Etwas of which the fragmentary phenomena will be the manifestation . . .[8]

Thus metaphysics is a function of an expanded notion of sexuality, in which, as for Brakhage, the macrocosm is a function of corporeality, of an anthropic system which Merleau-Ponty called the "flesh," encompassing the chiasmatic relationships between the flesh of our bodies and the flesh of the world. The body is the scene of the intertwining of inner and outer horizons; it is the fulcrum of the meaningful embodiment of the world. Yet the ideality of the holistic body underlies the reality of the fragmentainess of phenomena, as for Lacan the Ideal "I" interacts with the real "I" in the dialectic of existence. Lacan too subscribed to a microcosm/macrocosm ontology:

> I am led, therefore, to regard the function of the mirror-stage as a particular case of the function of the imago, which is to establish a relation between the organism and its reality or, as they say, between the Innenwelt and the Umwelt.[9]

It is at the mirror-stage that the body as gestalt is formed, where the consequent symbolic function arises. If for Lacan the representation of the subsequently fragmented body is a psychic aberration, for Merleau-Ponty the fragmentary, non-hierarchical and discontinuous nature of phenomena is an indication of the ruins of Being, of the end of onto-theology. Yet in both cases, the body is the principle of the symbolic distribution of attributes and forms; this entails the notion of the body as the paradigm of fascination. There are two basic modes of such fascination, structured according to the two primary corporeal structures: male and female. Whence the fascination with the maternal body, and the subsequent fascination with that which the maternal body lacks: the phallus. From corporeal arche to telos, from one fragmentation to another: the body gestalt is an ideal situtated by its own doubles, its own representations. If anatomy is indeed destiny, as Freud claimed, then there is a dual, bisexual order of destiny, structured according to the two modes of identification, the two types of object choice (narcissistic and anaclitic), and the two modes of fascination. Anatomy is destiny, but it entails a history of illusions, a dialectic without ends.

Such a transcendental illusionism is the foundation of both truth and the ego. Appearances do not dissimulate the truth: they are nothing but themselves, the ruins of Being. "Truth" is just a second order phenomenon, a distortion of distortion, a necessary illusion.[10]

> T.O.U.C.H.I.N.G.
> DESTROY que je sais d'elle
> Composite graffiti found on a blackboard in the Department of Cinema Studies, New York University.

Paranoia as art; art as criticism; criticism as paranoia. From surrealism through the "visionary" and abstract filmmaking of the American avant garde, there is a modernist hermeticism, gnosticism, orphism in the arts. The eroticized body is once again, as it was at the origins of art, the thematized foundation of an ontology, of an aesthetics. Through a confusion, a montage, of genres and styles, we approach that plenitude of presence which is the mark of utopia, a return of knowledge to its corporeal source. We discover that true knowledge is not rational order, but fascination.

13

Frampton's Lemma, Zorn's Dilemma

Copulation and mirrors are abominable. For one of those gnostics, the visible universe was an illusion or (more precisely) a sophism. Mirrors and fatherhood are abominable because they multiply and disseminate that universe.

Jorge Luis Borges

I do not believe there is such a thing as a perfect appearance. Even an epiphany is not in the theological sense a perfect appearance. . . . Appearance itself is imperfect.

Hollis Frampton

To the abominations of copulation and mirrors one might add cinema. In a world where error, as Nietzsche teaches us, is the very precondition of thought, truth and beauty are always proximate to sophism and illusion. Cinema disposes of yet another set of codes which are available for ideological misappropriation. This disposition by means of seriality, exemplification, listing, and cataloguing operates within the limits of two antithetical functions. Either such listing is a subversive activity, destroying all taxonomic schemes, or lists serve as formal imperatives, constituting structures and systems. In the former case, a hermeneutic schema entails a decentering and detotalizing logic of events, operating according to the aleatory conditions of existence. In the latter, a hermeneutics entails a centering and totalizing logic of structures and formal systems, constituting a determinate axiomatics.[1]

Hollis Frampton's film *Zorns Lemma* is structured according to a twofold axiomatic system. The first axiom is indicated by the film's title, which refers to mathematical set theory: "Zorn's lemma. The maximal principle: If T is partially ordered and each linearly ordered subset has an upper bound in T, then T contains at least one maximal element." The second axiom derives from the mystical philosophy expounded by Robert Grosseteste in *On Light, or the Ingression of Forms,* which offers a combination of neo-Platonic and Aristotelian philosophy to express a theology, ontology, and cosmology of light. A section of this text is read in the third part of the film.

These two axioms are already figured within the text recited in the first part of the film, the eighteenth-century Massachusetts elementary school lesson book called *The Bay State Primer.* The production of the sets and subsets in the second part of the film is determined by a system of substitutions and progressions ordered by the (abridged) twenty-four-letter alphabet of the English language used in the primer. The mathematical axiom is operative in the alphabetical order of the text; the theological axiom is operative in the biblical content of the text. Thus the twofold axiomatic system is articulated according to a double coding: structural and ontological.[2]

In both cases, the axiomatic systems postulate a maximally ordered universe and generate a maximally ordered film. We may compare the implications of Zorn's lemma and Frampton's theory of narrative in this respect. A corollary of Zorn's lemma is that "any set can be well ordered." This accords with Frampton's claim that narrative is one of the axioms of cinema, defined as Brakhage's Theorem: "For any finite series of shots ['film'] whatsoever there exists in real time a rational narrative, such that every term in the series, together with its position, duration, partition and reference, shall be perfectly and entirely accounted for."[3] This narrative ordering obtains not only on the cinematic and meta-cinematic levels, but also on the micro-cinematic level, wherein every shot is already an ordering of the very frames which constitute it. Recognition of this fact (already made manifest in the single-frame work of Robert Breer as well as in Frampton's own film *Ordinary Matter*) permits Frampton the radical conclusion that "a still photograph is simply an isolated frame taken out of the infinite cinema."[4] It is indeed the rare frame that does not meet the condition of a hapax.) This is the antithesis of Eisenstein's theory.

> Why do we use montage at all? Even the most fanatical opponent of montage will agree that it is not merely because the film strip at our disposal is not of infinite length, and consequently, being condemned to working with pieces of restricted lengths, we have to stick one piece of it onto another occasionally.[5]

For Eisenstein, cinematic montage necessitates a thematics, an ordering principle; otherwise montage is nothing more than an empiricism on the formal level. Montage theory is a special case circumscribed by the general theory of dialectical materialism: the central trope of both theories is antithesis. Thus Eisenteinian montage does not entail a formally heterodox film practice, but rather a cinematic orthodoxy in relation to the meta-theme of dialectical materialism.

Frampton's theoretical stance is the guarantor of intertextuality within the *de facto* open system of cinema. His filmic practice generates ordered systems which are subsets of a disordered universal cinema, wherein empirical conditions give rise to diverse metaphysics and metaphysics informs cinematic hermeneutics. Frampton's meta-thematic is the imaginary of individual consciousness; Eisenstein's meta-thermatic is collective revolutionary praxis.

The specific configurations of the unavoidable narrative algorithms are generated by diverse rhetorical strategies. The antithetical epistemological functions of such algorithms (that is, the detotalizing destruction of taxonomia or the totalizing construction of systems) find their prime structures in the respective figures of *accumulation* and *enumeration*. Accumulation is a mode of listing independent of any necessary formal or material connection between the constituent terms. Enumeration is a listing of attributes, a mode of predication, defining a central term by means of ancillary terms. Hence, enumeration implies a mode of subordination and determination, a systematization of terms. While the relation between terms in an accumulative list is *disjunctive*, the relation between terms in an enumerative list is *conjunctive*.

Within any enumerative system what must be determined is the central term. The importance of this determination for filmic practice was recognized by Eisenstein: "Just as in the case of a homogeneous ideology (a monistic viewpoint), the whole, as well as the least detail, must be penetrated by a sole principle."[6] Frampton expresses the same principle with a concrete example by explaining that in Japanese culture the supreme metaphor is Mount Fujiyama, because of its inevitable, central visibility. Thus, "all things were to be construed according to the number of qualities they could be seen to share with Fujiyama."[7] The ultimate ontological generalization of this principle is stated by Merleau-Ponty: "Any entity can be accentuated as an emblem of Being."[8] This claim may be emended with the corollary: any rhetorical trope or figure may serve as the organizational structure of a text.

Traditionally, in Western epistemology, there have been two such supreme metaphors: consciousness and God. Thus in a sense, all axiomatics are reducible to these terms: all accumulation is achieved in relation to them, and all enumeration is a determination and expression of their attributes. For Frampton, consciousness is the supreme mediator,[9] organizing the dynamic codes of cinema, a cinema which can thus be nothing other than the expression, sympton, and enumeration of the qualities of consciousness. What, then, is the central metaphor of *Zorns Lemma*?

Every day is the beginning of the world.
Hollis Frampton

. . . that harmony which makes every composition steadfast.
Robert Grosseteste

To determine the narrative characteristics of *Zorns Lemma* according to Brakhage's Theorem, we may account for the "position, duration, partition, and reference" of the shots, sequences, and segments by means of the film's rhetorical structure. The topography, chronography, and prosography of its terms must be determined. This will simultaneously reveal the contours of consciousness and a divine cosmology.

The film begins as darkness, with the first enunciation a statement of collective guilt and responsibility read from *The Bay State Primer*: "In Adam's Fall, we sinneth all." This text, read over a black screen, provides the zero degree of subordination of the sound track to the visual track. (This lack of subordination will be strangely reversed in the second part of the film, which is silent but which presents words visually, perhaps to be recited.) The text is read by a female voice, maintaining the authority of enunciation within the disquieting paradigm of a voice unmediated by the presence of a body, a paradigm central to biblical theology and the iconoclastic tradition. This particularly happy disquietude vis-à-vis the tradition is due to the fact that it is a female voice which speaks; but the scenario will become even more disconcerting when the recitation of Grosseteste's text in the third part of the film is performed in rondo, one word per second, by six different female voices. This destroys the illusion of homogeneity of the enunciation's source, just as the visual track of the second section achieves the fragmentation and heterogeneity of narrative structures.[10] Spectatorial pleasure is here a function of heterodoxy, where narrative is a function of secondary process ratiocination and allegory is a condition of truth.

The phrase, "In Adam's Fall, we sinneth all," bears as its referent both the Bible and the subsequent filmic texts and structures. Consequent to the Fall is the infinite distanciation of God from humankind, which entails a form of knowledge based upon sense perception in a world fragmented by the ordeals of Chronos. Henceforth, God was manifested only through the Divine Logos, which had the dual referent God/world: it is precisely the significative rupture between these terms that necessitated hermeneutic procedures, and which led to the reductio ad absurdum of a God with either an infinite number of names or the name of God as the most general tautology. Yet it is precisely this name which is lacking in the film, but which is revealed by *pronomination*, that is, the designation of a thing by means of its attributes, qualities, and actions rather than by its proper name. This structure of absence is also supported by the last enunciation from *The Bay State Primer*: "Zacharias, he did climb the tree, his Lord to see." This futile task, to see the invisible, provides the articulation of the film's three parts: from Zacharias's tree we do indeed see the forest depicted in the third part of the film. But before that we are presented with the transformational complex of the film's second section, which is composed of sequences of one-second-long shots, ordered according to the alphabetical system already provided by the primer. The first sequence depicts only words; in subsequent sequences a shot of a word will be replaced by a shot without words, of a person, place, thing, or event. This is the ultimate pronomination: God is represented by His creation, that is, by the world's diversity of Logos and Physis.[11] Such is precisely the cinematic representation of that "broken and scattered God" referred to by Borges in his tale, "Paradiso, XXXI, 108," which indicates that "something infinite had been lost."[12] The death of God is expressed in an epiphany of His partial representations. What remains is a disjunctive world and the set of arbitrary relations between words and things.[13]

The structure of the first two parts of the film, a system of ordering and substitution based upon the order of the alphabet, is also emblematic of the film's theological referent. It is homologous with hymns to God structured as an alphabetical litany: such litanies offer a multiplication of praise to God, with each letter of the alphabet used to begin a word of praise, a hyperbolic predication of the Divine Being. The particular words do not matter as much as the liturgical structure itself.[14] System as signifier; metaphysics as metaphor.

Thus the double codification of *Zorns Lemma*, of structural and ontological modes, respectively generates accumulative and enumerative sequences, which in turn refer respectively to the world and to God. Yet God, as the conflation of the systems of infinite accumulation and infinite enumeration, entails the breakdown of the ontological implications of rhetorical figures: the literalness of "nature" becomes the zero degree expression of truth.

Furthermore, within the primary transformational matrix of the alphabet is expressed a secondary transformational system:[15] in the second part of the film the first four images that replace shorts of words represent fire, water, air, and earth, that is, the four elements of which the cosmos is composed according to popular pre-Socratic belief, codified by Empedocles, incorporated into Platonism, and subsequently utilized by Grosseteste (in the text read in the film's third part). Every object is composed of a well-ordered combination of the four elements, and it might be noted that according to some mystical iconoclastic theologies these four elements will merge during the apocalypse. As the cosmos is structured between the composition and decomposition of its constituent elements, so this film is structured between the lack of light and the plenitude of light, between the blackness of the first section and the white light into which the snow scene of the third section fades. Between the darkness before creation and the pure white divine light of the apocalypse, we have the second part of the film, that is, the representation of the diversity of the world and language. The film is composed between the perfect antithesis, darkness and white light, the stuff of all cinema.[16]

So I asked him if he thought angels would speak in a language without images, purer and akin to light. "Angels must be very good to eat. I would imagine they are very tender, between chicken and fish."
Peter Kubelka interviewed by P. Adams Sitney

The heresies we should fear are those which can be confused with orthodoxy.
Jorge Luis Borges

The shot of the ibis (the final image of the second part of the film) is startling in its color, its placement as the maximal element in the transformational series, and its brevity: it alone among the nonlinguistic images in the film appears for only one second. (This is an eschatology not without humor: the shot of the ibis occurs immediately after the shot of an egg frying on a pan, thus reviving and reconstituting the myth of the phoenix.) The ibis was the Egyptian god of wisdom, symbolic of the spiritual, of the highest level of existence. It here serves as the articulation between the second and third parts of the film, and also serves as an analogue for the phrase articulating the transition between the first, second, and third parts: "Zacharias, he did climb the tree, his Lord to see." Both the ibis and the object of Zacharias's gaze indicate the subject of Grosseteste's neo-Platonic ontology/theology of light, which is related by the text of the film's third section. That object is God, made manifest in the purity of light, from which all else emanates, especially the cinema.

It is quite appropriate that the initiates of Gnostical and Kabbalistic knowledge are known as *illuminati*, those who have been enlightened. We find, for example, in Lurianic Kabbalism a theosophical cosmogony which explains the role of light in the creation of the universe. As Gershom Scholem explains in *Major Trends in Jewish Mysticism*:

> The first being which emanated from the [Divine] light was Adam Kadmon, the "primordial man." Adam Kadmon was nothing but a first configuration of the divine light which flows from the essence of En-Sof into the primeval space of the Tsimtsum—not indeed from all sides but, like a beam, in one direction only.

To the abominations of mirrors, copulation, and cinema, one might add God. We find here an expression of the infinite cinema of which Frampton writes: God is the infinite film projector; world and humankind and language are the film that is projected by means of the pure, white, Divine light. And my life, and yours, are partially ordered sets of that maximally ordered set. As is that synecdoche of the infinite film, Frampton's *Zorns Lemma*.

14

Between the Sign of the Scorpion and the Sign of the Cross

It is because the Scorpion is infinity that it must, to the contrary, encompass all of the real; those who say the contrary issue from the possessive infinite spirit's hatred of me, the Real.

Antonin Artaud
Cahiers de Rodez

In the sixth volume of the Surrealist journal *Minotaure*, (Winter 1935), is reproduced an illumination by Pol de Limbourg from the 15th century manuscript *Les Très Riches Heures du Duc de Berry*, entitled "L'Homme anatomique." Ironically, what is represented is neither anatomical nor a man: it is a dual representation of the posterior of a woman partially eclipsed by the anterior of another woman, bordered by the signs of the zodiac. Marked upon the front of her body are the twelve astrological symbols, each situtated upon the part of the body which it governs. Saliently located upon, and immodestly covering, the central position of her genitals is Scorpio, the scorpion. The scorpion, governing the genitals and the anus, symbol of sex, excrement and death, dweller in the shadows and hell.

Several years earlier, this symbol of anal-sadistic determinations was to serve as the prologue of the archetypical Surrealist film, *L'Âge d'or*, which opens with a quasi-documentary about scorpions, where we learn of their venomousness, agressiveness, unsociability and hatred of the sun. As we shall see, the function of this prologue must not be understood simply in terms of a startling diagetic anomaly within the film, but rather as a symbolic protasis in which is prefigured a Surrealist "theory" of culture where the established values of sublimation are consistently challenged by the disruptive effects of perversion.

The demons and the Devil are justified in always leading me towards Evil and towards being, for it is by dint of denying it and saying other than what actually is that God has completely fallen into the mud.

Antonin Artaud
Cahiers de Rodez

In 1930, the year in which *L'Âge d'or* was filmed and already a year after the great *succès de scandale* of *Un chien andalou*, Salvador Dali wrote "L'Âne pourri," in which he defended the ideality of Surrealist imagery as a revolutionary praxis, according to the laws of his "paranoic-critical" method of pictorial production. His claims could have served as the program for the film *L'Âge d'or*:

> And we don't really know if the desired "land of treasures" is not hidden behind the three great simulacra: shit, blood and putrefaction. Connoisseurs of simulacra, we have long known how to recognize the image of desire behind the simulacra of terror, and even the awakening of the "ages of gold" (*âges d'or*) behind the ignominous scatological simulacra.[1]

Indeed, the first major diagetical section of *L'Âge d'or*, culminating in the "founding of Rome" scene, is structured according to two parallel but antithetical excremental simulacra. The material foundations of symbolism engender images according to two modes of symbolization: sublimation and perversion, which in turn generate two types of phantasms. Yet it is precisely the perverse manifestations of desire that disrupt the established exigencies of sublimation and, as Dali claims, "contribute to the ruin of reality. . . lead us to the clear sources of masturbation, exhibitionism, crime, love."[2]

As is well documented in Bourke's *Scatologic Rites of All Nation*, excrement is often found as an ingredient in love potions.[3] This cultivated sign of a scatological eroticism, a remnant of primal symbolizations where the potentially dangerous excreta is transformed into a magical good object,[4] restoring to its possessor long lost powers of potency and omnipotence, is but a symbol of the perverse erotic syndrome of coprophilia. Shit, that zero-degree of matter, is erotized by the body,[5] mixing horror and desire in its object as is the case in all fetishism.

Whence the first moment of excremental vision in *L'Âge d'or*: the ceremony of the founding of Rome is interrupted by the screams of a woman wrestling with a man in the mud, in the throes of passion and ecstasy. They are quickly separated, and as the woman is led away, the first phantasm arises for the man: he first fantasizes the woman sitting on a toilet; then simply a toilet with a roll of burning toilet-paper beside it; then the bubbling, steaming lava of a volcano, with the sound of the toilet flushing. The coprophilic event of making love in the mud is doubled in his fantasy of her sitting on a toilet, which is further symbolized by the cosmic hyperbole entailed in the condensation of images of the toilet and volcano (excrement/lava, burning toilet-paper/fiery eruption). As Georges Bataille claims in "L'Anus solaire": "The terrestrial globe is covered with volcanos which serve as the anus."[6] This cosmic/corporeal metaphor, equivalent to that of the scorpion, signifies a perverse modality of eroticism which is intricately bound to a position of rebellion against societal and natural norms. If society is founded upon murder and power, and if, as Canetti claims, excrement "is loaded with our whole blood guilt. By it we know what we have murdered. It is the compressed sum of all the evidence against us,"[7] then it is apparent why during the period of the infant's socialization the anus become the place of possession and exclusion. If the individual is to be socialized, what must be excluded is this first sign of our guilt (bad object, weapon, stain), and this first sign of our power (good object, gift, magical object, artwork). Such exclusion is the destruction of our own sovereignty, the process whereby the body becomes the *topos* of its own rejection, *i.e.*, the very scene of sublimation. Death and agression are organized by the cultural machine of production within the symbolic, and all nonproductive expenditure is denigrated.

Excrement, as an image of death, as the formless, as pure heterogeneous matter, is excluded from the order of the symbolic. Excrement is a sign that is doubly threatening to cultural formations: first because it signifies a pure, wasteful expenditure, circumventing societal modes and organizations of production; secondly, because it is a sign of self-production, an autonomous, sovereign creativity which eludes the exigencies of the Oedipal situation, since the origin of the creation of excrement is the body, not the socius. Thus a non-sublimated return to anality in adult life (in art, dreams, delirium, or erotic perversion) breaks the significative chain of quotidian existence by inaugurating a return of the repressed. Yet while the scatological is a mode of ontological heterogeneity, an antimetaphysical subject position, the pervert is not (unlike the psychotic) outside the symbolic law. Perversion is the substitution of a personal law for the collective symbolic law, and is thus the substitution of desire for law.

Surrealism attempted to constitute one such set of sovereign, revolutionary laws, and utilized a perverse iconography to express its rebellious critique of culture. *L'Âge d'or* is a love story which is organized according to such a transgressive mode of eroticism. It recognizes, as Yeats understood, that "Love has pitched his mansion in the place of excrement." This is not only a specific expression of the coprophilic perversion, but a general truth about the very origins of love and culture.

> And I don't engender beings like glossolaliating turds, doublings arising from what?
>
> Antonin Artaud
> *Cahiers de Rodez*

The second moment of the excremental vision in the film is the ceremony of the founding of Rome. This ceremony, which was interrupted by the scatological events previously described, continues with the diminutive master of ceremonies enunciating a speech composed of glossolalic babble (in decidedly adult intonations and timbre), amongst which the only discernable words are ". . .*les matières primaires elles-même*" ("primary matter itself"). In this ironic babbling within a quite civilized event, the highly encoded metalinguistic term "*matières primaires*" is substituted for the primal infantile term "caca." Consultation of a dictionary on this matter is instructive. *Le Petit Robert: Dictionnaire de la Langue Francais* informs us that on the ontological level, "*matières primaires*" (primary matter) is that which is "not yet transformed by work," hence it is chaotic matter, pure potentiality. We also discover that by ellipsis, "*matières fécales*" becomes simply "*matières,*" a euphemism (a subset of irony) synonymous with excrement, feces, stool.

The "*matières primaires elles-même* " to which the orator refers is non other than the cement in the form of a turd which is placed upon the cornerstone of the foundation of Rome. (And we might note the visual pun: in French the word "*fondement*" means both "foundation" and "fundament," "ass.") Excrement is indeed the primal matter, serving as gift, tool, weapon, and as the prototype of the artwork. Sublimation is thus a function of the sublation of anal erotism in all activity; coprophilic perversion is the enunciation, the revelation, of the displaced and repressed origins of culture, an objective euphemism.

The history of the Western ontotheological tradition is the history of the disavowel of chaos, matter, the formless, the body proper. Where matter couldn't be fully disavowed (as is usually the case), it was thoroughly denigrated, so that, for example, within Manicheanism, stemming from the Neo-Platonic tradition, matter was equated with Evil. Within the Scholastic, Aristotelian tradition, "prime matter" is considered to be the lowest grade of sensible existence. And there occurs within the history of Scholasticism an ellipsis parallel to that of the etymological ellipsis from "*matières fécales*" to "*matières*." This shift is outlined in André Lalande's *Vocabulaire technique et critique de la philosophie* in the article on "*Matière* ":[8]

> B. In expressions of Aristotelian and Scholastic origin (and, in this case, always opposed to form): 1. that which, in a being, constitutes the potential, indeterminate element, in opposition to what is actualized; 2. every already determined physical or mental given that an activity receives and ulteriorly elaborates.
>
> Originally the terms "primary matter" and "secondary matter" were used to distinguish these two meanings, but the term "primary matter," passing into current use, has become the synonym of "secondary matter," which has fallen into disuse, in the same time that the Aristotelian idea of pure potentiality was effaced in the word "matter."

As in the case of the substitution of "*matières primaires*" for "*matières fécales*," and the ellipsis of "*matières*" for "*matières primaires*," the terms' original significance, especially the denotation of a primal lack of determination on the material level, is lexically suppressed. This is a function of cultural censorship, a mode of euphemism which emphasizes the transformative powers of sublimation: the cultural will to overcome and obfuscate its own material origins necessitates this transumption of terms, with all of its inherent ironies. Sublimation is a system of substitutions, deflections, deferrals and differences which function as a metamorphosis of desire. Within this systematic transfiguration of desire, this perpetual displacement of libido, all defenses are tropes which dissimulate the origins and aims of the libido. Eros is deflected from the body and the body's products onto cultural objects and formations, yet the meaning of these sublimated (sublime!) objects is always a function of the primary cathected objects. Thus culture provides a symbolic system of substitutions and representations which is nothing other than a system of symbols for the body. The civilized disavowel of these origins serves as a guarantor of the collective law of the Symbolic.

The orator's enunciation of the phrase *"les matières primaires elles-mêmes"* serves as a magical incantation, a *Logos Spermatikos* which effects an active reworking of the passive matter to which it refers: the excrement as the foundation of Rome. For, apparently inscribed on that foundation stone are the words: "In the Year of Our Lord, 1930, on the site of the last resting-place of the four Majorcans, this stone was laid as the first foundation for the city. . ." and we see an aerial view of modern Rome, ". . . Imperial Rome." Within this vast historical ellipsis effected by one cinematic cut, we find that Rome was indeed built, not in a day, but in an instant. Rome, founded circa 600 BC, was here instantaneously created in the year 1930 AD: an ellipsis of 2530 years! This cut produces a chronological ellipsis, a psychological prolepsis, and a narrative irony. Rome, Vatican City, St. Peter's, which are the highest points of Western civilization and the center of Christianity, are seen to be but a sublimation of the *"matières primaires"* of all creation, *i.e.*, a trope for excrement. Yet this trope is the effect of a peculiarly Surrealist mode of creation, where the temporality inherent in work is abolished within the causality of desire, where creation is instantaneous upon volition. Thus the founding of Rome is here a collective phantasm, where both power as simulacrum and history as phantasmagoria are inaugurated. It is an allegory for the process of sublimation itself. Yet it is diametrically opposed to the individual, sovereign phantasm which preceeded it, the hero's perverse excremental vision.

1930, the year of the "founding of Rome," follows the year in which André Breton wrote the *Second Manifesto of Surrealism*, where he reaffirmed the Surrealist desire to eliminate time and to transform reality according to the forms of our desire.[9] Perfectly in accordance with this project is Harold Bloom's recognition that eros is the will's revenge against time, which leads to the material transformations of all figuration.[10] This revenge, this desire to eliminate time, is manifested in the instantaneity of the founding of Rome. Yet if the "origins" of Rome are traced back to the babble and excrement of the magical incantation, we find that irony is the central trope of sublimation. History is hysteresis, a trajectory of symptoms, where there are only stories of origins and no real eschatology. History is the grand syntagma of sublimation, where the corporeal, material origins of existence are dissimulated. Historical mimesis is dissimulated by the abstractions of a *mathesis universalis* which is none other than the program of universal domination by means of rationality and the deflections of desire.

Psychoanalytic symptomatology teaches us that origins are the place of a loss: loss of truth, love object, even desire. Such loss necessitates a hermeneutic procedure to reinstate the lacking truth and desire. Yet if the central trope of sublimation is irony, then the central form of an appropriate hermeneutic, genealogical procedure must be parody. If ironic, carnivalesque reversals are the very trajectory of primary matter becoming cultural artefacts, then Bataille is correct in claiming, in "L'Anus solaire," that "the world is purely parodic,"[11] (in obvious contradistinction to Marx's claim that historical events occur twice, "the first time as tragedy, the second time as farce"), and Foucault rightly understands that "Genealogy is history in the form of a concerted carnival."[12]

Catharsis leads things to their own law.
Antonin Artaud
Cahiers de Rodez

Yet the founding of Rome entails a paradox about the formation of founding/founded relations, according to the rhetorical figure of fabulation. Rome, the collective phantasm, is not distinguished from perception: thus it becomes the scene of the diagesis which contains the very personages who founded the city. Such a visionary *mise-en-scène* is emblematic of the idealizing and sublimatory position of Surrealist creativity: origins are metaleptically dissimulated in their effects, and culture becomes a symptom. This is the very structure of ideology, where material heterogeneity is dissimulated by present cultural forms.

This mode of disavowal entails the fact, as Merleau-Ponty claims, that "every historical object is a fetish."[13] The originary, corporeal paradigm of such material heterogeneity is sexual differentiation, which is codified within the symbolic paternal Law. But it is the constitution of fetishism (the paradigm for all modes of perversion), that inaugurates a revulsive, contestatory set of "laws" outside the symbolic law of sublimation. Fetishism is the disavowal of representations of sexual differentiation, the condensation of contradictions whereby the lacking female phallus is instituted by metaphor or metonymy as a fetish object. This simultaneous affirmation and denial entails a radical questioning of the very basis of Oedipal law by the recognition that desire is the law. Such disavowal is a transgression of normative modes of sexual expression: within perversion, the enigma of sexual differentiation cannot be resolved by sexual union, but only by a series of substitutions. In a sense, the pervert cannot merely interpret the world, but must change it, since the very form of sexual difference is antithetical to the exigencies of desire. Thus, as a revolt against the Oedipal law, perversion entails the revolutionary position of either the murder or forgetting of the idealized father of whom the law is a symbolic tributary, or, failing that possibility, it entails the ascetic martyrdom of the pervert: one must either change the world or perish.[14]

Hence the radical role of the protagonists' passion in *L'Âge d'or*: the perverse is manifested not only in the coprophilia already discussed, but also by fetishism proper. After the protagonist is separated from his beloved, as he is led through the city he is aroused by the sight of an advertisement for a powder puff, which becomes animated as he phantasizes it as a woman's hand in the act of masturbation; then he is further aroused by the picture of a woman's stockinged legs on another advertisement; and immediately afterwards he sees a photograph of a woman's face in a bookshop window, which in his fantasy is transformed into his beloved lying on a couch, evidently having just masturbated, with a bandaged finger. This phantasm then becomes the next segment of the diagesis: as she arises from the couch, her mother asks her, *"Tu as la main bandée"*: (Have you got a bandaged hand?) - with the pun on the word *"bandée"*: "bandaged" or "erection." Thus her masturbation takes on the perverse tones of fetishism, with the finger *"bandée"* as the substitute phallus. And later on, as she is buffing her fingernails (unbandaged), she senses the approach of her lover and, as she becomes aroused, the bandage reappears—the substitute phallus is erect.

Thus the substitute gratifications and continual coitus interruptus which determine the course of the narrative must not simply be taken as a result of societal interference and disapproval: rather, it is an integral aspect of the logic of perversion.

When the state of the world exhausts you, new forces can be drawn from sexuality; such is an opium created by walking and sadness, which aids in ascending ever higher after a

thundering impregnation of the toes and heels
with shit, be this a revindicated torture.

Antonin Artaud
Cahiers de Rodez

Richard von Krafft-Ebing, in *Psychopathia Sexualis* (a book known both to the Surrealists and to Bataille), categorized foot fetishism and coprophilia under one heading: "Disgusting Acts for the Purpose of Self-Humiliation and Sexual Gratification—Latent Masochism—Coprolagnia." We learn, for example, that, "The beatified Marie Alacoque licked up with her tongue the excrement of sick people to 'mortify' herself, and sucked their festering toes."[15]

Hence the appropriateness of the apparent foot fetishism in the culminating love scene of *L'Âge d'or,* where the protagonists attempt to consummate their love in the garden, only to be interrupted yet again. They begin by sucking on the fingers of each others' hands; he then caresses her face with a hand that is missing its fingers: this is no longer a hand *"bandée,"* but now a hand *"castrée."* Immediately afterwards, the fetishistic substitution for this symbolic castration is indicated: he is distracted by the foot of a nearby statue, and as he is called away to the telephone, she (whether from perversion or sheer desperation) begins to erotically suck and kiss the toes of the statue. This is a substitution and sublimation of symbolic wounds, where apparently the perversions of fetishism and coprophilia are united.

In "Le gros orteil," Georges Bataille explains how the big toe is the most human part of the body: embarassing, ignoble, ignominous, filthy, cadaverous, fetishistic, deformed, idiotic, and associated with the lowness of mud. For Bataille, human existence is a perpetual exchange between the spiritual and the material, between the high and the low, between garbage and the ideal: the foot, the big toe, is the sign par excellence of material baseness.

> It is there that a seduction occurs which is radically opposed to that which is caused by beauty and the light. The two orders of seduction are often confused because we continually move between one and the other; being given this movement of coming-and-going with its termination in either one direction or the other, the more brutal the movement, all the more keen the seduction.[16]

It is precisely with the Surrealist aesthetic that this confusion is valorized: Breton claims in the *Second Manifesto of Surrealism*, following

Hegelian metaphysics and Freudian metapsychology, that the goal of Surrealism is to reach the point in the mind where contradictions cease to exist.

We may be seduced by the high or the low, or in psychoanalytic terms, seduced according to the formations of sublimation or perversion. While the act of kissing the statue's foot appears to be a combination of the scatological and fetishistic perversions which determine the protagonists' erotic activities, it is actually the culmination of ironic sublimation. What is kissed is not that lowest part of the human body, a filthy foot, but rather the cold, clean stone foot of a sculpture; the filthy fetish is replaced by an artwork, a cultural object of the highest order, symptomatic of the collective phantasm in which the protagonists find their erotic dissatisfaction. And this dissatisfaction is hyperbolically expressed in the reaction shot of the statue's unmoved, expressionless face: this is the ultimately ironic reaction shot, since there is no reaction at all.

Thus the statue's foot is not a fetish object, but the simulacrum of a fetish, a typically Surrealist conflation of the high and the low (foot as artwork; foot in stone.) Indeed, Dali himself, ceding to Breton's distaste for perversion, excused himself for a scatological image in his painting, *Le jeu lugubre*, by claiming that, "It was necessary that I justify myself by saying that it was only a simulacrum of excrement."[17] Mutatis mutandis, this explains why the pseudo-fetishism/coprophilia of this event is *L'Âge d'or* is emblematic of the Surrealist ethic and aesthetic, and serves as an allegory of the Surrealist theory of sublimation. It illustrates N.O. Brown's observation that, "Sublimation is a mortification of the body and the sequestration of the life of the body into dead things."[18]

In view of such an aesthetics, with its ironic reversals and extremely idealized sublimations, it might be well to consider the provocation of Bataille's admonishment, "I defy any art lover to love a painting as much as a fetishist loves a shoe."[19] Yet, in turning to consider the epilogue of the film, it might be well to remember that one also kisses the feet of Christ.

Do you know of anything more outrageously
fecal than the history of God and of His being:
SATAN?

The Holy Virgin will never rejoin the wife of
the Scorpion, never.

The science of Satan is never anything but
that of our own surplus.

Antonin Artaud
Le théâtre de la cruauté and
Cahiers de Rodez

The film's epilogue occurs after the final interruption of their lovemaking. The protagonist, in a rage of frustration, defenestrates several symbolic objects: a bishop, a plow, a burning pine tree, a giraffe, and finally the feathers of a pillow that he has torn apart. In a beautiful metaphor, these feathers metamorphize into snow falling on an isolated chateau which the intertitles identify as the Chateau de Selliny (sic), the site where four godless libertines, led by the Duke of Blangis, retired for 120 days to celebrate the most brutal of orgies. This is, of course, a synopsis of D.A.F. Sade's masterpiece, *120 Days of Sodom*,[20] which is an encyclopedic fictional compendium of the perverse manifestations of desire.

The dissolve from the feathers falling from the window of the Roman mansion (1930) to the snow falling on the Chateau de Selliny (18th century) takes place, as the intertitles inform us, simultaneously. While the ellipsis responsible for the founding of Rome establishes a progressive temporal shift, indicating a sublimatory activity, the reverse ellipsis from Rome to Selliny establishes a regressive temporal shift, indicative of desublimation.

The ironic reversals inherent in these temporal antitheses are paralleled by the differences in the symbolic *topoi* of the two scenarios: Rome, the site of the Vatican and St. Peter's, is the center of Christianity; the Chateau de Selliny, built on a volcano, is the site of the most horrendous atheistic orgies. This opposition is further inherent in the architectural structure of the chateau itself: as described in Sade's text, the tower of the chateau, which originally contained a chapel, was transformed into a privy.[21] This condensation of *topoi*, of high and low places, of theological and scatological, is yet one more comment on the relations between the sublimated and material conditions of existence. Thus, given the fact that coprophagy, the extreme limit of coprophilia, has both a theological (high) and a pathological (low) value, it is not at all surprising that Sade's text goes so far in its radical indictment of culture as to establish a scatological gastronomy!

This reconciliation, or rather, fusion, of sacred and profane *topoi* is prefigured and mediated by an object that appears earlier in the film: the monstrance which is placed at the feet of a woman leaving a limousine and arriving at the mansion. As reliquaries contain the putrified waste parts of some saint's body, monstrances exhibit the host, the flesh of Christ separated from his blood. Such monstrances thus mediate between St. Peter's and Selliny, between the divine and the diabolic, insofar as this corporeal relic is a sign of both the foundation of the sacred, and the evil inherent in the production of tortured, dismembered bodies. Thus the monstrance serves as a symbolic articulation of the two phantasmatic *topoi*.

This conflation of the sacred and the blasphemous is also a sign of the most scandalous figure in the film: the Duke de Blangis, organizer of the events at the Chateau de Selliny, appears at the door of the chateau in the form of Jesus Christ. Beyond its apparent shock value, this figure has the same semiotic value as the privy in the chapel, the duplicity of meanings of the monstrance, and the difference between Rome and Selliny; according to the Surrealist desire for the reconciliation of opposites, we have a primal psycho-theological identification of God and the Devil, a typically ambivalent expression of love and hate, desire and detestation of the absolute figure of authority. Indeed, as Luther had realized, the worst torment is when "one does not know whether God is the devil or the devil God."[22] Within the phantasm of Rome (that of Christian culture), God had been sublimated into a universal homogeneity, where He lost His terrifying, demoniacal character; in the perverse Sadian phantasm of Selliny (Silling in Sade's text), the demoniacal nature of God reappeared by means of desublimation, as also occurs in our nightmares and in the temptations of the saints. The devil, as a sublimated manifestation of anality, signifies the repressed aspects of the deity. Within such a desublimated position, which manifests the base material origins of existence, there are two possible alternatives. One may accept, for example, the position of the Cathar heresy, which does not recognize the possibility of a material manifestation of divinity. As one pious Cathar mother explained to her daughter: "Do not believe, daughter, that a man of flesh, who produces excrement, can save souls."[23] Hence the desacralization of the figure of Christ. The alternative is that of the Stercoranist heresy, which attests to "The grossly sensual conception of the presence of the Lord's body in the sacrament, according to which that body is eaten, digested, and evacuated like ordinary food . . ."[24] Hence the sacralization of excrement.

André Breton glorified Teresa de Avila's vision of her wooden cross transformed into a crucifix of precious stones.[25] This is hardly the image with which *L'Âge d'or* ends: we see here a Sadian cross with several scalps hanging from it. Rather than bearing the body of Christ, it bears parts of the dismembered bodies of the victims of Blangis' orgies. Yet in both symbols, the notion of the expiatory suffering of the innocent is the rationalization of death: within Christian theology, Christ's sacrifice was necessary for the expiation of humankind's sins; within the Sadian universe, the sacrifice of the innocent was necessary for the realization of the libertine's perverse pleasures. (Hence the exulation with which our protagonist exclaims, during the final love scene, "What joy! What joy to have murdered our children!")

This final symbol, of the cross with the scalps hanging from it, establishes the same signification as was figured by the symbol of the scorpions with which the film began: the anal realm of the devil, governing perverse sexuality, excrement, and death. (And we might remember that in Christian iconography, the scorpion appears on the shields of the Roman soldiers who assisted at Christ's crucifixion.)[26]

Writing of Sade's *120 Days of Sodom*, Georges Bataille, in a marginal note to the manuscript of *Le petit*, provides a gloss which may serve as an epilogue to the film *L'Âge d'or:*

> the age of gold is an infinite conflagration, but real eroticism leaves the age of gold to enter into chance . . .[27]

The problem is that the Sadian libertine cannot transform the entire world into a Sadian chateau. Thus, in relation to such erotic desires of mastery, an infinite conflagration would be nonsense. Hence the fall into a material heterology. And yet, isn't sublimated civilization itself the site of the loss of the "age of gold"? Isn't this precisely the reason for the film's tragedy and Sade's irony?

> The body is the first abstraction.
>
> Antonin Artaud
> *Cahiers de Rodez*

1930 was the year of the "founding of Rome;" it was the year in which *L'Âge d'or* was made; and it was the year after Breton wrote the *Second Manifesto of Surrealism*, which created the definitive rupture in the Surrealist movement, most notably the excommunication of Bataille and the reaffirmation of Artaud's ouster. In this manifesto, Breton criticizes Bataille insofar as, "M. Bataille professes to wish to consider in the world that which is vilest, most discouraging, and most corrupted . . ." hence, "It is to be noted that M. Bataille misuses adjectives with a passion: befouled, senile, rank, sordid, lewd, doddering. . . "Such monomania is explicated by a citation from Marx, which Breton presents in obvious reference to Bataille's "Le gros orteil": "Marx tells us how, in every age, there thus come into being hair-philosophers, fingernail-philosophers, toenail-philosophers, excrement-philosophers, etc." And in further reference to Bataille's article, "La figure humaine," Breton ridicules Bataille's supposed love of flies:

> The only reason we are going on at such length about flies is that M. Bataille loves flies. Not we: we love the miters of old evocators, the miters of pure linen to whose front point was affixed a blade of gold and upon which flies did not settle, because they had been purified to keep them away. M. Bataille's misfortune is to reason: admittedly, he reasons like someone who "has a fly on his nose," which allies him more closely with the dead than with the living, but he does reason.[28]

Thus Bataille, according to Breton, wishes to share his obsessions, and in the communication of such obsessions he is already within the realm of ideology; since his obsessions form a *de facto* system, he cannot be logically opposed to all systems.

In Bataille's response to Breton, "La 'vielle taupe' et le préfixe *sur* dans les mots *surhomme* et *surréaliste,*" Bataille counters with an epigram which is also from Marx: "In history as in nature, the rotten is the laboratory of life." Bataille accuses the Surrealists of "pretentious idealist aberrations" and utopianism, and elsewhere claims that they are "idealist nuisances" (*emmerdeurs idéalistes*).

> More exactly even, since Surrealism is immediately distinguishable by a share of base values (the unconscious, sexuality, filthy language, etc.), it is concerned with giving these values an eminent character by associating them with the most immaterial values.[29]

Thus the grounds of the rupture within Surrealism are precisely the terms of the irony in *L'Âge d'or, i.e.,* the relative position of the two phantasms. The question is whether revolutionary action is to be effected according to a sublimated or desublimated model, dialectical idealism or nondialectical materialism.

Indeed, Bataille loves flies. In a parodic critique of the metaphysical tradition, Bataille writes, in "La figure humaine":

It is impossible to reduce the apparition of a fly on an orator's nose to the supposedly logical contradiction between the self and the metaphysical totality (for Hegel this fortuitous apparition would simply be attributed to the "imperfections of nature.") But, if we lend a general value to the *improbable* nature of the scientific universe, it would be possible to proceed to an operation contrary to that of Hegel and to reduce the appartition of the self to that of the fly.[30]

We will remember that the condition of having a fly on the nose was depicted in *L'Âge d'or*, when during the party in the mansion the father is seen talking, quite nonchalantly, his face covered with flies. A typically Surrealist sardonic conciliation of opposites: the flies, associated with filth, excrement and garbage (base materiality), cover the face, which is the highest part of the human body, the mask that simultaneously hides and expresses the human soul. This contradiction is obviously "corrected," desublimated, in the acephalic condition of the women in the Chateau de Selliny whose scalps are seen fluttering on the cross.

It is not in Surrealism but in neo-Dadaism that we find an unambiguous expression of this base materiality: Marcel Duchamp's *Torture morte* (1959), which is a plaster cast of a foot covered with flies. The foot, the flies, and death are all characteristics of the lowest level of materiality, of the unformed. Such a desublimatory iconography is one of the centers of Duchamp's system of representations, and was already evident in his short film, *Anémic cinéma* (1925-26.) The titles of the film may be read as the refusal to sublimate; the form of the film, spiraling titles alternating with visual spirals, without representational images or narrative connection, make this film the antithesis of the Surrealist project (as Dada in most cases was.) Among the titles is: *"L'enfant qui tète est un souffleur de chair chaude et n'aime pas le chou-fleur de serre chaude"* (The nursing infant is a lover of hot flesh and doesn't like hot-house cauliflowers.) Here, the infant at the breast refuses a substitute breast, the cauliflower, and in doing so refuses the refined product of cultural creation—this condition is parodied in the visual spirals, some of which appear in the form of a breast. Sublimation is refused; the corporeal, material condition of erotic existence is valorized.

I am an anarchist, a pariah, a fanatic, a serf
of the heart and the soul.

Antonin Artaud
Cahiers de Rodez

Artaud played a brief but central role in the development of the Surrealist movement. In 1925 he was made the director of *Le Bureau des recherches surréalistes,* and in the third issue of *La révolution surréaliste* we find his report on the activities of the bureau. And yet, within that very report is a central theme of Artaud's work quite antithetical to the Surrealist ethic: "Surrealism enregisters a certain order of repulsions rather than beliefs." Just as was the case for Bataille, Artaud's excommunication from the Surrealist movement must be understood according to his basic desublimatory position. Breton first denounced Artaud in *Au grand jour,* a pamphlet published in 1927, where Artaud is characterized in terms of his "veritable bestiality," doubtlessly because of the vehemence, candor, and baseness of Artaud's diatribes against established values and institutions. Artaud's response, much like Bataille's, revolved around the nature of the politicization of the Surrealist movement. In "A la grande nuit ou le bluff surréaliste," Artaud explains that "all of the exasperations of our quarrel turn around the word Revolution." Artaud didn't believe that a collective social revolution could change the nature of existence, which could only be changed by a "metamorphosis of the interior conditions of the soul." Thus the Surrealists were "revolutionaries who revolutionize nothing," merely creators of "grotesque simulacra."[31] We must remember that by this time, surrealism was already *"au service de la révolution"*: while Artaud wished to inaugurate a psychical revolution, and Bataille wished, to the contrary, to recognize the revolutions material level, they both opposed Surrealist aestheticizations and idealizations.

While the vehemence and scatological vision did not reach its blasphemous limits until Artaud's *Cahiers de Rodez* (written during his incarceration in 1945-46), his central concern with desublimation was already manifested in his early Surrealist writings and especially in his theory of the "theater of cruelty", an antidialectical art of difference, transgression and forgetting. Such a theater is a mode of artistic production, and not reproduction or representation: it is the scene in which enunciation is no longer ruled by a metaphysical Logos. This was also to be the condition of his madness at Rodez. And it was, no doubt, one of the preconditions of his expulsion from the Surrealist movement. A vision of sovereignty, perversion and madness could never be in accordance with a vision of collectivity, sublimation and joy.

We must make reason shit.
[*Il faut faire chier la raison.*]

Antonin Artaud
Cahiers de Rodez

The irony of the "age of gold" is apparent. Freud reminds us that, "We know how the money which the devil gives his paramours turns to excrement after his departure,"[32] and in a more general sense Bataille explains the antithetical condensation of these terms:

> While in a dream a diamond has an excremental signification, this does not occur only through an association by contrast; in the unconscious, jewels as excrements are accursed matter which flow from a wound, from the parts of oneself destined to an ostensive sacrifice (they serve in fact as sumptuous gifts charged with sexual love.)[33]

This gift, this stain of love, may originate in either sublimatory or desublimatory phantasms, may be either romantic or perverse. The symbolic wound, the sacrifice, may be a sign of either a *Liebestod* or a totem. Two dreams may illustrate this difference. "In one dream a priest reached into the patient's rectum and pulled out an arabesque fecal piece to be used in a ceremony."[34]

This is an expression of a process of self-repair, of a cure, of the renewed self-realization of value. Hence the trajectory of the object in question: from worthless excrement to valuable, albeit perhaps still fetishistic, sacred object. This dream signifies the same phantasm as that of the "founding of Rome": it is an allegory of sublimation.

The second dream is recounted by Bourke in his *Scatologic Rites of All Nations*:

> . . .which represents Zador as making a compact with his satanic majesty whereby in exchange for Zador's soul the devil discloses a gold mine in a graveyard, from which the poor dupe extracts enough for his present needs, and then marks the locality by an ingenious method, only to be awakened by his angry wife to the mortifying consciousness that he has defiled his own bed. . .[35]

If the object of a ceremony is subsequently maintained as a relic, as is the case in fetishism and totemism, then it is particularly appropriate that this goldmine is to be found in a graveyard: the trajectory of the object's devaluation (from gold to excrement) is a sign of the recognition of the corporeal origin and limit of existence, as well at the teleological limit of limits: death. Whence the impossibility of living in the "Age of Gold."

In the *Cahiers de Rodez* Artaud explains how he too was driven from Paradise, and that this was doubtless a result of the fact that, "my consciousness is not in my mouth but in my cunt."[36] Here, consciousness is not a function of human or divine Logos, but rather of the corporeal *topos* of sex and excrement. And that this place be his own *female* genitalia reveals that his rebellion, his quest for self-engenderment at Rodez, his madness, led him to discover the very secrets of sexual differentiation, and led him to live this difference. Within that psychiatric cloister, Artaud lived as a man and woman, God and Devil, Christ and Anti-Christ. Rather than excluding the representations of sexual differentiation from consciousness, as is the case in fetishism, he lived this difference in seriality, in alternating subject positions which marked the multifarious possibilities of psychic delirium.

But what are we to make of Artaud's delirium, his solution—we, whose very presence here attests to the extent to which we value the objects, rituals and effects of sublimation!? Bataille provides one possibility:

> From the moment that the effort of rational comprehension ends in a contradiction, the practice of intellectual scatology requires the dejection of the inassimilable elements; this amounts to saying, crudely, that a burst of laughter is the only imaginable, definitively final, outcome, and not the means, of philosophical speculation.[37]

Such a laugh is a nonmaterial excrement, an expulsion of the exigencies of reason, a valorization of the material heteronomy of existence. This is a Nietzschean laugh of affirmation and celebration, of parody and irony: it is meant to shatter the silence imposed by the theological and ontological infinity of the cosmic void which for Pascal was God. Such laughter is the sign of an atheological certainty, where we finally recover both language and the body, liberated from metaphysical closure. Eros is no longer a metaphysical supplement, but an originary disruption of existence. Yet such a laugh nevertheless remains vocal, and is always in danger of being appropriated by the cultural system of linguistic signifiers which it purports to disrupt. Hence one more contradiction; hence we must laugh again.

Notes

Preface

1. *Oulipo: La littérature potentielle* (Paris, Gallimard, 1973).
2. Abbé Dinouart, *L'Art de se taire* (1771), edited and with an introduction by Jean-Jacques Courtine and Claudine Haroche (Paris, Jérôme Millon, 1987).
3. See my, *Iconology and Perversion* (Melbourne, Art & Text Publications, 1989).
4. Friedrich Nietzsche, "On Truth and Lie in an Extra-moral Sense" (1873)
5. Sigmund Freud, *The Interpretation of Dreams* (1900)
6. Bernard Pautrat, *Versions du soleil* (Paris, Seuil, 1971); pp. 49-80.
7. Friedrich Nietzsche, Letter to Jacob Burckhardt, January 6, 1889.
8. Ironically, after the French Revolution Saint-Just proposed that in the French *lycées* the prize for eloquence be given for laconism.

Chapter 1

1. Friedrich Nietzsche, *The Birth of Tragedy*, trans. Walter Kaufmann (New York, Random House, 1967); p. 66.
2. *Ibid.*, p.71.
3. Georges Bataille, *Sur Nietzsche*, in *Oeuvres Complètes*, vol. VI (Paris, Gallimard, 1973); p. 79.

4. *The Birth of Tragedy, op. cit.;* p. 65.

5. *Sur Nietzsche, op. cit.;* p. 42.

6. Friedrich Nietzsche, *The Will to Power,* trans. Walter Kaufmann and R.J. Hollingdale (New York, Random House, 1968); p. 421.

7. *Sur Nietzsche, op. cit.;* p. 17.

8. *The Birth of Tragedy, op. cit.;* p. 40.

9. Friedrich Nietzsche, *Twilight of the Idols,* in *The Portable Nietzsche,* trans. Walter Kaufmann (New York, Penguin Books, 1968); pp. 518-520.

10. The Birth of Tragedy, *op. cit.;* p. 63.

11. Georges Bataille, "Nietzschean Chronicle," in *Visions of Excess,* trans. Allan Stoekl (Minneapolis, University of Minnesota Press, 1985); p. 206.

12. *Ibid.,* p. 207.

13. *Sur Nietzsche, op. cit.;* p. 23.

14. Georges Bataille, "The Obelisk," in *Visions of Excess, op. cit.;* p. 220; (slightly altered translation.)

15. Marcel Detienne, *Dionysos à ciel ouvert* (Paris, Hachette, 1986); passim.

16. Georges Bataille, "Le rire de Nietzsche," in *Oeuvres Complètes* vol. VI, *op. cit.;* p. 313. For a further study of Bataille's desublimatory epistemology and his reading of Nietzsche, see "Impossible Sovereignty," (supra).

17. Georges Bataille, "Méthode de méditation," in *Oeuvres Complètes,* vol. V, *op. cit.;* p. 221.

18. "Nietzschean Chronicle," *op. cit.;* p. 210.

19. *Twilight of the Idols, op. cit.;* p. 519.

20. Gilbert Rouget, *Music and Trance,* translation revised by Brunhilde Biebuyck and the author (Chicago, University of Chicago Press, 1985); p. 322.

21. *Ibid.,* p. 206.

22. *Ibid.,* p. 209.

23. *Dionysos à ciel ouvert, op. cit.;* p. 91.

24. *The Birth of Tragedy, op. cit.*; p. 64.

25. *Ibid.*, p. 40.

26. *Ibid.*, pp. 46-47.

27. *Dionysos à ciel ouvert, op. cit.*; p. 42.

28. *Ibid.*, pp. 33-35.

Chapter 2

1. Georges Bataille, "Le bas matérialisme et la gnose." *Oeuvres Complètes*, Vol. I. (Gallimard, Paris); p. 225.

2. Georges Bataille, "Sacrifices." O.C., I; p. 92.

3. Pierre Klossowski, "La messe de Georges Bataille." *Un si funeste désir.* (Paris, Gallimard, 1963); p. 132. Klossowski makes this claim for Bataille's tale, *L'abbé C.* but it remains true for Bataille's general notion of an atheology, as well as perhaps, for the formation of the secret society *Acéphale* which they founded together.

4. The progression of Bataille's interpretation of Nietzsche, as well as his notion of community, is traced out in Allan Stoekl's, "The Death of *Acéphale* and the Will to Chance: Nietzsche in the Text of Bataille." *Glyph* #6, 1979. Note that the community in question diminishes from that of a heterogeneous proletariat in *Contre-attaque*, to the secret community of *Acéphale*, finally to the isolation of the inner experience, where Bataille is in community with Nietzsche himself, as described in the texts of *La somme athéologique.*

5. Pierre Rosenstiehl, "The *Dodécadédale*, or in Praise of Heuristics." *October* #26, Fall 1983.

6. Paolo Santarcangeli, *Le livre des labyrinthes.* (Paris, Gallimard, 1974); pp. 51-54.

7. Denis Hollier, *La prise de la Concorde.* (Paris, Gallimard, 1974); p. 112; and Gaston Bachelard, *Le terre et les rêveries du repos* (Paris, José Corti, 1948); p. 240.

8. Georges Bataille, "L'anus solaire." O.C., I; p. 81. The notion of thought as catastrophe may be circumscribed by mathematical models of catastrophe theory (such as those proposed by René Thom) which deal with the stabilities and transformations of systems and their points of rupture. But this would, of course, belie the sovereignty of the inner experience by placing it within a *mathesis universalis*, thus quantifying a qualitative process.

9. Maurice Blanchot, *La communauté inavouable.* (Paris, Minuit, 1983); p. 30.

10. Georges Bataille, "La conjuration sacrée." O.C., I; p. 445. Pierre Klossowksi's article, "Le Monstre," immediately follows this text of Bataille's in *Acéphale.*

11. Bachelard, *op. cit.;* pp. 254-255.

12. Friedrich Nietzsche, *Thus Spoke Zarathustra.* in *The Portable Nietzsche,* ed. Walter Kaufmann. (New York, Penguin, 1968); pp. 257-259.

13. For Klossowski's position, see "A Logic of the Simulacrum," (supra).

14. Georges Bataille, *Sur Nietzsche.* O.C. VI; and Pierre Klossowski, *Nietzsche et le cercle vicieux* (Paris, Mercure de France, 1969). Passim.

15. *Sur Nietzsche, op. cit.;* p. 20.

16. *Ibid.,* p. 131.

17. Georges Bataille, *Méthode de méditation.* O.C., V; p. 221. See also *La souveraineté,* O.C. VIII; p. 401.

18. *Sur Nietzsche, op. cit.;* p. 23; cf. also p. 159.

19. Sigmund Freud, *Jokes and Their Relation to the Unconscious.* (New York, Norton, 1963), Especially pp. 140-158.

20. *"L'Anus solaire," op. cit.;* p. 81.

21. *Méthode de méditation, op. cit.;* p. 204.

22. Georges Bataille, "La valeur d'usage de D.A.F. Sade (1)." O.C., II; p. 64.

23. Pierre Klossowski, "Nietzsche, le polythéisme et la parodie." *Un si funeste désir, op. cit.;* p. 226.

24. We must here note a central difference between Bataille and Nietzsche; while Bataille's thought has certain affinities with mysticism, Nietzsche's position may be summed up by considering section #126 of *The Gay Science:* "Mystical explanations are considered deep. The truth is that they are not even superficial."

25. *Thus Spoke Zarathustra, op. cit.;* p. 339.

26. Roman Jakobson, "Two Aspects of Language and Two Types of Aphasic Disturbances." (The Hague, Mouton, 1956).

27. *Méthode de méditation, op. cit.;* pp. 227-228.

28. Georges Bataille, *Madame Edwarda*. O.C., III; p. 22.

29. Friedrich Nietzsche, *The Will to Power*. (New York, Vintage, 1968); p. 270.

30. Georges Bataille, *Le coupable*. O.C., V; p. 327.

Chapter 3

1. Jean Lalande and J.B. Pontalis, "Fantasme originaire, fantasmes des origines, origine du fantasme." *Les Temps Modernes*, no. 215, March 1964; p. 1854.

2. Pierre Klossowski, "Sade et Fourier." in *Les Derniers travaux de Gulliver suivi de Sade et Fourier*. (Fata Morgana, 1974, Montpellier) p. 34. Trans. by Paul Foss and Paul Patton as "The Phantasms of Perversion: Sade and Fourier," in *Phantasm and Simulacra, Art & Text* #18 (1985).

3. Pierre Klossowski, *Nietzsche et le cercle vicieux*. (Mercure de France, 1969, Paris); p. 58.

4. Laplanche and Pontalis, *op. cit.*; p. 1868.

5. *Nietzsche et le cercle vicieux; op. cit.*; p. 67.

6. Cf. "The Errant Text," (supra).

7. Cf. "Structures of Exchange; Acts of Transgressions." (supra).

8. Pierre Klossowski, "Du tableau en tant que simulacre." in *La Ressemblance*. (Editions Ryôan-ji, 1984, Marseille); p. 77.

9. Jean-François Lyotard, *Economie libidinale*. (Minuit, 1974, Paris); p. 97.

10. Roman Jakobson, "Why Mama and Papa?" in *Perspectives in Psychological Theory* (New York, 1960), pp. 124-134.

11. Lyotard, *op. cit.*; p. 29.

12. *Nietzsche et le cercle vicieux*; p. 156.

13. Cf. my, "The Body Dionysian: Nietzsche, Freud, Merleau-Ponty in *The Great Year of Zarathustra* edited by David Goicoechea. (Lanham University Press of America, 1963).

14. Pierre Klossowski, *Sade mon prochain*. (Seuil, 1967, Paris); p. 34; Cf. also Guy Rosolato, "Etude des perversions sexuelles a partir du fétichisme." in *Le désir et la perversion*. (Seuil, 1967, Paris); passim.

15. Gilles Deleuze, *Loqique du sens.* (Minuit, 1969, Paris); p. 346.

16. Michel Foucault, "Nietzsche, Genealogy, History." in *Language, Counter-Memory, Practice.* Trans. Donald F. Bouchard (Cornell University Press, 1977, Ithaca); p. 151.

17. Pierre Klossowski, "La décadence du nu." in *La ressemblance.* p. 66.

18. Pierre Klossowski, "Nietzsche, le polythéisme et la paradie." in *Un si funeste désir. (Gallimard, 1963, Paris); p. 217.*

19. *Ibid.*, p. 195.

20. *Ibid.*, p. 209.

21. "La décadence du nu." *op. cit.;* p. 70.

22. "Du tableau en tant que simulacre"; *op. cit.;* p. 77.

23. *Economie libidinale; op. cit.;* p. 107; Cf. also Pierre Klossowski, *La monnaie vivante* (Eric Losfeld, 1970, Paris); passim.

24. Jacques Derrida, "Force and Signification." in *Writing and Difference.* Trans. Alan Bass (University of Chicago Press, 1978, Chicago); p. 11.

25. Pierre Klossowski, *Roberte ce soir.* (Grove Press, 1969, New York); p. 143.

26. Cf. "The Art of Fascination," supra.

27. Guy Rosolato, "La dormition, destin de l'imago maternelle." in *Elements de l'interpretation.* (Gallimard, 1985, Paris); p. 291. On the problems of iconoclasm and iconology, see my monograph, *Iconology and Perversion* (Melbourne, *Art & Text* Publications, 1989).

Chapter 4

1. *New York Times,* July 1, 1986, p. A18. If there is anything "heinous" in this matter, it is the Supreme Court ruling itself, which is blatantly antihomosexual. Briefly stated, this ruling results in the fact that there is now no constitutionally protected right to engage in homosexual activity, and the protections afforded heterosexual choice of sexual activity (including sodomy), shielded by a "zone of privacy," are not extended to homosexuals. Thus not only is this a flagrant invasion of privacy, but even more distressing, it givers a clear sign to lower courts to rule against homosexual rights in other matters, such as cases of job discrimination, child custody, medical care, etc. This rulling—superficial, illogical, insensitive, and based on a distorted use of historical precedents—must be carefully examined for what it is: an outrightly prejudicial

act. Such a study is beyond the scope of this article, which is rather concerned with some considerations of a genealogical analysis of the symbolic structure of sodomy, and its particular utilization in Sade's text. Though the notion of sodomy in Sade is not directly related to issues of homosexuality, I nevertheless hope that this study might in some way aid in posing a new facet of a critique of current prejudices. On these issues, see *October* #43 (1987), a special issue on AIDS, edited by Douglas Crimp.

2. D.A.F. de Sade, *Philosophy in the Bedroom*, Trans. Richard Seaver and Austin Wainhouse, (New York, Grove Press, 1966); p. 359.

3. *Ibid.*, p. 363.

4. *Ibid.*, p. 360.

5. Claude Lévi-Strauss, *The Elementary Structures of Kinship*, trans. James Harle Bell, John Richard von Sturmer, Rodney Needham, (Boston, Beacon Press, 1969); p. 497.

6. For Klossowski's analysis of Sade, see *Sade mon prochain*, (Paris Seuil, 1967); *La monnaie vivante*, (Paris, Losfeld, 1970); and "The Phantasms of Perversion: Sade and Fourier" trans. Paul Foss and Paul Patton, in *Art & Text 18: Phantasm and Simulacra*, (July, 1985), pp. 22-34. For some current readings of Klossowski on Sade, see Paul Foss, "On the 'Difficulty' of Picturing the Emotions of Pierre Klossowski," Alphonso Lingis, "The Incommunicable," Chantal Thomas, "The Indiscreet Gaze," all in *Art & Text* #18.

7. "The Phantasms of Perversion," *op. cit.*; p. 31. Needless to say, as Madison Avenue advertising agencies know so well, simulacra can also be used to *create* such phantasms, as well as being their external sign.

8. *Ibid.*, p. 31.

9. *Ibid.*, p. 31.

10. On the Breton/Bataille debate, see especially Breton's *Second Manifesto of Surrealism;* and Bataille's "The Use Value of D.A.F. Sade," in *Visions of Excess*, trans. Allan Stoekl, (Minneapolis, University of Minnesota Press, 1985); for some current theoretical studies of the history and aesthetics of surrealism in regard to Bataille's exclusion from the movement and his subsequent influence, see Rosalind Krauss, "Corpus Delicti" in October #33 (Summer, 1985) and "Antivision" in October #36 (Spring, 1986); see also Paul Foss, "Eyes, Fetishism, and the Gaze," in *Art & Text* #20 (February-April, 1986); on the theoretical paradigms behind Bataille's

position, see Annette Michelson, "Heterology and the Critique of Instrumental Reason," in October #36 (Spring, 1986).

11. This project will be followed by another publication in six volumes forthcoming from Fayard, edited by Thibault de Sade (a descendent of the "Divine Marquis") and Maurice Lever, consisting of Sade's previously unpublished tales, poetry, theater, letters, and essays. Also, two new biographies, by Pauvert and Sade/Lever. Finally, Sade's literary canonization will be complete when the three volume critical edition of Sade appears in *La Pléiade*, scheduled for 1989. All of this was deemed of sufficient interest for the Parisian daily *Libération* to publish a 16 page dossier on Sade (May 23, 1986).

    It is certainly interesting to note that the publication of Le Brun and Sade coincided, in France, with three major exhibitions of Surrealist art: (1) *André Breton et l'art surréaliste* at Artcurial gallery in Paris; (2) *La planète affolée* in Marseilles; (3) *Explosante fixe* at the Centre Georges Pompidou in Paris. (The latter was the Paris manifestation of the exhibit *L'Amour fou*, organized by Rosalind Krauss and Jane Livingston, which originated at the Corcoran Gallery in Washington, D.C.) As would have been expected, only *L'Amour fou/Explosante fixe* took into account the critical role played by Bataille in relation to surrealism. The other exhibitions were organized according to the stereotyped, "official" history of surrealism, in which Bataille *et al.* are excluded, and the 1930 rupture discounted for the sake of a continuous, homogeneous history.

12. Annie Le Brun, *Les châteaux de la subversion*, (Paris, Pauvert, 1982); p. 70.

13. *Ibid.*, p. 72.

14. *Ibid.*, p. 80.

15. *Ibid.*, p. 57.

16. Annie Le Brun, *Soudain un bloc d'abîme, Sade*, (Paris, Pauvert, 1986). The page numbers of all quotations from this book appear in parentheses in the text.

17. See the epigraph to this essay.

18. *New York Times, op. cit.*; p. A18.

19. Ernest Jones, *On the Nightmare*, (New York, Liveright, 1971); p. 172.

Chapter 5

1. Foucault, Michel, "Nietzsche, Genealogy, History." in *Language, Counter-Memory, Practice,* trans. Donald F. Bouchard, (Ithaca, Cornell UP, 1977); p. 162.

2. Lyotard, Jean-Francois, *Discourse/figure.* (Paris, Klincksieck, 1974; p. 289.

3. Sade, D.A.F., *Juliette.* (N.Y., Grove Press, 1968); trans. Austryn Wainhouse, p. 1175; My corrections to the translation are added, from *Histoire de Juliette,* (Oeuvres Complètes IX; Paris, Cercle du livre precieux, 1966); p. 569.

4. Hénaff, Marcel, *Sade: l'invention du corps libertin.* (Paris, PUF, 1978); p. 126.

5. Sade, D.A.F., *Philosophy in the Bedroom,* trans. Richard Seaver and Ausryn Wainhouse, (N.Y., Grove Press, 1966); pp. 202-203.

6. Hénaff; *op. cit.;* p. 127; (Cf. also Gérard Genette's *Figures I).*

7. *Foucault, Michel. Discipline and Punish* trans. Alan Sheridan, (N.Y., Vintage, 1979). passim, esp. pp. 195-228 One should also note here the psychoanalytic insights of the relation between sadism and the scopic drives.

8. Barthes, Roland, *Sade, Fourier, Loyola,* trans. Richard Miller, (N.Y., Hill and Wang, 1976.); p. 32.

9. Foucault, Michel, "Language to Infinity." in *Language . . . op. cit.;* p. 62.

10. Lacan, Jacques, "Le stade du miroir comme formateur de la fonction du Je." in *Ecrits I;* (Paris, Seuil, 1966); pp. 89-97.

11. Merleau-Ponty, Maurice, *The Visible and the Invisible,* trans. Alphoso Lingis, (Evanston, Northwestern U. Press 1960); p. 217.

12. *Ibid.,* p. 217.

13. *Ibid.,* p. 137.

14. *Ibid.,* p. 215.

15. *Ibid.,* p. 215.

16. *Ibid.,* p. 136.

17. *Ibid.,* p. 125.

18. *Ibid.,* p. 270.

19. Maurice Merleau-Ponty, "Eye and Mind," in *The Primacy of Perception*, trans. Charleton Dallery, (Evanston, NWU Press, 1964); p. 168.

20. *Ibid.*, p. 256.

21. *Ibid.*, p. 201.

22. *Ibid.*, p. 266.

23. *Ibid.*, p. 270.

24. Hénaff, *op. cit.*; p. 128.

25. Lyotard, *op. cit.*; p. 257.

26. Foucault, "Nietzsche . . ." *op. cit.*; p. 162; Cf. the writings of Pierre Klossowski, especially his novel *Roberte ce soir* and *Nietzsche et le cercle vicieux*, which have as their central themes the problem of the dissolution of subjectivity after the death of God. Nietzsche and Sade were the inspiration for these works, which in turn inspired Foucault.

27. Foucault, "What is an Author?" in *Language* . . . *op. cit.*; p. 130n.

28. Barthes, *op. cit.*; p. 37.

29. Lyotard, *op. cit.*; p. 22.

Chapter 6

1. Jan Kott, "The Sexual Triangle" in the *Partisan Review* Vol. XLIV, no. 4; pp. 589 ff.

2. Idem.

3. Michel Leiris, "Du temps de Lord Auch" in *L'Arc* #44, 1971; p. 5.

4. Roland Barthes, "La métaphore de l'oeil" in *Essais critiques*, (Paris, Seuil, 1964); p. 241.

5. Leiris, *op. cit.*; p. 9.

6. Georges Bataille, *Story of the Eye*, trans. Joachim Neugroschel (New York, Urizen, 1977); pp. 69-70; 73-74.

7. Ernest Hemingway, *Death in the Afternoon*. (New York, Scribner's, 1960); p. 247.

8. *Ibid.*, p. 96.

9. Bataille, *op. cit.;* pp. 79-80. The paintings referred to by Bataille are Valdès Léal's *Hieroglyphs of Our Last Days* (circa 1670) which are to be found in the chapel of the Hospital de la Santa Caridad in Seville. Bataille uses some poetic license in his description of these paintings, since it is a roach, and not a rat, which is seen crawling near the empty eye socket of a corpse in one of the paintings. Also appropriate is the fact that in the other painting is to be found the inscription: *"in ictu oculi"*, "in the blink of an eye" or, more literally, "in the cut of an eye"! Hence this *vanitas* might serve as an ironic allegory of Bataille's story.

10. *Ibid.*, p. 90.

11. *Ibid.*, pp. 86-87. Note that in *Scatologic Rites of All Nations* (New York, Johnson Reprint Co., 1968), Bourke reports that the heretical Manicheans, Cathars and Albigensians celebrated Communion such that their "eucharistic bread was incorporated or sprinkled with human semen, possibly with the idea that the bread of life should be sprinkled with the life-giving excretion." (p. 220).

12. *Ibid.*, p. 96.

13. Gilles Deleuze and Félix Guattari. *Anti-Oedipus.* trans. Robert Hurley, Mark Seem, and Helen R. Lane (New York, Viking, 1977); pp. 111-112.

14. Idem.

15. Hemingway, *op. cit.;* pp. 24-25.

Chapter 7

1. Richir, Marc, "Phénonémalization, distortion, logologie." *Textures,* 1972/4-5; p. 111 (my translation.)

2. Minkowski, Eugene, *Lived-Time,* trans. Nancy Metzel, (Evanston, Northwestern University Press, 1970); p. 181.

3. Merleau-Ponty, Maurice, *The Visible and the Invisible,* trans. Alphonso Lingis, (Evanston, Northwestern University Press, 1968); p. 270.

4. Rubin, William S., *Dada, Surrealism, and their Heritage.* (N.Y., Museum of Modern Art, 1968); p. 53.

5. Merleau-Ponty, Maurice, "On the Phenomenology of Language," in *Signs,* trans. Richard C. McCleary, (Evanston, Northwestern University Press, 1964); p. 91.

6. Merleau-Ponty, Maurice, *The Prose of the World.* trans. John O'Neill, (Evanston, Northwestern University Press, 1973); p. 60.

7. Merleau-Ponty, Maurice, *The Visible and the Invisible, op. cit.*; p. 270.

8. Malraux, André, *Picasso's Masks,* trans. June Guicharnaud, (N.Y., Holt, Rinehart & Winston, 1976); p. 151.

9. *Ibid.*, p. 32.

10. Arsan, Emmanuelle (pseudonym of Marayat Rollet-Andriane) *Emmannuelle,* trans. Lowell Bair (N.Y., Grove Press, 1971); p. 140.

11. "Tlön, Uqbar, Orbis Tertius" trans. James E. Irby, in *Labyrinths.* (N.Y., New Directions, 1964); p. 10.

12. Lyotard, Jean-François, *Discours/figure.* (Paris, Klincksieck, 1964); p. 284.

13. Freud, Sigmund, "Psychoanalysis and Religious Origins," in *Character and Culture,* (N.Y., Collier, 1972); p. 225 (my emphasis).

14. Thévoz, Michel, *Art Brut,* trans. James Emmons (N.Y., Skira/ Rizzoli, 1976); p. 119.

15. Barthes, Roland, *A Lover's Discourse,* trans. Richard Howard, (N.Y., Hill & Wang, 1978); p. 153.

16. Foucault, Michel, *The Order of Things,* (N.Y., Vintage, 1973); passim, esp. p. xv ff.

17. Hartman, Geoffrey, (ed.), *Psychoanalysis and the Question of the Text.* (Baltimore, Johns Hopkins University Press, 1978); p. 88.

Chapter 8

**L'Amour fou* (1937) is the title of a classic Surrealist text by André Breton. It is also the title of the exhibition of Surrealist photography curated by Rosalind Krauss and Jane Livingston, which opened at the Corcoran Gallery, as well as the catalogue of this exhibit, *L'Amour fou: Photography and Surrealism* (New York, Abbeville Press, 1985).

1. Note that Breton entitled one of his books *Arcane 17* (1944), referring to the seventeenth major enigma of the Tarot, the Star, which symbolizes hope, predestination, abandon to immortality, idealism, a taste for beauty, and the moral influence of ideas over forms. As we shall see, this Tarot card is particularly indicative of Breton's idealizing model of Surrealism.

2. Max Ernst carried with him to Paris, as a gift for Paul Eluard, a copy of the book which remains the *locus classicus* of works on

the art of the mentally ill, Hans Prinzhorn's *Bildnerei der Geisteskranken* (1922) *(The Art of the Mentally Ill)*, a text which has recently been translated into English and French. Selected works from the Prinzhorn collection of the Psychiatric Clinic at the University of Heidelberg were recently on display in the exhibition *Selections from the Prinzhorn Collection: The Art of the Mentally Ill*, which opened at the Neuberger Museum of the State University of New York at Purchase, curated by Stephen Prokopoff. One should also consider the superb collection of *Le musée de l'Art Brut* in Lausanne, Switzerland.

3. For a more detailed exposition of Bataille's position, see my article, "Between the *Will to Power* and the *Will to Chance*," (supra).

4. Rosalind Krauss already presented a study of the influence of Bataille on the dissident Surrealists in her article on "Giacometti," which appeared in the catalogue of the Museum of Modern Art (New York) exhibit, *"Primitivism" in 20th Century Art*. See also Jean Clair, "La pointe à l'oeil d'Alberto Giacometti," *Cahiers du Musée National d'Art Moderne* #11 (Paris, 1983), pp. 64-99.

5. The major such revision was inaugurated by the *Tel Quel* group, which valorized the works of the dissident Surrealists, Bataille and Artaud, against the official history of Surrealism based on Breton's position. This moment of contemporary French culture culminated in the conference organized by Philippe Sollers at the Centre culturel International de Cerisy-la-Salle in 1972, *Vers une Révolution Culturelle: Artaud, Bataille*. Most of the papers presented in this colloquium were anthologized in two volumes published by the Union Générale d'Editions, in the series 10/18, #804 *Artaud* and #805 *Bataille*.

6. On the relation between tropes and hermeneutic systematization, see my "The Errant Text," (supra).

7. Two excellent recent studies dealing with the iconography of hysteria, and the relation between seduction and mastery in the hysteric scenario, are, Joan Copjec's, "Flavit et Dissipati Sunt," in *October* #18, fall 1981; and Georges Didi-Huberman's *Invention de l'hystérie* (Paris, Editions Macula, 1982).

8. In terms of the psycho-poetic typography of Surrealism, Gilles Deleuze's claim that Dadaism is a schizophrenic/active art while Surrealism is a paranoid/reactive art is a schematic over-simplification of the issue, as we have seen. What must be determined are the historical, rhetorical and iconographic conditions which determine the rupture within the Surrealist movement itself. It might be suggested that this will lead to a

psycho-typology in which Breton instantiates the paranoid, Artaud the schizophrenic, and Bataille the perverse, thus indicating the three major modes of Surrealist madness.

Chapter 9

1. For historical information about Shih Huang Ti, see Karl A. Wittfogel's *Oriental Despotism* (NY, Vintage, 1981); Jorge Luis Borges, "The Wall and the Books," in *Labyrinths* (NY, New Directions, 1964).
2. This paper is an attempt to examine the structure of narcissism as constitutive of subjectivity, and not the notion of narcissism as a type of character disorder. And yet, the Emperor Shih Huang Ti may certainly be thus categorized. Drawing upon Nathan Schwartz-Salant's *Narcissism and Character Transformation* (NY, Inner City Books, 1982), we may match the following characteristics of the narcissistic character disorder with some of the deeds and personality traits of Shih Huang Ti: (a) *lack of psychological penetrability and defense against relatedness to others:* the Emperor not only protected his nation behind the enclosure of the Great wall, but he also secluded himself within a vast palace, and took the advice of nobody except his Prime Minister, Li Ssŭ. (b) *extreme self-reference:* the Emperor wanted to found an eternal dynasty, with himself as the First Emperor, and his heirs to be known as the Second Emperor, Third Emperor, etc.; he constructed enormous monuments for himself, palaces and a tomb, (in addition to the Great Wall), using vast work crews of over 700,000 workers. He also began construction of the great hydraulic systems. (c) *rejects interpretation:* he implemented standardized and objective laws which pertained to everyone without discrimination (this was the supremacy of Legalism.) He thus consolidated the centralization of power, which was accomplished by the destruction of the feudal barons and the suppression of local customs (*i.e.*, of different worldviews.) (d) *cannot tolerate criticism:* all of the positions of power previously held by the feudal barons were given to his own functionaries, so as to avoid dissension. (e) *grandiose self-image (megalomania) and quest for perfection:* he spread the rumor that he was God. (f) *low empathetic capacity; given to anger, rage, and envy:* he was known to have "the heart of a tiger or a wolf," and was completely "without beneficience." He even forced his father to suicide and persecuted his mother. (g) *power drive:* he ascended the throne at the age of 12, and began to conquer and unify the states at the age of 25. (h) *lack of sense of history:* The historical process is assimilated only to the extent that it aggrandizes the

ego, and (i) *the desire to know ahead of time:* he insisted that history begin with him; in his old age, he wished to deny death, and not only forbade anyone to mention death in his presence, but also sought the elixer of immortality.

3. From Elias Canetti's *Crowds and Power* (NY, Continuum, 1981), the section on "Rulers and Paronoiacs;" p. 417. In this regard, also consider the following lines of W.H. Auden:

   Perfection, of a kind, was what he was after,
   And the poetry he invented was easy to understand.
   He knew human folly like the back of his hand,
   And was greatly interested in armies and fleets.
   When he laughed, respectable senators burst with laughter
   And when he cried, the little children died in the streets.

4. In Maurice Merleau-Ponty, *The Visible and the Invisible,* trans. Alphonso Lingis (Evanston, Northwestern University Press, 1968); p. 217.

5. Julia Kristeva, "Place Names," in *Desire in Language* trans. Leon S. Roudiez (NY, Columbia, 1980); pp. 289-291 and passim.

6. On the role of garbage in modernism, and in *Merz* in particular, see my "The Errant Text," (supra). On the glossolalic structure and the materiality of the text in modernism, see Annette Michelson's "De Stijl, Its Other Face: Abstraction and Cacaphony, or what Was the Matter with Hegel?" in *October* #22. It should also be noted that in the first *Manifesto of Surrealism* (1924) André Breton suggests that echolalia and the Ganser syndrome responses, techniques utilized in the Zen *Koan* (question and answer exercise) as methods of enlightenment (Satori), are also typical of the Surrealist enterprise. Yet, the difference between Schwitters and Breton, between Dadaism and Surrealism, must be noted. If the gutter with its garbage was the *topos* of discovery for Schwitters and the Dadaists, Paris with its bourgeois flea-markets and artifacts was the *topos* of discovery for the Surrealists. Hence the claim of Deleuze-Guattari in *Anti-Oedipus* (NY, Viking, 1977) that Dada was a schizophrenic-revolutionary art, while surealism was a paranoid-oedipal-reactionary art.

7. Merleau-Ponty, *op. cit.;* pp. 118-119.

8. *Ibid.,* pp. 255-256; For a further investigation of the "flesh" as mirror phenomenon, and the rhetorical structure of the

"chiasm" in Merleau-Ponty, see my "Structures of Exchange; Acts of Transgression" (supra). The *locus classicus* of psychoanalytic studies on narcissism is Sigmund Freud's "On Narcissism: An Introduction" (1914), in *General Psychological Theory* (NY, Collier, 1970). A major recent analysis of the Freudian theory of narcissism is André Green's *Narcissime de vie, narcissime de mort* (Paris, Minuit, 1983). For an in-depth study of the constitution of the self and the ontology of Freudian metapsychology, see Marcel Gauchet's "Freud: Une psychanalyse ontologique," in *Textures* 72/4-5 and 73/6-7. Also see Jacques Lacan's "The Mirror Stage as Formative of the Function of the I as Revealed in Psychoanalytic Experience," in *Ecrits* trans. Alan Sheridan (NY, Norton, 1972). Finally, for a critique of all of the above positions from the point of view of post-structuralist libido theory, see Deleuze-Guattari's *Anti-Oedipus.*

9. Sigmund Freud, *The Ego and the Id* (NY, Norton, 1962); pp. 15-16.

10. Jacques Lacan, *op. cit.;* p. 2.

11. Sigmund Freud, "On the Mechanism of Paranoia" in *General Psychological Theory* (NY, Collier, 1970).

12. All information on Schreber is from his *Memoires d'un nevropath* (Paris, Seuil, 1975). The locus classicus of the psychoanalytic interpretation of this case is Freud's "Psychoanalytic Notes Upon an Autobiographical Account of a Case of Paranoia" (1911) in *Three Case Histories* (NY, Collier, 1973). See also Lacan's "On a Question Preliminary to Any Possible Treatment of Psychosis," in *Écrits.* See also W.G. Niederland's work on Schreber. Still the classical text on the structure of the paranoiac mechanism is Victor Tausk's, "On the Origin of the 'Influencing Machine' in Schizophrenia" in *Psychoanalytic Quarterly* Vol. II, 1933. An interesting account of these issues in relation to art can be found in Joan Copjec's "The Anxiety of the Influencing Machine" in *October* #23.

13. Santiago or Carthago
Chineseness or Jesus Christum
twilight or dyspnoea (difficulty in breathing)
Ariman or laborer
paperweight or Mr. Examiner swears
See also Louis Wolfson's *Le schizo et les langues* (Paris: Gallimard, 1970) for the internal structures of schizophrenic language and homonomy and the rejection of one's own language ("mother tongue").

14. From Brisset's "La grande loi ou la clef de la parole," in André Breton's *Anthologie de l'humour noir* (Paris: Pauvert, 1972)

    The teeth, the mouth.
    The teeth plug it
    helping the mouth.
    Help the mouth.
    Ugly (teeth) in the mouth.
    An ugly mouth.
    Milk in the mouth.
    Painful in the mouth.*
    The teeth—hidden there**

    * *j'ai mal aux dents* (I have a toothache)
    ** *cache des dents-là, ferme la bouche* (hide the teeth there, shut the mouth

15. Franz Kafka, "The Great Wall and the Tower of Babel," in *Parables and Paradoxes* (New York: Schocken, 1975)

16. Phillip Wegener, *The Life of Speech* (1885), trans. and edited by D. Wilfred Abse in *Speech and Reason: Language Disorder in Mental Disease* (Charlottesville: University of Virginia Press, 1971), p. 172.

17. *Ibid.*, pp. 177-178.

Chapter 10

1. This section is indebted to Jacques Lacarrière's, *Les hommes ivres de Dieu* (Paris, Fayard, 1975).

2. In 313 A.D. the Edict of Milan established religious tolerance and permitted open Christian worship, prior to Constantine's ultimate proclamation of Christianity as the state religion of his Empire; in 392 A.D. paganism was prohibited in the Empire by Theodosius I.

3. Cited in Jean Dubuffet, "Messages et clichés de Jeanne Tripier la planétaire in *Prospectus et tous ècrits suivants* Vol. I (Paris, Gallimard, 1967): p. 410. The classic texts on Art Brut, including detailed studies of the works of Jeanne Tripier, are: Roger Cardinal, *Outsider Art* (New York, Praeger, 1972); Jean Dubuffet, *Prospectus et tous écrits suivants,* vol. I & II (Paris, Gallimard, 1967); Michel Thévoz, *Art Brut* (New York, Rizzoli, 1976); Michel Thévoz, *Le langage de*

la rupture (Paris, Presses Universitaires de France, 1978); and *Les Fascicules de l'Art Brut* (the publication of the Collection de l'Art Brut, Lausanne.) See also, *Art Brut: Madness and Marginalia,* a special issue of *Art & Text* #27 (1988), edited by Allen S. Weiss.

4. For a further consideration of this text, see "The Errant Text." (supra).

5. William J. Samarin, *Tongues of Men and Angels* (New York, Macmillan, 1972); p. 253. For the biblical sources on speaking in tongues, see *Acts of the Apostles* and *The First Letter of Paul to the Corinthians.* For linguistic and psychological readings, see: David Christie-Murray, *Voices from the Gods* (London, Routledge & Kegan Paul, 1978); Antoine Compagnon, "La glossolalie: une affaire sans historie?" *Critique* #387-388, August-September 1979; Felicitas D. Goodman, *Speaking in Tongues* (Chicago, University of Chicago Press, 1972); see also *Le Discours Psychanalytique* #6 and #7, March and June 1983, especially Michel de Certeau, "Utopies vocales: glossolalies," and Jean-Jacques Courtine, "Des faux en langue?" and *Langages* #91 (Paris, PUF, 1988) a special issue on glossolalia edited by Jean-Jacques Courtine.

6. Courtine, *"Des faux on langues?" op. cit.;* pp. 43-44.

7. On the relation between mediumism/Spiritualism and Art Brut, see Michel Thévoz, *Le langage de la rupture. op. cit.;* pp. 64-80.

8. All quotations from Artaud are from the *Oeuvres Complètes* Volumes I-XXI (Paris, Gallimard). Citations will be noted with the volume number in Roman numerals, followed by the page number in Arabic numerals. The *Cahiers de Rodez* appear in volumes XV-XXI. (It might be interesting to note that Artaud's first visitor from Paris at Rodez was Jean Dubuffet.)

9. The quite notable decline in the production of Art Brut in psychiatric institutions over the last quarter century is accounted for by the increased use of electroshock and later chemotherapy.

10. It might be of interest to compare Artaud's theological deliria with those of Daniel Paul Schreber in *Memoirs of My Nervous Illness,* on which Freud based his theory of psychosis. See the collection of critical studies of the Schreber case, *Psychosis and Sexual Identity* edited by Allison, Roberts, de Oliveira, Weiss. (Albany, SUNY Press, 1988).

11. In the *Cahiers de Rodez* Artaud states that, "Mary the Egyptian will not make my way easier, I will make it easier, *me.*" (XVI,161) Mary the Egyptian was a late 4th century saint, roughly contemporary with Saint Anthony, who, after a youth of debauchery, converted to Christianity after experiencing a holy

vision, and henceforth exiled herself to the Palestinian desert where she suffered the greatest mortifications of the flesh until her death.

12. On early Christian iconography, see Pierre du Bourguet, *Early Christian Painting* (New York, Viking, 1966) and André Grabar, *Christian Iconography: A Study of its Origins* (Princeton, Princeton University Press, 1968).

13. Claude Lévi-Strauss, *The Raw and the Cooked* (New York, Harper & Rowe 1970), pp. 339-340. On the relation between glossolalia and the arts, see Annette Michelson's "De Stijl, Its Other Face: Abstraction and Cacaphony, or What Was the Matter with Hegel?" *October* #22, Fall 1982; on Artaud's glossolalia, see Laurent Jenny, *La terreur et les signes: Poétiques de la rupture* (Paris, Gallimard, 1982).

14. Florence de Mèredieu, "La pensée émit des signes, le corps émet des sons" *Traverses* #20, November 1980; p. 50.

15. The name of Artaud's mother was *Euphrasie*, which in her mother-tongue, Greek, means "good cheer" or "fine phrasing" (*euphrasia*), "to gladden" (*euphrainein*), and is directly related to the word "frenzy" (from the Latin *phrenesis*). Such frenzy accurately describes Artaud's own relation to his "mother-tongue," which is often a highly marked factor in schizophrenic discourse. [Cf. Louis Wolfson, *Le schizo et les Langues* (Paris, Gallimard, 1970)]. It is perhaps not without interest that the given name of the mother of the present article's author is *Eulalia Barbara:* this would oppose "good babble" (*eulalia*) to the *lingua barbara* of the Barbarians. Such a *coincidatio oppositorum* might in fact describe the rhetorical strategy of this article. Furthermore, the diminutive of *Eulalia* is *Lala*, which is not only a stereotypical expression of musical sounds, but is also a type of echolalic primal linguistic opposition described earlier, structurally congruous with the words *mama, papa*, etc.

16. Romain Goldron, *Byzantine and Medieval Music* (Stuttman Co., 1968); pp. 21-22.

17. *Ibid.*, p. 28.

18. *Ibid.*, p. 17.

19. This text by Maurice Ohana is to be found on the dust-jacket of the 1981 recording of his *Messe* and *Lys de Madrigaux* on the French label ERATO, STU71482. For a contemporary musical work based on religious glossolalia, consider Richard Felciano's treatment of the 150th Psalm in his 1967 piece, *Glossolalia* (recorded on Cambridge Records, CRS 2560.) For a nonreligious contemporary musical investigation of the disarticulation and distention

of the vocal signifier, listen to Cathy Berberian's performance on Luciano Berio's *Visage* (1961) (VOX-TURNABOUT, TV 331 027).

20. On the history and trial of Gilles de Rais, see George Bataille *Le procès de Gilles de Rais* (Paris, Pauvert, 1979), which includes the transcript of the trial, translated from the Latin by Pierre Klossowski.

21. One of the productions that Artaud planned under the rubric of his Theater of Cruelty was the tale of Blue-Beard (IV,119), which is believed to have been based in part on the story of Gilles de Rais.

22. *Les hommes ivres de Dieu, op. cit.*; p. 192. Coincidentally, monophysitism—the heretical doctrine that the human and divine aspects of Christ constitute only one nature—is emblematic of Artaud's own "heresy."

23. Alfred Jarry, *Le Surmâle, suivi de: Gestes et Opinions du Docteur Faustroll, Pataphysicien* (Paris, Editions Les Humanoïdes Associés, 1979); p. 119.

Chapter 11

1. Gershom Scholem, *Major Trends in Jewish Mysticism* (New York, Schocken, 1973); pp. 349-350.

2. René Descartes, *Meditations* trans. F.E. Sutcliffe (New York, Penguin, 1968); p. 110.

3. *Ibid.*, p. 113.

4. Jacques Derrida, "Force and Signification," in *Writing and Difference* trans. Alan Bass (Chicago, University of Chicago Press, 1978); p. 27.

5. Gérard Genette, *Palimpsests* (Paris, Seuil, 1982); p. 80.

6. Roland Barthes, *La chambre claire* (Paris, Gallimard/Seuil, 1980); p. 165.

7. *Ibid.*, p. 141.

8. Note Chantal Thomas' claim, in "La photo du jardin d'hiver," (in *Critique* #423-424, August-September 1982) that this reduction or sublimation of the figural to the textual was in fact the very case in Barthes' own *La chambre claire,* where he accomplished, ". . . the elimination of the image, and more precisely of the photographic

image . . . for there is an incompatibility between the imaginary of the image and that of writing." On this problematic, specifically within Frampton's cinema, see Annette Michelson, "Frampton's Sieve," in *October* #32 (Spring 1985), a special issue entirely devoted to Frampton.

9. Hollis Frampton, *Circles of Confusion* (Rochester, Visual Studies Workshop Press, 1983); p. 111.

10. Maurice Merleau-Ponty, *The Visible and the Invisible* trans. Alphonso Lingis, Evanston, Northwestern University Press, 1968); p. 223.

Chapter 12

1. Leroi-Gourhan, André, *Le geste et la parole II* (Paris, Albin Michel, 1964) p. 214.
2. Brakhage, Stan, *Brakhage Scrapbook.* (N.Y., Documentext, 1982), p. 139.
3. Sitney, P. Adams, *Visionary Film.* (N.Y., Oxford U. Press, 1979) p. 175.
4. Dali, Salvador, "Objets psycho-atmosphériques-anamorphiques." in *Oui I: La révolution paranoïaque-critique.* (Paris, Denöel/Gonthier, 1971) pp. 201-207 passim.
5. Lacan, Jacques, *The Four Fundamental Concepts of Psychoanalysis,* trans. Alan Sheridan, (N.Y. Norton, 1981) pp. 87-88.
6. Lacan, Jacques, "The Mirror Stage as Formative of the Function of the I as Revealed in Psychoanalytic Experience," in *Écrits,* trans. Alan Sheridan, (N.Y., Norton, 1977), p. 4.
7. Merleau-Ponty, Maurice, *Phenomenology of Perception,* trans. Colin Smith (London, Routledge & Kegan Paul, 1970), p. 237.
8. Merleau-Ponty, Maurice, *The Visible and the Invisible.* (Evanston, Northwestern U. Press, 1968), p. 205.
9. Lacan, Jacques, "The Mirror Stage . . ." *op. cit.;* p. 4.
10. Richir, Marc, "Phénoménalisation, distorsion, Logologie" *Textures* 1972/4-5; pp. 77 and passim.

Chapter 13

1. Apropos of this gross schematization of lists, consider the following set of analogies: closure: overture = conjunction:

disjunction = homogeneity: heterogeneity = fusion: diffusion = parity: disparity. On the relation between categorizaiton and epistemological structures, see especially Michel Foucault, *The Order of Things*, New York, Pantheon, 1970. On textual and libidinal subversion, see Gilles Deleuze and Félix Guattari, *Anti-Oedipus*, trans. Robert Hurley, Mark Seem, and Helen R. Lane, New York, Viking, 1977.

2. Thus Annette Michelson is correct to claim that in this film Frampton "translated the contradistinctions between lyric and analytic modes" (Annette Michelson, "About Snow," *October*, no. 8 [Spring 1979], p. 116). Here, the lyrical is an expression of the mystical praise of God, a poetic mode of knowledge; the analytic is an expression of the mathematization of sign systems, a "scientific" mode of knowledge. Both modes are expressed by Grosseteste's transformational onto-theology, and the rhythmic and transformational system is further delineated by the mathematical exigencies of Zorn's lemma. Both are subsumed by the all-encompassing province of Brakhage's theorem.

3. Hollis Frampton, "A Pentagram for Conjuring the Narrative," in *Circles of Confusion: Film, Photography, Video Texts 1968-1980*, Rochester, Visual Studies Workshop Press, 1983, p. 63.

4. Hollis Frampton, "For a Metahistory of Film," in *Circles of Confusion*, p. 111. As a corollary to this claim, consider Peter Kubelka's statement, "Cinema is not movement. Cinema is a projection of stills—which means images which do not move—in a very quick rhythm. And you can give the illusion of movement, of course, but this is a special case, and film was invented originally for this special case" (Peter Kubelka, "The Theory of Material Film," in *The Avant-Garde Film*, ed. P. Adams Sitney, New York, New York University Press, 1978, p. 40).

5. Sergei Eisenstein, "Word and Image," in *Film Sense*, trans. Jay Leyda, New York, Harcourt, Brace & World, 1947, p. 4.

6. Sergei Eisenstein, "A Dialectic Approach to Film Form," in *Film Form*, trans. Jay Leyda, New York, Harcourt, Brace & World, 1949, p. 48.

7. This fascination with Mount Fujiyama is of broader interest within American experimental film. One may note Robert Breer's film *Fuji*, as well as Harry Smith's avowed desire to have Andy Warhol make a film of the mountain (see Frampton, "A Pentagram for Conjuring the Narrative," p. 61).

8. Maurice Merleau-Ponty, *The Visible and the Invisible*, trans. Alphonso Lingis, Evanston, Northwestern University Press, 1968, p. 270.

9. See Hollis Frampton, "Notes on Composing in Film," in *Circle of Confusion,* p. 124.

10. The split-screen image of a woman speaking (in the second part of the film) serves as a figuration of the subsequent multiplication of voices in the third part.

11. That the words *god, angel, divine, church,* and *bishop* appear by no means negates the argument for pronomination (antonomasia): these are merely more signs lost in the plethora of words and images, from which no centering term may be established except *Deo favente.*

12. Jorge Luis Borges, *Labyrinths,* trans. James E. Irby, New York, New Directions, 1964, pp. 238-239.

13. Such disjunction would become the subject of other films by Frampton, as well as a great part of the avante-garde cinematic tradition. The disjunction between voice and image (as the voice's source) is investigated in Frampton's *Critical Mass;* and while *Zorns Lemma* discloses the world's disjunction in a mode of filmic discontinuity achieved through editing, *Travelling Matte* discloses the world's disjunction in a mode of filmic continuity, where the shifts from abstract to representational images are determined by the variable framing and camera motion within what appears to be one long, unedited shot. Furthermore, the visual series of *Zorns Lemma* are the formal equivalent of the textual lists of *Poetic Justice.*

14. For example, in *Major Trends in Jewish Mysticism* (New York, Schocken Press, 1973), Gershom Scholem shows how the Hebrew alphabet was found by the mystic Abraham Abulafia to be the perfect, absolute object of mystical meditation. This is the case because the name of God reflects the hidden meaning and order of existence, and the name of God is contained within the alphabet. This notion was derived from the earlier Merkabah mysticism (which had direct ties to neo-Platonism), in which we find hymns structured as alphabetical litanies, such as:

    Excellence and faithfulness—are His who lives forever
    Understanding and Blessing—are His who lives forever
    Grandeur and greatness—are His who lives forever
    Cognition and expression—are His who lives forever
    Magnificence and majesty—are His who lives forever
    Counsel and strength—are His who lives forever
    Luster and brilliance—are His who lives forever
    and so on, following the sequence of the Hebrew alphabet.

15. These two transformational systems are expressed by Grosseteste's text. (1) Numerological transformation (homologous with the alphabetical system): "Nor are all bodies of the same form though they have their origin in a simple light. Just as all numbers are not of the same form, though they are greater or lesser multiples of unity. Whenever the number one of form and the number two of matter and the number three of composition and the number four of entirety are added together they make up the number ten. Ten is the full number of the universe because every whole and perfect thing has something in itself like form and unity, and something like matter and the number two and something like composition and the number three and something like entirety and the number four, and it is not possible to add a fifth beyond these four. Therefore every full and perfect thing is a ten. But from it it is clear that only the five ratios from between the four numbers, one, two, three and four, are fitted to that harmony which makes every composition steadfast." (2) Ontological transformation: "Matter for the four elements was assembled in the ninth sphere which is the sphere of the moon. The ninth sphere engendering daylight from itself and resembling the mass within itself has brought forth fire. Fire engendering light has brought forth air. Air engendering from itself a bodily spirit has brought forth water and earth. But earth is all the higher bodies because the higher daylights were compressed together in the earth and the light of any sphere may be drawn forth from the earth into acts and operations."

16. Peter Kubelka's *Arnulf Rainer* is one of several films composed within the strict limits of this antithesis of black and white. As for the narrative structure of *Zorns Lemma,* it must be said that, appropriate to its apocalyptic metaphor, it is highly teleological. The substitutive shots are often those of (necessarily fragmented) brief events (such as tying a shoe, painting a wall, changing a tire), whereby the end of the second section is indicated by the progress of these events towards completion. These true teleologies find their counterpart in Frampton's film *Special Effects,* where the electronic soundtrack provides the anticipation of numerous (false) endings by producing sounds that seem to run down.

Chapter 14

1. Salvador Dali, "L'Ane pourri" in *Oui* vol. I; (Paris, Denöel/Gonthier, 1971); pp. 158-159.

2. *Ibid.,* p. 160.

3. John G. Bourke, *Scatologic Rites of All Nations.* (N.Y., Johnson Reprint Co., 1981); p. 216.

4. Melanie Klein, "On the Relation Between Obsessional Neurosis and the Early Stages of the Super-ego" in *The Psychoanalysis of Children,* trans. Alix Strachey, (N.Y., Delacorte Press, 1975); p. 165.

5. Marcel Hénaff, *L'Invention du corps libertin.* (Paris, Presses Universitaires de France, 1978); p. 238.

6. Georges Bataille, "L'Anus solaire" in *Oeuvres complètes* I; (Paris, Gallimard, 1970); p. 85. Note that in *Story of the Eye* (N.Y., Urizen, 1977; p. 25) Bataille likens the cunt to a volcano: this establishes an inverse but equally cloacal and scatological equivalence to that of anus and volcano. Cf. Artaud's reference to the "solaire anus roulant." (*OC* XIX; p. 11.) The symbolically transgressive role of the volcano in Sade is also of interest.

7. Elias Canetti, *Crowds and Power,* trans. Carol Stewart, (N.Y., Continuum, 1981); p. 211.

8. André Lalande, *Vocabulaire technique et critique de la philosophie.* (Paris, PUF, 1972); pp. 595-596.

9. André Breton, *Second Manifesto of surrealism* (1930). in *Manifestoes of Surrealism,* trans. Richard Seaver and Helen R. Lane, (Ann Arbor University of Michigan Press, 1969); p. 128.

10. Harold Bloom, "Freud's Concepts of Defense and the Poetic Will." in *Agon.* (N.Y., Oxford University Press, 1982); p. 136.

11. Georges Bataille, *op. cit.;* p. 81.

12. Michel Foucault, "Nietzsche, Genealogy, History" in *Language, Counter-Memory, Practice,* trans. Donald F. Bouchard, (Ithaca, Cornell University Press, 1977); p. 161.

13. Maurice Merleau-Ponty, *The Visible and the Invisible,* trans. Alphonso Lingis, (Evanston, Northwestern University Press, 1968); p. 275. Cf. Artaud's question: "What is being? A totem . . ." (*OC* XIX; p. 80).

14. Guy Rosolato, "Etude des perversions sexuelles à partir du fétichisme" in *Le désir et la perversion.* (Paris, Seuil, 1967); passim.

15. Richard von Krafft-Ebing, *Psychopathia Sexualis,* trans. Franklin S. Klaf, (N.Y., Bell, 1965); pp. 123 ff. Such foot fetishism is also noted by Bataille, *op. cit.;* p. 204. The dual meaning of the fetish as symbolic object and displaced nonexistent body part, is made

evident in René Magritte's painting *Philosophy in the Bedroom*, (a reference to Sade's novel of the same name) where a shoe is partially metamorphized into a foot.

16. Georges Bataille, *op. cit.*; p. 204; Cf. Artaud's similar assertion that "the toes are sexual." (*OC* XIX; p. 149).

17. Salvador Dali, *La vie secrète de Salvador Dali;* p. 202. The polemic between Breton (especially in the *Second Manifesto of Surrealism*), and Bataille (especially in "Dossier de la polémique avec André Breton," *OC* II) is of special interest here.

    Such ironic reversals of high and low are elsewhere apparent in this scene: during the internal "dialogue" between the two lovers, one asks the other, "where is the light switch?" and the response is, "At the foot of the bed;" hence through a gross catachresis, what controls the light (pure, high) is to be found at the *foot* of the bed (low, base, fetishistic.) Furthermore, when the Minister of the Interior commits suicide as a result of the protagonist's political incompetence, we see a blood stain, a revolver, and his shoes (!) on the floor, and the camera pans up to show that his body has hit the ceiling: this reverse the prevailing belief that after death the soul ascends and the body becomes part of the earth. Here it is the body that rises.

    The interplay of spirituality and materiality, sexual and sublime, is doubled by the signification of the music played during this scene, from *Tristan und Isolde.* We should note that this opera is a tale of passion being worked and diverted through substitution and interruption. While the kissing of the statue's foot serves as an allegory of Surrealist iconography, the diagetic background music serves as an allegory of Surrealist narratology, and of sublimation in general. Also note that the attempt to perform this music is continually interrupted.

18. Norman O. Brown, *Life Against Death.* (Middletown, Wesleyan University Press, 1959); p. 298.

19. Georges Bataille, "L'esprit moderne et le jeu des transpositions." (*OC* I; p. 273.)

20. It should be noted that Sade was taken to be one of the precursors of Surrealism, as noted by Breton in the *First Manifesto of Surrealism.* Sade is also central to Bataille's atheological project, as is made evident in his "Dali hurle avec Sade" (*OC* II), and "La valeur d'usage de D.A.F. Sade" (which is part of his polemic with Breton), "Sade et Platon," as well as sections of his major works *Death and Sensuality* and *Literature and Evil.* Sade was also included in Breton's later *Anthologie de l'humour noir.*

21. N.O. Brown, *op. cit.;* p. 203. Brown also informs us that as for Luther's recognition that one's life must be justified by faith, Luther says that, "This knowledge the Holy Spirit gave me on the privy in the tower."

22. Ibid, p. 217; It might be remembered that just as the figures of Christ and Blangis are conflated in this film, Nietzsche, as he entered into madness, identified himself in his last letters variously as Dionysus and The Crucified; Artaud, during his incarceration at Rodez, identified himself variously as Christ and Anti-Christ, God and Devil.

23. Emmanuel Le Roy Ladurie, *Montaillou,* trans. Barbara Bray (N.Y., Vintage, 1979); p. 299.

24. Bourke, *op. cit.;* p. 54. Bakhtin, throughout *Rabelais and His World,* discusses the scatological aspects of the carnivalesque reversals of power and symbols. In particular, consider that during the medieval festival of fools, the elected bishops utilized dung instead of incense.

25. Ferdinand Alquié, *The Philosophy of Surrealism,* trans. Bernard Waldrop, (Ann Arbor, University of Michigan Press, 1969); p. 130.

26. In a 14th century gradual, illuminated by Silvestro dei Gherarducci, (in the collection of the Morgon Library), there is an illuminated letter "C" which contains a scene of the Last Supper, where Judas is distinguished by a black halo with scorpions inscribed on it.

27. Georges Bataille, Notes to *Le Petit* (*OC* III; p. 498).

28. Breton, *Second Manifesto . . . op. cit.;* pp. 181-185.

29. Georges Bataille, "La 'vielle taupe' et le préfixe *sur* dans les mots *surhomme* et *surréaliste.*" (*OC* II; p,. 103.)

30. Georges Bataille, "La figure humaine." (*OC* I; p. 184.) This view was also expressed by Nietzsche in "On Truth and Lie in an Extra-Moral Sense," where he writes: "But if we could communicate with the mosquito, then we would learn that it floats through the air with the same self-importance, feeling within itself the flying center of the world."

31. Antonin Artaud, "A la grande nuit ou le bluff surréaliste." (*OC* I); p. 363 ff.

32. Sigmund Freud, "Character and Anal Erotism" in *Character and Culture.* (N.Y., Collier, 1972); p. 31.

33. Georges Bataille, "La notion de dépense" in *La part maudite précédé de La notion de dépense.* (Paris, Minuit, 1967); p. 29.

34. Michael Eigen, "Musings on Freud and Schreber: Breakthrough and Failure." (Unpublished manuscript, presented at the conference *Schreber and Contemporary Thought,* held at SUNY Stony Brook, April 1984; p. 14.)

35. Bourke, *op. cit.;* p. 401.

36. Antonin Artaud, *Cahiers de Rodez.* (OC XVII) (Paris, Gallimard, 1982); p. 74.

37. Georges Bataille, "La valeur d'usage de D.A.F. Sade." (*OC* II); p. 64.

Index of Names